THE POMEGRANATE
a memoir

Copyright © 2018 by Elizabeth Stoll. All rights reserved.

No part of this book may be used or reproduced in any manner without written permission from the author, except in the case of brief quotations embodied in critical articles or reviews. For more information, please send correspondence to this address: query@vivaobscurapress.com

ISBN 978-0-578-47159-4 (print edition)

Printed in the United States of America.

Published by Viva Obscura Press, USA.

Author's Note: All recollections described here are true as best as I can remember, although names and personal details have been changed to protect the privacy of certain individuals. In addition, a number of conversations recounted here took place over longer time periods and have been consolidated for readability purposes. However, the overall content remains accurate and key facts can be verified.

Cover Design: Cover photo by Nicolas Livingston: 'Overripe Pomegranate'. Used here with permission from the artist under the statutes of creative commons licensing (Version 2.0): www.creativecommons.org/licenses/by/2.0/

For Professor Rheba de Tornyay, who always had faith in me.

And for Sister Marie, who didn't.

THE POMEGRANATE
a memoir

BY IZI STOLL

Viva Obscura Press
Denver

Chapter 1
Growing Up

On my seventh birthday, I was given a diary as a gift. It was white, covered with pink and purple flowers, with a little latch along the side. For my first entry, I chronicled the hours I spent watching a spider one evening, in a corner of the upstairs hallway of my parents' house. I was engrossed in documenting the spider – its appearance, its behavior, the strange alien way it moved – when my mother caught me.

"Are you writing about me?" she demanded.

"No, I'm writing about this spider."

"Stop lying to me. Let me see that book."

"No!" I slammed the book shut, latched the lock, and ran into my room.

A little while later I went into the den to say goodnight to my parents. My mother always lay across the sofa while watching tv, with my dad sitting in the corner at the other end. Instead of looking at me, my mother turned to my father and said, "She's been writing about me in her diary."

"No, I haven't," I said. "I'll prove it."

I left the room and returned with the diary. I handed it over, then knelt by the sofa at my mother's side. She flipped open the latch, which had no lock after all, and opened the diary to the first page. She read about the spider and handed the diary back.

"Why would you write about a spider?" She asked, disgusted.

"I thought it was interesting."

"Spiders are not interesting."

"OK," I said. "I understand. Goodnight."

Like everyone, I was a scientist from the day I was born, taking in sights and sounds and smells and learning how my hands could make things happen and how my legs could get me around so that my hands could touch more things. Most people stop being a scientist at some point, choosing more practical and immediate concerns to worry about. But I kept asking questions, kept trying to learn more basic principles about the world, and kept trying to find new ways to have an effect on the world around me.

I wanted to know the nature of the universe, and our place in it.

"These things don't really matter," people often say. But it's no fun just to skim the surface of existence, never digging for the deeper truth. Thinking more than we have to is what makes us human. It uniquely defines our consciousness.

Consciousness has several levels, each with increasing complexity. The simplest level is perceptual awareness, which we share with every member of the animal kingdom. I gained sentience at some point in preschool: my first memory is sitting in that warm room filled with scattered toys and noisy children, reflecting how wonderful it was to spend the days with a kind and gentle grown-up, Demetra, and two large green plastic turtles with wheels that I was allowed to ride around on.

The next level of consciousness is self-consciousness: being aware of being aware. This happened when I was nine years old: a dawning cognizance of my own waking existence and how deeply strange it was that I, and the world, and everyone else in it, were real and existed at all.

"What are we made of?" I asked my father, as he was tucking me into bed.

"Atoms," he said. He worked at the World Book Encyclopedia and he knew a lot of facts.

"What are thoughts made of though?" I asked.

"That's a good question," he replied. "No one really knows."

I asked my mother the same question. She often had a better handle on abstract issues because of her deep and abiding Catholic faith. She had my brother and me attend church every Sunday, rain or shine. We were also enrolled in parochial school the next town over.

"What are we made of, Mom?" I asked.

"We are both body and soul," she answered.

"Are they two separate things?" I asked. "Or are they connected somehow?"

"They're two separate things," she explained. "At the moment of conception, your soul enters your body, and when you die, your soul leaves your body and goes to heaven."

"Does that just keep happening over and over again, with your soul entering new bodies?"

"No!" she rushed to say. "No, no, no, no. Your soul spends an eternity on either side of life."

"Oh," I mumbled despondently. That sounded really boring. An eternity, stretched out on either side of life? The thought was unbearable. I found it difficult enough to wait through the drive home from school in the afternoon before I could get a cookie. The void stretched out in front of me and behind me, and an existential dread set in.

I went for walks to the park in our little suburb, Deerfield. I just wanted to get some fresh air, to move around, sit on the swings or play on the jungle gym. Each time, my mother called the police.

"Ma'am, the child has to be missing for more than 24 hours to make a report," they said.

Each time I arrived home, my mother yelled and hit me. And when my father returned from work in the evening, my mother would tell him what I had done and he would slap one hand hard across my face. At night, as I was starting to fall asleep, my mother would enter my room and share the feelings she had worked up while fuming downstairs after a long day. I stopped going outside.

I cried at night, restless and unable to fall asleep. My mother gave me a rosary to calm my nerves but repeating the Hail Mary ten times, the Our Father ten times, the Hail Mary ten more times, the Our Father ten more times, and then the final little prayer just wore me out and made me sadder, instead of comforting me to sleep.

I just wanted to stop thinking about the emptiness of existence and be happy like other kids. But I just could not will myself to feel happy. I tried a more direct prayer. "God, if you're out there," I thought, "Please take away this pain. Make me feel better."

Nothing. I felt nothing.

"Please, show me some sign that you exist," I begged silently. "I need to know that everything is not just emptiness. I want to feel there is some meaning out there, not just a complete void."

Nothing. Still nothing. I lost my faith.

Chapter 2
Nerds

In high school, I had two groups of friends. One was a large, unwieldy crowd of people with diverse backgrounds and interests. They were friendly, sociable kids. The other was a small group of nerds: deeply intelligent and thoughtful and introverted individuals who were generally mocked by others at the school. I didn't get fantastic grades like they did, but they included me because I did not judge their interests and I often facilitated them.

Patrick built electric guitars with his dad, and he needed another pair of hands to start a Beatles cover band. Ophelia sewed elaborate, historically-accurate costumes, and she needed another body to wear her masterpieces to the Renaissance Faire. Dave was into debating and needed someone to argue every subject under the sun. Zachary wrote amateur screenplays, and he needed actors who would help recreate an eerie Hitchcockian atmosphere or unsettling Lynchian transposition without asking too many questions about the purpose or meaning of his high-concept art. I was the type of person who would learn to play guitar for a friend, delight in wearing a homemade gown, argue night and day, and agree to walk towards a camera covered with chocolate sauce without laughing.

My best friend, though, was Kimberly. She had long, thick hair, stunningly blue eyes, and was cool as hell. She was an only child, and lived with her parents in a big empty house far into the suburbs of Chicago. She listened to Metallica and Tori Amos. We spent a lot of time complaining about our mothers. I thought hers was not so bad. She thought mine wasn't either.

"We could trade," I suggested.

"No," she said, citing the fact that she could watch tv on weekends while I had to clean the house.

We mostly hung out during school hours, in the hallway by her locker. She was friends with people in that big crowd. She was also dating a football player. His name was Freddy. They spent a lot of time together, which of course didn't include me.

One day the whole dynamic with that big crowd changed. When I approached the group, sitting in a chatty cluster in the foyer of the school, no one spoke to me or even looked at me. Like a silent herd, the entire group of people had agreed to ignore my presence. It was sudden and complete, this cut-off. I had no idea what was going on.

I found Kimberly by her locker. Before I could even ask a question, she grabbed me by the hair and slammed my head to the ground.

"What the hell is going on?!" I yelled.

"Stay away from my boyfriend!" she screamed.

"What do you mean? I haven't been near him!" I exclaimed, trying to free myself from her iron grip.

"You stay away from him!" she screamed again, dragging me down the hallway and throwing me in the corner. I was honestly baffled, and I stared at her as she turned and walked away.

Later that day I found Freddy in the cafeteria between classes.

"What's going on with Kimberly?" I asked. "She's really mad at me, and it seems to have something to do with you."

"Um, OK," he said. "I might have said your name at an inopportune time."

"What?!" I shrieked. "Why is this my problem?!"

He put his arms around me, and looked me deep in the eyes. "I think I'm in love with you."

I pushed him away. "You're dating my best friend. Or the person who used to be my best friend. She's mad at me, and no one else is speaking to me either. Set it straight. Tell everyone the truth."

But he never set everything straight. Our sophomore year ended a few weeks later, and my friends were still not talking to me. Everyone remained under the impression I was trying to steal my best friend's boyfriend, and no one would hear out my side of the story. My life was lonely and quiet.

I went in search of my other group of friends. Patrick was engrossed in a project for the summer. Zachary was engrossed in a project for the summer. Ophelia was engrossed in a project for the summer, which would get her extra credit at school. Dave was free.

Ophelia and Dave had grown up next door to each other, in small houses on the north side of Chicago, in St Juliana's Parish. They were close friends and even closer competition for the position of valedictorian, vying only with each other in both grade school and high school. Both times, Ophelia won. They both had the spark of brilliance, but she had more discipline and sense.

Dave was spending his summer watching films on VHS,

which he rented from the library. When I called him up, he was happy for me to join him.

"Yeah, just come over," he said. My mom dropped me off on her way to work, the special-ed school a few blocks away from St Juliana's, where she was the technology coordinator.

Dave and I hung out all day, walking over to the burger joint nearby for lunch. On the way back, he told me it would be cool to hang out all summer, but he was really attracted to me, so it would drive him nuts to be around me unless we were dating.

I grew upset, subconsciously clocking this statement as the emotional blackmail it was, although I could not articulate it at the time. He knew no one from my other group of friends was talking to me, so if I wanted companionship he was my only chance. He had leverage, and he used it. My mother picked me up that afternoon after she finished work, not noticing that I was silent on the way home and cried when I got there.

I went back to babysitting and programming software for adaptive computer equipment, both of which I had been doing since I was ten. With my earnings, I would walk to one of the only two restaurants in Deerfield to buy a chocolate cream pie, which I would eat over the ensuing days while I earned money to buy another pie. The fifth time I went in, the manager asked if I wanted to work there.

"You'll get lots of free pie," he said. That piqued my interest. But you had to be sixteen to work in food service and I was still only fifteen. "It's OK," he said. "We just won't put you on the books. You make most of your money from tips anyway."

That was true, and I can attest that, for the following twenty years, I never had a job that paid as much as waitressing at that little suburban diner, even well into my post-doctoral research identifying new drug targets to treat cancer. But it was hard work – walking continuously for eight hours a day, having to act extroverted without reprieve and having to remember arbitrary information such as which strangers wanted mayonnaise and which did not.

Nevertheless, the job was great – I met interesting people and I did get to eat a lot of pie. But I missed my friends. I called up Dave and agreed in principle to his proposal. The next day I went to his house to watch a movie, and we made out. After that, we were boyfriend and girlfriend.

Dave had been given the nickname "Quasi Modo" in school. [Kids can be cruel. But it was true. Dave was not a conventionally attractive teenager, and he did have a slight hunch on account of scoliosis.] He had soft brown hair and soft brown eyes, but underneath that lackluster visage his mind was a raging wildfire which left every person and idea ravaged in his wake. He was always gentle with me, though, and allowed me to calm him down whenever his debating got him too agitated.

We would argue all the time, about everything and nothing. It wasn't out of animosity and it wasn't out of any major disagreement. It was just intellectual exercise. We argued about space and time and god and the nature of the universe. We argued about books and bands and art and film. We argued about liberty and justice and the way society should be run.

His parents bought him a car and we were set free. We raced other cars along the Edens expressway, giddy with the danger. We lingered on roads winding through the ravines in the north suburbs and spent drawn-out afternoons by the lake. We drove for miles and miles just to go to a different burger joint. We searched for the best tacos across the tri-state metro area, and we went to concerts. We saw all kinds of bands, from Cheap Trick to Pearl Jam to Blonde Redhead to Run DMC.

I had to be home in time to help cook dinner each evening, but for a few glorious hours each afternoon, and some weekends, we were without restrictions and we enjoyed that liberation.

We grew to love each other deeply. We were best friends, and more, we were partners. We fooled around a few times a day, with the joyful energy of teenagers. He always respected my boundaries. We talked and talked. We ran everything past each other, and we decided everything as equals.

We built our personalities together. We were a united front - physically, emotionally, philosophically, politically, and critically, regarding art, music, and film. We pushed each other in new directions and, no matter where we went, we stood by each other along the way.

One time, after I won an argument, he changed the car radio to WBBM Newsradio 78: traffic, weather, and financial reports on hog futures from the Chicago Mercantile Exchange. He knew the station annoyed me because it reminded me of my parents' house. We didn't care about traffic; we weren't going anywhere anyway. We didn't care about the weather; we were always warm in each others' arms. We didn't care about the price of hogs or the future; money didn't seem very real yet.

"Change the station. I want to listen to music."

"OK," he relented, and let me choose Motown.

"I wish I had a boyfriend who would write me a song."

"But you got me instead," he said, and I lay my head on his shoulder.

"If you wrote me a song, I would marry you and love you forever and ever."

He snorted. "Neither of us wants to get married. Let's not go down that route."

We were non-conformist. Just like me, he was an atheist – the only other one at our school. We sat out communion one time, very noticeably not getting in line with every single other student in the auditorium on a holy day of obligation. We felt the eyes of two thousand people on us together and we served detention together later that day too.

The non-conformist streak only deepened with time. We learned about the division of labor and capital, and started to attend communist party meetings. We learned about the practice of factory farming and decided to become vegetarian. We learned about social anarchy movements, and stopped going to communist party meetings.

Then we got into punk music – Fugazi, Shellac, Minor Threat, Henry Rollins. The shows were not only very political, but very physical too. That was clearly a pull for him. He would get right into the fray at those concerts, while I stayed near the wall. And for the first time, I realized he needed something I could not provide.

After we graduated from high school, we broke up but stayed close. We both voted for Ralph Nader in the 2000 election debacle, both certain the two major political parties were too similar and too attached to the status quo to enact any meaningful change in our world. We felt neither would do what was desperately needed to address inequality, injustice, environmental concerns, or the power of corporations in our society. We were young, and we did not lean toward compromise.

The first cracks in our friendship appeared when we went our separate ways to college. Dave went to Northwestern, Zachary went to Notre Dame, Ophelia went to Harvard and Patrick went to Stanford. I went to the University of Illinois, in Urbana-Champaign, because I could afford to live there without getting financial help from my parents. I applied for and received federal subsidized loans to cover the in-state tuition, and I lived in cheap housing using my savings from my waitressing job. When the savings waned, I got another job, working behind the counter at a pharmacy.

Dave and I kept up, but more cracks fissured our relationship. When I went to college, I began to smoke weed. His punk rock seriousness had taken a straight-edge turn that was not compatible with regular college life. He yelled at stoners at parties. I no longer had the ability to calm him down.

My vegetarianism remained steady, but his turned to veganism. He grew his hair out long and shaved the sides, using vegan wax and vegan dyes to style a mohawk. I visited him in Evanston, where he lived at a co-operative, and one morning at breakfast, he criticized my choice to use honey as a sweetener. He roared that I was stealing the labor of the bees. I could not bring myself to care about the exploitation of bees while there were so many other problems in the world. Also I was pretty sure that bee farming helped bees to flourish more than anything. Meanwhile, he was angry that I did not follow his logic. He accused me of moral laziness, conforming to society and betraying our principles – particularly our vow that we would never cause harm to others.

The fissures in our relationship became gaping chasms. His new friends seemed to travel a lot to attend pro-animal rights and anti-WTO rallies, although no one had any jobs, so it wasn't clear where their money was coming from. They all objected to working, on principle. They had more important things to do. They spoke of direct action, the necessity of destroying property to save lives – not just human lives but animal lives as well.

I was growing up, and growing apart. Part of that

process is deciding which societal norms you will adopt and which you will skirt. That in turn determines what moral stands you will take. You cannot be alive and remain morally neutral, because everything you do affects someone or something else.

I did not like this pressure. I just wanted to understand the world more, by meeting new people and by doing scientific research. I thought that would be a low-impact way to live, without causing great damage to the world. But it did mean action, and therefore was not a morally neutral stance.

The next time I saw Dave, we met for lunch and I told him I would be joining an animal research lab.

"You know that means I can never see you again."

I nodded. "We each have to do our own thing."

I started dating another guy named Dave. He was studying to be a mechanical engineer. He didn't care about vegetarianism or animal research or politics. He loved money and nice things, and he thought he was morally neutral because he didn't consider it too much. I called him "Bourgeois Dave" to differentiate him from my ex, whom my friends and I now called "Proletariat Dave".

Bourgeois Dave enjoyed high-fidelity audio, and the appeal of nice sound systems started to grow on me too. He saved his money carefully to purchase Martin Logan speakers and a Sony amplifier, methodically building his assembly by elaborate plan, while I made random finds, picking up thudding Klipsch speakers at a garage sale and a solid-state Technics amplifier sitting on a dumpster. We would sit and evaluate each other's choices. Our relationship was less an alliance than a competition; when we went out to clubs we challenged each other to get other people's phone numbers instead of just dancing together. After a while, we broke up.

"You have terrible taste in men," my roommate Hélène observed. Her criticism was always right on target, and immensely helpful.

"What should I do, Hel?"

"Try dating European guys."

Hélène and I had met at college orientation and stayed up all night talking about our philosophies and our futures. We knew we would be lifelong friends from that first day.

She studied French and Greek, and had an effortless style in everything, from her clothing and jewelry to her laid-back and confident demeanor. She flirted easily but did not hook up. She was sure of herself, and she did not need anything from anyone. I admired her immensely – still do.

"Hel, teach me how to flirt," I pleaded with her one day, sharing a long story about an embarrassing encounter that had ended with me driving away a potential suitor.

She was happy to oblige. "Well, your wording and body language can be awkward. You're too serious. Just relax."

"OK," I said. "I'll try. Anything else?"

"Well, you could work harder on your appearance. You're pretty. But did no one teach you to put a brush through your hair and use makeup?"

"Hairbrushes were for spanking and makeup was strictly forbidden in my household."

"Oh, dear," Hélène said. She took me to the store to pick out a hairbrush, then showed me how to apply makeup.

"Anything else, Hel? I need constructive criticism."

"Well, you sometimes tell long stories with lots of tangents and no discernible point."

"But I have to provide all the different strands of information in detail. That way, the connections between things become apparent."

"Sometimes it can be difficult to see where you're going, that's all I'm saying. It puts people off."

"Maybe I should just date people who are as weird as me," I suggested.

"Maybe," she said doubtfully. "I'm not sure what that would look like."

"Helène," I asked. "Tell me again, what do you get out of our friendship?"

She shrugged. "You're different from me. It keeps things interesting."

Chapter 3
Electrophysiology

I began working in a neuroscience lab on the second day of January in 2001. The previous autumn I had enrolled in a class on psychopharmacology. Covering the variety of natural and synthetic drugs that affect the function of the brain, the course attracted the expected mix of stoners and nerds. A studious yet fun-loving undergraduate, I fell into both categories. I was taking this graduate-level course for credit towards my double major in biology and psychology and as a scholarly supplement to my extracurricular life of toking marijuana and listening to jam bands. [I wasn't interested in other drugs, though, except in an intellectual sense. My mind was wild enough merely alternating between sobriety, the occasional wine cooler, and stinky low-strength midwestern weed.]

The course was thorough, and in fact one of the most interesting agents presented with an effect on the central nervous system was not a drug at all: it was the placebo. That is, nothing at all but the idea there might be a drug present that was supposed to have an impact. Professor Jacob Isaacson, who ran the course, had made great strides in understanding the placebo effect by systematically studying how long human research subjects could withstand pain in the form of freezing water.

He presented the topic with great clarity – explaining the pain pathways in precise detail, from temperature sensors in the skin to spinal circuits and cortical regions activated by painful stimuli. Then he pointed out that placebos cannot have any physical effect on these neural pathways. Yet the empty pills still relieve pain about a third of the time, a significant effect. Therefore, he said, placebos are at the nexus of understanding neuroscience. They are the link between our biological makeup and our psychological experience, and proof that something must link the two.

I fell in love with neuroscience all over again that day. After the lecture, I went up to Professor Isaacson and asked to work in his lab.

"Aw!" he exclaimed. "I'd be very happy to take on a new research assistant, but I'm moving to Canada next month."

My heart sank. "You might be able to work for my friend Raphe though," he said helpfully. "Are you interested in learning and memory?"

"Yeah, definitely," I said, intrigued again. "Do you mean Professor Raphael Raziel? He taught us the principles of learning and memory in the intro to neuroscience course."

"Yes, exactly," he said. "Here's his email address. I'll let him know about your interest."

So I emailed Raphe and set up an interview. We had a nice chat and he agreed to let me work in his lab, studying how the patterns of neural activity changed during learning events and the recall of memories. The idea was to record electrical activity in the brains of bunny rabbits.

I was nervous, not at all sure how to start doing such a thing.

"Is there anything I can do to help out?" I asked the graduate student, Philippa, on my first day.

"Well," she said. "I have to put down a rabbit today. If you're okay with that, you can watch."

"OK," I said. I went with her. It was a very controlled, veterinary procedure. Philippa was calm, her hands capably holding the rabbit, anesthetizing him, loading the syringe with the drug that would slow the heart to a stop, and administering it smoothly. Later, I went home exhausted, thinking what a challenging, highly-skilled, intense job this would be.

"Is there anything I can do to help out?" I asked the exchange student, John, on my second day.

"Uh, I'm making teflon guides," he said in a thick Scottish brogue. "They position the electrodes during surgery. You're welcome to join me." He was whittling thick pieces of teflon material into tiny three-dimensional diamonds, with a pin stuck through.

"Thanks, I will," I replied, sitting down at the worktable.

He stopped whittling and stared at me. "Can you understand me?" he asked, in his strong dialect.

I looked around, confused. "Yeah," I responded. "Why?"

His jaw had dropped open and he held an expression on his face like he had just been transported to Brigadoon. "I've been living here for weeks and no one has understood a word I've said."

"Oh my gosh, I'm so sorry," I said in a gushingly sincere midwestern way. I couldn't believe the loneliness and isolation that must entail. "Where are you from?"

"Glasgow," he said. "And I thought the winters were bad there, until I came to Illinois."

I laughed.

"Seriously, how are you understanding me?" he asked, incredulously. "You're the first person I've come across who actually seems to hear the words coming out of my mouth."

"Um," I hesitated, considering the question. "I guess I've watched Trainspotting twice?"

It was his turn to laugh. "That's brilliant. I'm going to make my roommates watch that film."

On my third day of work, I went up to the post-doctoral research fellow in the lab, Thomas. "Is there anything I can do to help out?" I asked, for a third time.

"Sure," he said. "Make some electrodes for surgery."

"OK," I said, and he showed me how to coat an insect pin with epoxy, zap it at the tip with a salt solution to make a single point of electrical contact for recording, and test it using a meter.

"This is old-school!" I exclaimed. I liked vintage anything and I liked making things with my hands.

"Yeah, it is the old way of doing things," Thomas said, clearly disappointed. "I'm trying to get funding for a new system called Neuralynx, with much smaller recording electrodes."

"Well, I'm happy to learn this system in the meantime," I said, pretending to be cool about it.

In an hour I had made a dozen pin electrodes that were satisfactory. Thomas gathered them into a jar and we moved to the next lab.

"OK," he said. "The next thing you do is solder each of these pins to a bare wire, then solder the other end of the wire into one of these headstages." He handed me what looked like a plastic plug with holes punched in it.

"I've never soldered anything before," I said. He showed me how and I got to work. After several tries over the next few days, I had a fully-operational headstage, complete with a ground wire, that would sit snugly against the skull. I learned quickly, and the next one only took a couple hours to make.

The bunny rabbits would undergo anaesthesia and wake up none the wiser they were carrying preamplifiers wired to recording electrodes in their brain tissue, just like the human patients who get that kind of surgery. Afterwards, the bunny rabbits got a few days off, then spent a few days hanging out in the lab getting petted (a process known as habituation). Then they began training on a task. There were a number of different experiments happening in the lab; each of the graduate students and post-docs had their own project.

"The undergraduate research assistants are each getting paired up with a graduate student or post-doc," Thomas told me the following week. "I've put dibs on you."

"OK," I said. "What are we doing?"

Thomas took a deep breath. "Have you heard of Pavlovian conditioning?"

"Sure," I said. "It's when a tone is paired with something nice, like food, or something aversive, like a shock, and then, after a while, the tone alone prompts the response, like drooling in expectation of food or getting scared of the oncoming shock."

"Right," he said. "So we're going to do something slightly more complex, called operant conditioning. It's based on the same principles, but while the animal has to learn to respond to one predictive tone he also has to learn to ignore another tone with no predictive value."

"What constitutes predictive value?" I asked.

"The tone has to be very close in time to the pleasant or aversive stimulus for an association to be made. It's called temporal contingency. That link is the basis for the formation of memories, and it causes changes in the connections between neurons. And that's what we're going to track."

"OK," I said. "Sounds good."

We ran two types of experiments over the next three and a half years, both modifications of Pavlovian conditioning tasks. One involved actually recording during the habituation period, to find out how the neuronal activity was dampened as the bunny rabbit got accustomed to a new location, to understand why our brains can learn associations better in a novel environment than in an environment we're used to. That series of experiments was successful – Thomas and I identified alterations in the electrical potentials in prefrontal cortex and other cortical regions during the task. These areas are known to be involved in attention, so that made sense. The other series of experiments involved a task called sensory preconditioning, which is simply the association made between two neutral yet novel stimuli, such as a tone and a white noise. Thomas and I showed that an association was made when the two sounds were presented close in time to each other, but we never really did figure out what neurological changes occurred during that learning task.

Thomas was from Texas but he didn't have a southern accent. He always listened to NPR during surgeries, and he spoke very little. "Are you okay?" I asked one day, after hours of silence.

"I'm going through a divorce," he said.

"I'm sorry," I said. "That sucks." I switched the subject to science.

Thomas may have been quiet, but he did a good job of being my first mentor. I figured I was doing my part by completing experiments, so I felt comfortable asking for advice in return. I questioned him all the time. I asked him how people discovered electrical potentials in the brain and he told me about Hodgkin and Huxley, the Nernst equation, and other pioneering work in the field. I asked him how long it took him to get a PhD (about seven years), where he went to graduate school (Princeton), whether he had met the big scientists in our field, like Elizabeth Loftus and Eric Kandel and Joe LeDoux (some of them, but not all), what his previous research was about (learning and memory, of course), and how he trained in animal surgery and the manufacture of preamplifiers (the same way you're doing now, he said, laughing).

The lab was quite productive but also quite sociable. One day I walked into the histology lab to process some brain tissues and came across a blonde girl my age, dancing with heady abandon as music blared from the radio and a blue formal-thionin solution bubbled away in the fume hood.

"Hi, I'm Beth," I shouted over the music. "Do you work here?"

"Yep, I'm Kara," she said, turning down the radio. "I usually work Mondays and Wednesdays, but I'm here Tuesday and Thursday this week, trying to get some extra hours in."

"I like your taste in music, Kara. We should get on the same schedule."

She laughed. "Yeah, I like this band. I'm going to see them in a couple weeks, at Bonnaroo."

I stared at her. "Seriously? I'm going to Bonnaroo too. With my brother and his friends."

"Yeah, I'm going with my boyfriend and his crappy friends. We should drive together instead."

"Yeah," I agreed. "I'd like to hear about your projects. It's crazy we've been working in the same place and we've never run into each other."

And just like that, I had made a fast friend in science. A couple weeks later, we were piled into her Chevy with loads of CDs and camping gear, singing all the way to Tennessee.

After a couple of years, we started doing surgeries together, and the post-docs let us because we had built up the necessary skills and it gave them more time to write. We listened to FM radio, not NPR, and every time a new song came on we would tell each other what people and places and memories were kindled. It was a great way to get to know a person.

Our senior year of college, we were done with the grueling core courses in calculus, physics, and organic chemistry. Most of our credits came from hands-on lab work, which was easier and more fun than lectures. On weekdays, after work or classes, we would go to the Canopy Club or some other dive bar to watch music and drink $1 beers. On weekends, I worked at the pharmacy and she helped her mom with her home business. Sometimes we drove to Madison or Indianapolis, and one New Year's Day, after staying up most of the night, we drove all the way to Newport News, Virginia, for the Phish reunion. We had all the energy in the world, and music fueled us.

One Friday afternoon that year, I had settled into some data analysis in Lab 2, slumped in a chair with my headphones on. Kara popped in.

"What are you doing?" she asked.

I took off the headphones and gestured at the MatLab window open on the computer. "Spike sorting," I replied.

"You gotta come over. Everyone's in Lab 1. Elise says she's about to get married, but not to her boyfriend."

Elise was another undergraduate research assistant in the lab. She had previously asserted that she was named after the Cure song Elise, which came out six years after she was born. It wasn't always clear where the truth lay with her.

I stood up and followed Kara down the hall to Lab 1. I walked in after her, crossed my arms over my chest, and said "What's going on here?" as if I were a grown-up.

Everyone turned to face me. "Elise?" I prompted. "Are you getting married?"

"Yeah, well, that's the plan," she explained. "My family's going on vacation to Las Vegas, and I get to take a friend, so I'm taking my oldest friend and we're going to sneak off to get married."

I looked at Kara and shrugged. "But it doesn't make sense," she complained.

I looked at Elise. "OK, I do have a boyfriend," Elise admitted. "But I promised this other guy years ago that he would be the first person I would marry."

"You don't have to keep that promise," I said.

"There's your first problem, that's not how marriage is supposed to work," Kara said at the same time.

We looked at each other and shook our heads.

"I'll tell you who should be getting married," said Diana, the senior technician. "Me. I've been with my man for five years, and we have a three-year-old kid."

We all sat down at her corner desk. Diana was our den mother. She kept tabs on everyone and kept things running smoothly in the lab. She showed us several browser windows open on her computer: One was an offer on two tickets to Las Vegas with seven nights hotel stay at Circus Circus, for a total of $250 per person. The other was a wedding dress, unworn, for sale on eBay.

"Have you spoken with him about it?" Kara and I asked.

"Sure," she said. "I'm just gonna run it past him again." She picked up the lab phone and dialed her boyfriend's cellular phone number. He was at the pool with the kid. It was 2002, and cell phones were still new at the time. His cut out before the question was fully popped.

"He'll go along with it," Diana said casually, hanging up the landline. "I'm not gonna *not* book tickets at this price." She clicked purchase and turned to us with a huge grin.

"Kara, that's a really good deal," I said slowly.

"Should we go to Vegas too?" she suggested.

We sat down in front of Kara's computer, shut down her data analysis project in SPSS and opened a browser window to search for the same deal. Elise looked disappointed.

"This is gonna be great!" Diana exclaimed, putting an arm around her. "It'll be a double wedding, and we'll have two bridesmaids too!" Elise looked like she was about to throw up. Kara and I purchased the tickets and high-fived each other. We tried to talk Philippa, the graduate student, into joining us.

Thomas walked in and noticed the atmosphere. "What's going on?" he said.

"The whole lab's going to Vegas," Kara replied, leaning back in her chair.

"Awesome," he said. "Listen, can any of you guys work this weekend?"

Weeks later, Kara and I arrived in Las Vegas and hit the strip. But she was still not 21, neither of us were interested in gambling, the shows were out of our price range, and random men followed us down the street, asking if we were prostitutes. We decided we would rent a car bright and early on the morning after the wedding and get the hell out of town.

"$10 a day for a car!" I said. "We can't feel bad about paying for our hotel room at the same time."

"Gas is cheap now too," Kara noted. "This is gonna be awesome."

We attended the wedding, at a cute little chapel down the strip. The event turned out to have only one bride, Diana, and three bridesmaids including ourselves and Elise. One set of proud parents was there, the other set was watching the three-year-old kid at home. We took photos for them.

Two groomsmen arrived on the day of the wedding, fresh from Burning Man. Brad and Dylan were not in favor of wearing suits or really any restrictive clothing. They had been convinced to dress appropriately for the wedding, but they complained about it at dinner afterwards. One of them, Brad, expressed curiosity about our road trip. He offered us a national parks pass if we met him at his hotel room. Kara and I discussed it, and we decided it couldn't hurt if we went up there together and didn't go inside.

But when the two of us arrived at their hotel room in The Flamingo, Brad was not there. Dylan, who had seemed completely disinterested in us at dinner, asked us in. He said Brad was downstairs gambling and would be doing so for a while. We stayed in the doorway and inquired if we could just have the national parks pass. He asked us into the room again and suggested it would be fun if he tied us up, because he had just learned some erotic rope-play at Burning Man.

"No, thanks," we told him. "We just came over for the national parks pass."

"Suit yourself," he replied. We left The Flamingo and returned to Circus Circus.

The next morning, we got on the road. A couple hours

into the drive, while listening to Everything But the Girl, we got a phone call from Brad, who was wondering if it was too late to get in on things.

I was in favor of swinging around to pick him up. "He's pretty attractive," I said.

Kara groaned. "He's a total froot loop. You know he won't stay clothed for long. And his friend was really weird."

"It's an adventure! Let's pick him up!" I argued. She agreed, and we turned the car around at the next exit. Turned out, Brad was good company, paid part of the gas, took over some of the driving, and brought his national parks pass. Kara continued to call him Froot Loop, even in his presence, which he didn't seem to mind. In fact, he seemed tickled by it.

He did take off his clothes every chance he got, but it didn't really matter since no one was around to care. And at one point we all took our clothes off to go skinny dipping in the icy waters of the river running through Zion National Park. We arrived on the north rim of the Grand Canyon one morning at dawn to watch the sun rise, and over breakfast decided to drive fast enough to watch the sun set over the Pacific Ocean. That same evening we made it to Santa Monica in time to watch the colors change across the sky, then drove up Pacific Coast Highway before returning to Vegas.

After returning to Chicago a few days later, Brad drove back with us to Urbana-Champaign, then asked me if he could stay the night. "Ugh, you're never gonna get rid of this guy," Kara muttered under her breath.

He ended up staying in the spare loft room for a week before my roommate Helène said something about the situation. I went upstairs and told him he had to go back to wherever he came from.

"Where is that, anyway?"

"Peoria," he replied.

"What do you do there?" I asked. I realized this point of conversation had not come up until now.

"I'm in med school."

"You really ought to go back there. The school year must have started, and you can't stay here."

"OK," he said, and gathered his things.

"Keep in touch, buddy," I told him. I had enjoyed making out with him several times during our trip.

"Will do," he said. I understood it must be tough to go back to reality after the freedom of Burning Man. Sometimes people just need a kick in the pants.

He called me a few times over the following year. The final time, he reported that he was in a barn, playing poker with some farmhands. I asked why he was calling me and he said he was looking for some direction in life.

I reminded him that he had been happy out west and suggested that maybe he should move to California. It seemed like the perfect place for him, his natural spiritual home. After chatting a while, he hung up. I never heard from him again.

I did see Dylan one other time however. The week I was leaving Illinois, I was at the bank to cash my last paycheck and there he was: the guy who had offered to tie us up. With his mother. He introduced me to her, saying we had been in a wedding party together, which of course was the truth.

"What are you up to?" I asked. Dylan's mother burst into tears.

"I'm moving to California," he said. "Brad's already out there."

"That's awesome," I said. "Best of luck to both of you. And say hi for me."

The following spring Kara and I graduated from the University of Illinois. We had both decided to take a year off after completing our undergraduate degrees. We would continue living in Urbana-Champaign, and work as technicians in the lab before pursuing graduate school.

Professor Raphe was kind enough to hire us as full-time staff, but during the year we learned that he would be retiring his faculty post. His new priority as Emeritus Professor would be sailing his boat across the Great Lakes, up into Hudson Bay, then hugging the Atlantic Coast all the way down to Florida, where he would live happily ever after.

That was great for him. Unfortunately, that meant the sharks began to circle back home. Our lab space was to be downsized and we would have to squeeze all the rigs into Lab 1 and the small room adjoining it. We received the news at short notice. Diana had left her post as senior technician a few months back and things had grown chaotic.

On the evening before the big move, as I was leaving work, I told the new senior technician, Tiffany, not to touch my two rigs and behavioral setup and the dozens upon dozens of cables. I had a plan. I would arrive at 8am, label the wires with different-colored tape, unplug them, move all the equipment into that small adjoining room, and then replug all the cables into the right places.

When I arrived at work at 8am the following morning, I found two electrophysiology rigs, amplifiers and tone producers, a large behavioral learning box, several computers and a massive pile of cables in the hallway. Great, I thought. So much for my plan. This will take me at least a week to sort out.

"Why did you do this to me, Tiffany?" I asked.

She just shrugged and sipped her coffee.

I got to work moving the equipment, and surprisingly finished setting up the first rig and the behavioral learning box that same morning. I had lunch before attacking the other rig – the Neuralynx system. It was an entirely different recording setup – instead of the thick pin electrodes coated with epoxy, it recorded from much smaller populations of cells through microwire tetrodes, which I made by placing a metal bar through two loops of hair-like nickel wire securely taped to the cabinet above the worktable, spinning the metal bar until the four wires were tightly braided, and gently supergluing the braid before soldering each wire tip into a headstage that would be secured to the animal's skull during surgery (with the skin and fur closed up around it). So while the animals always sat in the same behavioral box to learn their associations between tones, the systems for recording their brain signals were completely different for the separate experiments. The simple problem was, both rigs would not fit into the new little room. I only realized that once the learning box, the computer, a desk chair, and the first rig were already inside.

Thomas showed up in the afternoon. By that point, I already had the second rig partly set up, but it had become apparent that bit of equipment would have to be situated apart from the rest of the system, in the big lab. I was standing there wondering if I could just string the wires from the little room through the adjoining doorway to the big lab next door.

"No, no, no," he said. "You'll need to drill through the wall and thread the wires through."

"OK," I said. "Do you have a drill?"

"Hold on," he said, and returned moments later with a large electric drill. I'd never seen one in person, much less used one. It looked pretty cool.

"Do you think there's any electrical stuff in the wall already that we need to worry about?" I asked, fiddling a large drill bit into the opening and locking it. It seemed like the thing worked similarly to the smaller drills we used for brain surgeries.

"No, almost definitely not," Thomas said, watching me test out the drill in the air. "You'll be fine."

I should have worried then. But I was lucky, there were no live wires in that part of the wall. My problem was a different one. A few minutes later, I was standing on a chair, concentrating on keeping the drill steady as it forcefully drove through the plaster wall between the two labs, when I realized that Thomas had returned with a bag of popcorn and was eating it as he watched me.

Suddenly I was aware of myself – skin glistening with sweat from the hours of work, lavender tank top tucked into my hip-hugger jeans, the entirety of my upper-body musculature pressing the electric drill into this wall – and I realized I was a cliché. I was a photo in a calendar, some random young woman with a machine, stripped of my own autonomy of purpose, merely acting as entertainment by juxtaposing two things that men like – the female body and a power tool.

I felt like I'd been tricked. Did we even need to drill through the wall? We probably could have strung the wires through the open doorway – they would not have blocked passage. But the hole was finished. I pushed the wires through and plugged each one quickly into the rig I had pushed against the wall on the other side, then stepped back to evaluate the situation. I had to admit the whole thing was a rather elegant, space-efficient, and (most importantly) fully operational setup.

And hell, I thought, there's no shame in looking good in a tank top. Although, if that's what I had set out to do that day,

I probably would not have also set up two electrophysiology rigs. I was quite proud of myself, and I convinced Kara to knock off early and join me for a beer. I was going to celebrate my accomplishment – not let someone, even my mentor, make me feel self-conscious.

Chapter 4
Grad School Interviews

Naïvely confident, I only applied to a couple graduate programs. I knew that I wanted to study neuroscience and I knew that I wanted to move out west, so I focused like a laser on the University of Washington.

I arrived in Seattle for the interview in February, counting the mountains as the plane circled and lowered altitude for the landing. That same evening, all of the candidates were taken to dinner at Ivars, a seafood restaurant located on the canal between the two lakes which divide the city north to south. The view was gorgeous, the light from the setting sun dappling the gray-blue water with pink and yellow hues. I was more certain than ever I wanted to live there.

We were told there had been 170 applicants to the program that year, 17 candidates were invited to interview, and half of us would be offered a place. I realized I had vastly underestimated the pressure I was under.

The following morning, I was shown into my first interview and introduced to Professor Frank Foldero. He had curly gray hair and wore a very well-tailored black suit. He shook my hand brusquely and motioned for me to sit in a comfortable chair positioned on the opposite side of his desk.

"Now, tell me about your research project at the University of Illinois," he started, and I jumped right in.

As I was speaking, there was a knock and a wild-haired professor with a shabby sweater walked into the office, turning to close the door behind him.

"Frank, I've got to tell you something," he announced in a loud stage whisper.

"I'm in a meeting here, Bill."

"It'll just be really quick," the man insisted.

"What is it, Bill?"

"Frank, one of these PhD applicants wrote in his cover letter that me and Bertil Hille are two of the greatest neuroscientists alive today."

Damn. I wish I'd thought of that.

"That's great, Bill."

"It's a good crop this year, don't you think, Frank?"

Professor Foldero sighed impatiently. "Maybe it is, Bill."

"Do you have any interviews, Frank?"

My interviewer gestured toward me. "I'm actually in the middle of one right now, Bill."

"Oh!" the other professor exclaimed, noticing me for the first time. He pushed his glasses down his nose and peered at me as if I were a specimen.

"Is it a good one, Frank?" he asked, still looking at me over his spectacles.

"I don't know yet, Bill. I'll have to finish the interview and let you know."

I was thoroughly terrified now.

"OK, I'll leave you to it then." The intruder pushed his glasses back, turned around and walked out the door.

"Where were we?" my interviewer asked.

"Uh," I replied. My throat was dry. "I think I had just

finished telling you about my current research."

"Right," he said, checking his notepad. He set it down on his desk and looked at me intently. "Have you done any interesting drugs?"

I was sort of starting to wonder if I was high right then, but I didn't say so. "Just weed," I replied.

"You really should try LSD at some point," he said, scribbling something on his notepad.

I shifted uncomfortably in my seat. This had to be the first time anyone had lost points at an interview for *not* doing drugs.

"How did you become interested in neuroscience?"

"Uh," I stammered. That seemed like the sort of question that had a correct answer, but I wasn't sure what it was. All I had was the truth, so I went with that. "I guess I was a depressed little kid and I just thought a lot about the emptiness of the universe and the vastness of time. And then I thought it was cool that we could even start to comprehend that stuff, so I became interested in how the brain operates. Like how we process information from the world, and how we direct the action of our limbs."

He nodded. That messy answer seemed to make up somewhat for my inadequate response to the drug question.

"You mentioned time. What do you think about time?"

"Uh," I said again. "It seems to move only in the forward direction. And our neural processing speed determines how we experience it."

I paused. "I don't really understand it much more than that."

"That's alright," he said. "What concerts have you been to lately?"

I beamed. I'd been to tons of concerts lately. I had this

one in the bag.

At my next interview, I was asked to summarize the professor's own research accomplishments. And at the interview after that, I was given raw data in the form of a western blot to evaluate critically. I had never seen a western blot before.

By mid-afternoon, around my sixth interview, I was starting to feel weary. I presented myself to Professor Louis Simmons. He asked how I was doing, the first time anyone had done so that day. I said I was holding up.

He smiled. "I am going to read all of the adjectives in your letter of recommendation from your current supervisor," he said.

My jaw dropped open.

For the next few moments, I thanked Raphe and my lucky stars for this break. I could not have been more relieved. This was actually going well.

"That's an impressive list," Louis said when he finished reading. "It seems like you'd make a good researcher. Do you want to hear about my lab?"

"Yes," I said. "Yes, I do."

Chapter 5
Moving Out West

Back in Urbana-Champaign, I had fallen in love.

Or rather, I had taken interest in a graduate student who worked in the same building as me. My heart fluttered whenever we passed in the hallway, but my shyness prevented me from speaking. He studied human perception, and his research involved testing whether people shared the same experience of colors.

One day we shared an elevator. I was nervous and unable to control the actions of my limbs. My pen and notepad dropped on the floor, and awkwardly I bent to pick them up. Remembering Helène's advice, I gave a quick wink and a smile as I straightened up. It worked like magic. He asked for my phone number, and afterwards always maintained I was a smooth operator, having arranged a flirtatious encounter on purpose.

Ivan was three years older than me but seemed far more mature. He had the posture and assurance of someone who studied martial arts. He was Russian, and he had completed his undergraduate degree in psychology at Moscow State University. We'd talk for hours over dinner and then we'd talk more in bed at night. Despite all our differences, we found our commonalities. Although we had grown up in separate hemispheres, we had listened to much of the same music and had similar dreams of traveling the globe.

We danced, watched movies, went for long walks together, met each other's friends, took trips to Chicago, camped under the stars, and fell in love.

We enjoyed cooking together, and he taught me how to make traditional Russian foods like Borscht and vinaigrette salad and piroschki dumplings.

After the lab closed down and I was left adrift, I visited his family in Moscow. I felt right at home, again surprised to find little similarities in the vast expanse of cultural difference that separated us. His father was enamored of facts like mine was; his mother had the same wine glasses as my mother; his sister reminded me of my school friends when we were younger.

In the mornings, we lazed around watching music videos on Russian MTV. In the afternoons, we wandered neighborhoods connected by the vaulted underground system. In the evenings, we went out to bars with his childhood friends, who were all making their lives in the city.

We drove out of town to stay at the family dacha, in the forested outskirts of Moscow. We took along the dog (sabaka) and the cat (nye-sabaka, in my terrible Russian). Ivan and I pretended to sleep in separate bedrooms. His dad played ping-pong with us in the rec room, his mother showed me how she tended her rose garden, and his sister practiced her English by entertaining me with stories of her friends at school. We made meals together and sat outside eating in the cold sunshine.

I was reminded not to whistle indoors and not to open an umbrella in the house to let it dry after a walk in the rain. Superstitions were taken seriously in this household.

"But you have a black cat," I complained, pointing to

not-dog, whose name was Santana.

"That means you are immune to the bad luck that comes from crossing any black cat."

I shrugged. I had no need for that stuff.

When I returned from the trip, I learned my plan had worked and I was accepted into the Neurobiology & Behavior program at the University of Washington. I was exhilarated about my future. But now I realized that I had grown a connection that pulled me east rather than west. Maybe it would be better to stay in Illinois for a while longer, then decide my next step based on the best place on the globe for my boyfriend to go. After all, he was further ahead in his career.

But I was young and selfish. I decided to chase my dreams and move to Seattle.

I had a car. Earlier that year, my parents and I had shared the purchase of a ten-year-old lavender Ford Taurus. In return for them covering half of the $5000 car, I drove upstate to see them in Deerfield every weekend. My father had been diagnosed with prostate cancer and he had a full resection. The surgery was successful, and he didn't need chemotherapy or radiation, but he needed a lot of help at home during his recovery. My mother was not able to do the shopping or cooking or laundry or dishes, so most of that year I sorted things out for them each weekend before returning to Urbana-Champaign. My father recovered easily, and they were back to taking care of themselves. Since I still had the car, I decided to take it to Seattle.

My college roommate Helène would be driving out there with me – she was excited about the adventure. Ivan would be staying in Illinois to continue the psychology experiments needed to complete his dissertation – he didn't want to drag our goodbye across a ten-day journey. On the evening before I left, he was helping me to pack up the car, when I broke a mirror.

"Oh no," he said quickly. "Don't touch anything." He immediately called his mother in Moscow, disregarding the massive time difference. I couldn't figure out why this accident constituted a transatlantic emergency.

But I was alone in that. Awakened with an unexpected and expensive phone call from the states, his mother rose to the urgency of the situation and gave extensive instructions for properly disposing of the broken mirror.

After a few moments, my boyfriend sighed as he hung up the phone. "The timing is bad, and the damage has already been done," he said. "But we can reduce your bad luck if we act quickly and carefully." I started to feel uncomfortable. He was a sensible guy, and yet he was taking this very seriously. It was hard not to feel nervous with his own nerves jangling beside me.

We couldn't follow the directions exactly, because the type of soil and tree which were specified for the burial of the glass were not available in the area, but we did our best approximation. Later that night, after returning from our hasty ritual, we held each other and said goodbye.

Helène and I arrived in Seattle over a week later, dirty from camping and euphoric from our adventure. We hit Pike's Place Market, the Space Needle, Alki Beach with its view of the snow-capped Olympic Mountains through the summer haze. She wished me luck and placed me in the hands of my new roommates, Rose and Lila. I immediately became part of their family, like another sister.

Rose was studying to be a doctor; Lila to be a lawyer. We spent time together like it was nothing, hanging out in the house or at the park nearby.

I loved Seattle, and I felt safe there. Men didn't grab me on the street like they did in the Midwest. We women were free to go about our business, and so we did.

The three of us lived in Greenlake and we took the 48 bus to the university whenever we had classes or work. I had managed to start my lab rotation with Professor Simmons early. He had gotten wind of the lab closure back in Illinois and had kindly asked if I needed a job for the late summer months before grad school started. I had spent the past couple of months selling wedding dresses at a family-owned shop, and I was eager to switch back to brain surgery. So, once again shocked by my lucky stars and Professor Simmon's kindness, I said yes, grateful for both the much-needed money and an opportunity to start my lab work earlier than expected.

The job flowed smoothly into my first rotation, and then classes started as well. My classmates were all Ivy Leaguers, except for one guy, Jack Fadden, who had attended a public university as well. We became fast friends, and he introduced me to all the people he knew in Seattle.

Jack had been working on campus at the University of Washington for a few years already, as a research assistant in the primate center. That lab used electrical signals recorded from the brains of monkeys to drive the movement of robot arms. The monkeys used the robot arms to feed themselves M&Ms. The setup was high-tech but less terrifying than it sounds on paper. And the monkeys seemed quite happy.

In the lab, Jack was paired up with a post-doctoral research fellow named Andy. Andy was tall, good-looking, British, charming, brilliant, and almost always drunk.

"Are you still dating that Russian guy?" he would say, at parties or when I saw him on the bus.

"Yes," I would say, even after it was no longer true. I

had given up on our long-distance relationship, and Ivan had decided to move to Europe to pursue his post-doctoral research there.

"Just let me know if you become available and you want to go on a date."

"OK," I'd say, although I was somewhat repulsed by his confidence.

One day, I saw Andy at the park, reading a book under a tree. I had come there intending to do the same thing, so I joined him. Afterwards we went for a drink and dinner.

We didn't start dating right away, but I started to catch him on the bus more often. We had both moved from Greenlake to Capitol Hill, and now we were both heading the other direction to the university every morning on the 43. After a while Andy admitted he had noticed I always took the 8:30 bus, so he had started to wake up in time to catch that one so he could sit with me. He mentioned that, as a result, he was getting a lot more work done in the lab.

Andy was working on publishing a paper that described his invention of the first wireless neural prosthetic, which connected neural pathways in the brain which had not previously been connected. It could in theory be used to help people with spinal cord injury recover limb function. But the first thing he had used it for was to prove Hebb's principle of neural plasticity, the law of neuroscience that states 'cells that fire together, wire together.'

It was what I had learned in Professor Raphe Raziel's lab: that temporal contingency could force the remodeling of neural pathways, simply through the miracle of coincident timing. In Illinois, we had observed it happening; in Seattle, Andy showed he could make it happen.

My interest was piqued. We started dating.

Through 2006, Andy and I grew closer. We danced, watched movies, did karaoke together, went to parties with our friends, took trips to Oregon, had sex on the beach, and fell in love.

I enjoyed cooking for him, and he enjoyed cooking for me too. He liked spicy food, and so early in our relationship I purchased a fiery red chili pepper plant and kept it on my windowsill. Every time I made a meal, I picked a pepper from the plant and used it to spice up the dish.

At the end of the year, Andy wrapped up his post-doctoral research, published his findings in *Nature* and moved back to the United Kingdom. He had done the same thing I had done to Ivan: set a plan in motion, fallen in love while it came to fruition, then stayed the course with the plan despite it all.

At the airport, on a cold November morning, we held each other and said goodbye.

That winter, the chili pepper plant on my windowsill shriveled and died.

Chapter 6
Floundering

During my first year of graduate school, I became smitten with stem cell research.

They always say, you should choose a supervisor not a project. But I was young, brash, and certain of myself. I didn't think it mattered if I had a good support system and I didn't listen to advice.

Professor Simmons had been an excellent supervisor for my first rotation project. He was considerate. He was engaged in his students' progress and their career plans. His post-docs were happy, with both the independence and the support they needed. We studied the effects of hormones on gene expression in the brain. My rotation project was well-planned, part of a larger study, and when it was published, I was included as a co-author. It's a highly-cited paper to this day.

In short, I should have joined that lab.

Alternatively, I could have joined the lab of a prominent geneticist who had developed the first transgenic mouse and published this seminal work the year before I was born. He was a great supervisor too – many of his graduate students and post-docs had continued in academia, acquiring their own faculty positions. My project there was interesting – I had shown that rescuing production of the neurotransmitter dopamine in a specific region in the brains of parkinsonian mice allowed them to move around more freely. The research was exciting. It would have made sense to join that lab too.

But one time, while we were conversing in the hallway, this prominent geneticist reached over and tucked the tag into my shirt, his hand momentarily sliding gently along the back of my neck. It was nothing, really. Yet this acknowledgement of our mutual physical presence revealed that we did not exist only in the realm of ideas – there were so many more possible routes for our interaction to take. I admired this man deeply, as a scientist and as a mentor. That touch, and the confessingly awkward smile that followed it, gave me a certain kind of despair. It told me that I would always be a woman in his eyes before I was a scientist. And if he ever decided he wanted something from me, I would not be in a position to refuse as his PhD student. So I didn't join that lab either.

It was 2005 and the prospect of neural regeneration had grabbed my interest in a big way. I joined a third rotation lab, under the supervision of Dr Addison Epsilon. Addison wanted to discover the molecular switch that changed a stem cell into a neuron – the key that would unlock the door to regenerating the central nervous system. She was young and determined. Unlike the other two professors, she had not received tenure yet. But she was on her way up, and I wanted to go with her.

Like I said, I was smitten. I followed my heart.

During my second and third years of graduate school, I dug into the molecular biology of the cell.

My experiments progressed well – each week I started a fresh cell culture, carefully extricating the brain tissues from the membrane surrounding them with a pair of tweezers in each hand, loosening the attachments between cells with a series of enzyme-containing solutions, mechanically dissociating the cells from each other by pipetting up and down with a long thin glass tube I had shaped under a gas flame, collecting the cells by spinning them in a centrifuge, and finally placing the cells, spread out delicately, in a petri dish. The whole process was slow, deliberate, and sterile. During the following week, I would feed the cells and watch them grow.

These cells were neural stem cells. They were not capable of becoming any cell in the body, but they could become any cell type in the brain – excitatory neurons, inhibitory neurons, star-shaped astrocytes, ostentatiously convoluted oligodendrocytes. In the meantime, the stem cells divided and created more of themselves. Sometimes, after producing a number of progeny, a cell would stop being a stem cell and grow into a beautiful neuron, with an arbor of dendrites to receive electrical impulses from other cells and an axon to send messages of its own.

I infected the cell cultures with engineered viral vectors that would deliver a gene. The gene encoded a protein that would bring messages from the surface of the cell to the nucleus of the cell. We hoped this little signal, called a kinase, would affect the cell's decision to remain a stem cell or to become a neuron. We had a few viral vectors – one carrying a functional copy of the gene that was active all the time and one with a copy of the gene that was mutated in such a way that its encoded protein was non-functional. We also had a viral vector that did not contain any version of the gene at all. All three viral vectors also contained another gene – the green fluorescent protein which had been isolated from the jellyfish and had recently won its discoverer the Nobel Prize.

The cells that were transduced with a viral vector

contained an extra bit of DNA – the gene we had introduced. They also glowed green under the microscope, because of the green fluorescent protein. I mixed each batch of transduced cells with naïve cells at a ratio of 1:100. That way, individual cells could be picked out for observation, but the cells would be dense so there was physical contact and nourishing factors to support the whole population. At the end of the week, I would stain the cells with markers that identified stem cells and neurons and astrocytes and oligodendrocytes. Then I would count the number of each cell type under the microscope, in the small clusters of green cells that had grown around a single glowing stem cell.

The goal was to test whether neurotrophic factors determined the fate of the stem cell, prompting it to become a neuron, and whether our little kinase carried that message from the surface of the cell to the nucleus.

I studied neurotrophic factors – their chemistry, the receptors that captured them on the surface of cells, their history in the annals of science. Rita Levi-Montalcini had studied the development of frog limbs in her home lab in rural Italy during the second world war, ignoring the chaos around her. She was fascinated by the development of sensory pathways that linked the skin to the brain, and she dissected them. The following decade, after the war, she moved from Europe to St Louis, Missouri, to isolate the chemicals that caused neurons to form and link up, thus discovering the neurotrophins. She won the Nobel Prize for this work. Yet decades later it still remained a great mystery, how much of neuronal fate was genetically encoded to be activated during development and how much influence the neurotrophic factors had in determining the switch from a growing stem cell to a fully-differentiated neuron.

I wanted to take another step in solving this mystery. I counted the stem cells and I counted the neurons, and I did a statistical test to evaluate whether adding neurotrophic factors could increase the number of neurons in each little cluster of cells.

The numbers didn't change. I couldn't find a difference in any of the experimental conditions.

"Do the experiment a few more times," instructed my supervisor.

But nothing changed as the data piled up. I went back to her office and sat down glumly.

"The hypothesis isn't true," I said.

"Of course it is," she said.

I didn't know how to respond. I could tell Addison did not want her elegant hypothesis to be thrown into the dustbin. "I think maybe the neurons that are there are more neuronal when treated with the neurotrophins," I said helpfully. "Their dendrites are more elaborate, with more branches reaching more extensively to find other neurons. That's something I could quantify instead." I described the kind of software that would allow me to trace the outlines of each cell and measure the total extent of branches a neuron had, which essentially determined its processing power.

"It doesn't matter if the neurons that are there are more neuronal. I want to make more neurons."

I just looked at her. We weren't really in a position to decide what we wanted. We were just there to discover what nature had made true.

"I am interested in neuronal fate commitment, not small changes in neurons that are already neurons," she stated.

"OK," I said. "But the neurotrophic factors are not affecting that process. There are no changes in neuron number in any of the experimental conditions. The hypothesis is just not true."

Addison looked me in the eye. "Maybe you're just too stupid to prove the hypothesis."

I leaned back in my chair. We couldn't turn around now. There was no going back to a time when she had not said that.

Obviously, things took a turn for the worse after that. Addison told me she was removing me from the project I had developed the skillset for. She would give it to a new student, who would surely prove the hypothesis correct.

My general exam was coming up. This test would decide whether I would become a PhD candidate or fail out of the program. I presented the neurotrophin project as my thesis proposal, even though I knew it would have to change. I gave a fifteen-minute talk and then answered questions for another hour. To my shock, my committee was satisfied with the proposal. I was so stunned, in fact, that when we entered the next phase of the exam, the general knowledge questions, I could not speak. The esteemed professors looked at me sadly. I had been able to open my mouth and form words just a moment previously, and now I stuttered, unable to complete a sentence.

They failed me but then kindly offered me the opportunity to try again. I heard the first part and it stuck me like a knife in the heart. I walked outside, into the sunlight, and continued walking, until I reached the closest bar. My friends met me there later. We drank as much beer as we could, and I cried.

Addison called me later that night. I don't know why I even answered the phone. I was very drunk. Unexpectedly, she tried her best to comfort me.

"Once there was a person who failed their general exam, and they still went on years later to get a faculty position," she alleged.

"That sounds like an urban legend," I said sadly. This person she spoke of had no name and I did not believe 'they' existed. "You're just making that up to make me feel better."

"You're gonna be okay," she said. "We'll make sure of it." It didn't look good for a supervisor to have a student fail the general exam. She wanted me to get through this part at least.

Over the following weeks, I brushed up on my general knowledge, knowing the next go-around would only be tougher. Addison took pity and helped me, organizing quizzes each week so the entire lab could test my knowledge. The practice sessions were tough and humiliating, but they worked, and I passed my general exam on the second try.

But I had to face it – I could not continue to work in that lab. Trust had broken down completely between me and my supervisor, a mutual feeling on both sides. I had to find another place to go.

Chapter 7
Switching Labs

In the weeks that followed, I visited every member of my thesis committee in turn, asking to make a fresh start on my dissertation research. I told each man about the demise of my previous project and I begged each for a chance to work with him instead. But no one had space in his lab or the time to accommodate another graduate student, especially a struggling one.

I finally managed to arrange a meeting with the fifth and final member of my thesis committee, Dr Steve Heckler, who had been unavailable for a couple weeks while he was attending conferences.

I met him in his office. He was relaxed, at ease. I was exhausted, with few options left. I cut to the chase.

"Long story short, I need a new lab to join. And I want to stay in stem cell research, if I can."

He leaned forward, put his elbows on his desk and said, "I like adopting strays because you have to work hard to prove yourself. Because you know that if you fail here, you won't get another chance. As a result, you'll work your ass off."

I had to agree with his logic.

"Now, tell me about your expertise."

I explained how setting up cultures of rodent neural stem cells had become second nature to me, after doing it on a weekly basis in my previous lab. He asked if I had ever tried to isolate this cell type from adult brain tissue, and I said no. It was easier to get proliferating, multipotent, neural stem cells from the embryonic brain. Few people in the world had isolated these cells from the adult brain.

"Well, we have a protocol for that," he said, smiling. "You'll be able to do it. The hard part will be growing stem cells from the aged brain."

I nodded. I was up for a challenge.

"Do you know how to clone DNA?" he asked.

I recounted some site-directed mutagenesis projects I had done in the previous lab, to make constitutively-active and non-functional versions of the genes for our little kinases. But I had never copied an entire gene and stuck it into a larger bit of DNA so that it could be delivered to cells.

"You can learn that too," he said, with an assuring manner. "We aim to modify the genome in adult neural stem cells, using the same kind of viral vector you were using as a delivery system before. That way, we can work toward achieving better stem cell therapies in people after disease or injury."

"Sounds good," I said. "I'm in."

But Steve had a slightly different project in mind for me than regenerating neural tissue after disease or injury. He had just been to a conference in Texas, where he had met a neurosurgeon originally from there but currently living in Seattle. His name was Dr William Bromley, and he was the Director of Gamma Knife Neurosurgery at Harborview Medical Center downtown. Will and Steve had hit it off, then abandoned the conference to drive around east Texas trying all the best

BBQ joints.

In the course of their adventure, they decided to start a collaboration together, teaming up as a stem cell biologist and brain tumor specialist to identify the cellular origin of malignant brain tumors. All they needed was a grunt worker, someone who could isolate and culture neural stem cells and who could genetically modify them in a systematic way to figure out what triggered the cancer. They had come up with a broad plan. And when Steve returned from the trip, I was on his doorstep with the exact set of skills needed for the job.

Steve introduced me to Will. He was a large man, with silvery-gray hair and a grizzled silvery-gray beard, piercing blue eyes and a gruff voice. He wore a white lab coat with his full name and the initials of his degrees embroidered on the left side. He barked a prescription into the phone while I seated myself. Steve arrived a few moments later, with a lanky sort of ease and a cup of coffee.

Will hung up the phone. "OK, I've got some start-up funds and I'd like to do some science here."

"Cool," I said. "What do you want to do exactly?"

Will explained, in a booming voice, that he had spent two decades digging brain tumors out of people, without coming any closer to understanding why it was that people got brain tumors. So now, he wanted to identify the cell of origin of these tumors, isolating key cell types from the mouse brain, altering them genetically to predispose them toward tumor formation, and transplanting them back into the mouse brain. Hopefully, that would reproduce the tumors he had observed in humans.

It was a very novel idea. Until this point researchers had only created tumors by introducing carcinogens into the diets of unsuspecting rats or by transplanting human cancer cells into mice with no immune system to reject the graft. Neither strategy created anything that appeared, histopathologically speaking, to be a true brain tumor. You just got rodents with awkward lumps in their sides.

If we could isolate the true cell-of-origin which caused malignant brain tumors and introduce clinically-relevant mutations into that cell type, we might create a more realistic starting point to replicate human cancer. Then we could transplant the altered cells into the brain of a normal mouse – the host mouse just had to be genetically identical to the donor mouse, or similar enough to reduce the risk of graft rejection. At that point, we should have a better laboratory model of malignant brain tumors. If all went well, then we could study what caused the brain tumors to grow.

"So have you done small animal surgery?"

"Yep, lots of it," I replied.

"And you have some molecular biology experience."

"Some. I would need to learn a lot more."

"And I hear you know how to culture stem cells."

"Yes, I do."

"Great, can you get both neural and glial stem cells?"

"I think so," I said. "But it will be a challenge to separate them out and modify them independently." I understood what Will was getting at. What we call neural stem cells can either become neurons, continuing to divide for several days as their progeny commit to that cellular identity and mature into anatomically complex, electrically active cells, or they can become an even more limited type of stem cell, a glial stem cell, which continues to divide but produces only glia, a broad category of cells in the brain which includes the star-shaped astrocytes and elaborate oligodendrocytes that I mentioned earlier. Most malignant brain tumors in adults look like they are made of glia, which is why these tumors are called glioma. The cancer looks to be made of normal astrocytes (a type of glioma called astrocytoma) or normal oligodendrocytes (a type of glioma called oligodendroglioma). But the cells that make up these tumors are not normal glia. Instead, they proliferate uncontrollably, which is why the three of us thought it was likely the tumors arose from a rogue stem cell. We just didn't know at which point along the path of lineage commitment the stem cell tended to become cancerous, and what molecular switches were responsible for triggering this process. But we aimed to find out.

The previous year, I had been awarded a training grant in stem cell biology, funded by the National Institutes of Health but administered locally through the university.

In order to join a new lab, I needed to have that funding. In order to keep my funding, I needed to have a lab in which to work. So I had to call everyone's bluff, assuring my new supervisors that I had the funding and assuring the funders that I had a lab to go to.

Sensibly, all parties asked for proof that everything was in place, in the form of a new thesis proposal that would be acceptable to both my supervisors and my funders.

I spent the following month, July 2007, in my apartment on Capitol Hill, writing the proposal. I read all I could about adult neural stem cells and the more limited, fate-restricted glial stem cells; about oncogenic transformation and genetic models of cancer; about the many semi-redundant mechanisms suppressing tumorigenesis in normal stem cells; about the types of genetic mutations known to cause glioma and other cancers. I thought about my DNA cloning plans and my experimental design — which genes would I choose to manipulate, how would I target the individual cell types, in what ways could I measure the malignant potential of the transformed cells?

One day I decided I needed some plants to provide more decoration for the room and more oxygen for my thinking brain. So I got in my car and drove to the Home Depot on Aurora Avenue.

I was browsing the shrub section when a woman came up to me, holding a tomato plant. She tapped me on the shoulder and asked if it was sunny enough to grow tomatoes in the city of Seattle. I thought of my disappointment the previous summer when the little fruits on my windowsill remained hard and green, refusing to ripen in the weak light, and I remembered my disgust when finally in autumn I fried the damn things, seasoned them with salt, and still had to spit them out. They had never acquired even a streak of red or a hint of sweetness after many months.

"No, don't bother with them," I said, distractedly. I went on searching for a giant houseplant, and a few minutes later the same woman approached me again.

I noticed her coming over. "You know, I don't work here," I mentioned.

"I realize that," she replied. "But I hope you don't mind if I ask your opinion."

I noticed her voice. It was tinged with familiarity — like home, like people I had loved. Like Ivan and his family.

I said to her, "I recognize your accent. Are you from Moscow?"

She looked stunned. "Wow, to come half-way around the world," she murmured, "And for someone to recognize where you are from, down the very city."

I looked down at the plant she was holding. It was a chili pepper plant, identical to the one I had kept on my windowsill the previous year. I thought of all the ripe red chili peppers my plant had produced and all the spicy dinners I had shared with Andy that happy summer when we were together.

I pointed. "That plant will grow well here."

She smiled. "I think I might buy it then."

I stuck out my hand and introduced myself. "My name's Beth," I told her.

"My name's Luba. It's short for Lubyet, which means-"

"Love." I murmured softly. "Ja znayoo. I know."

I did know that word, and I recognized it emanating from her. I felt like I was in a trance, or a dream. The series of coincidences had hypnotized my brain and short-circuited something. Her accent, the plant she was holding, her name – it was all too much. I felt dizzy.

She looked at me closely, holding my gaze. "The reason I kept coming up to you is because you look like my daughter, Anna. She died 3 years ago, when she was 23."

"I am 26 right now," I spoke slowly, the feeling of entrancement deepening further.

"She died of a brain tumor, a glioma," Luba said.

"I am studying gliomas for my PhD," I said, feeling like I was moving but not of my own accord.

We stared at each other, gripping each other's wrists, locked in a strange embrace.

Very slowly and deliberately, with her eyes wide, Luba asked, "Do you believe in God?"

I sighed, still meeting her eyes but feeling sad, like the spell was broken.

"No," I said firmly, looking into her face. "But that doesn't make this moment any less amazing."

"I hope one day you will believe in God."

"That's really unlikely," I replied. "I have no more intention of changing my mind than you have of changing yours."

She looked disappointed. "Well, I hope one day you will find a new treatment for glioma."

I didn't know what to say to that. I couldn't just say no. I managed to say, "I will do my best." Once it was out of my mouth, I realized it sounded like a promise.

We exchanged email addresses. I gathered some houseplants and returned to my apartment on Capitol Hill. The summer light streamed through the windows into my dining room and living room, reflecting on the panes of the French doors which linked the space. The rays settled on my new greenery and my new chili pepper plant. I sat down, breathed in the fresh air, and began to write.

After Labor Day weekend, I began my fourth year of graduate school and started work in the new lab.

During the following years, as I pursued the work on the new mouse model of glioma, Will provided tissue samples from patients as well. He and the team of nurses and residents would resect the tumor and I would receive it in a little conical tube. These samples were more challenging; an ultracentrifugation step was required to remove all of the extra vasculature and myelin from the adult human brain. It was hard for another reason too. Even though I knew the patients had consented to the use of their cells for research, it was emotionally difficult to process tissue samples that I knew had been inside someone's brain just hours before.

Those nights — it was night-time when the samples

finally arrived from neurosurgery – I imagined that Luba's daughter Anna was standing next to me, looking over my shoulder at the microscope or sitting just beyond the edge of my vision as I worked in the hood. This woman, this stranger in the plant section at Home Depot, had created a ghost. How strange – she believed in the afterlife, as an Orthodox Christian, and I didn't – but by telling me about her daughter, she ensured the girl existed in my mind. Anna was as real a person to me as anyone I had ever met or heard about. But the difference was, I only grew to know her and be affected by her *after* she had passed away. So Luba had actually created an afterlife for her daughter in that emotionally charged moment.

I realized there can be meaning to life – we just have to create it. Even without a god, we have each other, this amazing world, and our brains to appreciate it all.

There are many different directions my stem cell research could have taken that summer, but as it happened circumstances took me in the direction of studying glioma. Still, the focus was on basic research to understand the underpinnings of the disease. When it became apparent later that my studies were yielding a potential new drug target to slow the growth of these tumor cells, I grew hopeful and I pursued that side of the research. I drew meaning from that encounter, and I chose to let it fuel my actions.

Chapter 8
Gathering Data

Soon after I started work in the new lab, I got scooped.

Another group published a conclusive study identifying the cell-of-origin of glioma. They had carefully traced the accumulation of genetic mutations that led to the formation of these malignant brain tumors and learned the neural stem cell was the source.

These results were in line with previous findings: genes that act as critical tumor suppression mechanisms in neural stem cells are often lost or mutated in glioma, and growing cells within the tumor contain similar proteins as normal neural stem cells. The problem was essentially solved.

Will had another idea. He had noted that age was the single biggest predictive factor in glioma occurrence. Glioma, like many cancers, is an age-related disease. Will wanted to discover how exactly age contributed to increased incidence and increased malignancy of these tumors.

He could have stayed in his comfortable position as a clinician, doing neurosurgery and prescribing post-op treatments for patients, but he decided to become a scientist as well. He wanted to understand why people got malignant brain tumors, so he could find a way to stop them from occurring or recurring.

I watched his steady hands in the operating theater, under the lights – the scalp of a human being pulled down over the forehead and a section of the skull cut away. I watched as Will calmly and carefully repositioned the normal brain tissue, methodically excising the tumor and nothing else, cauterizing each rogue blood vessel before it could spurt, then setting the normal tissue back into place and counting the calipers before fitting the square of skull back in its place.

"If you're gonna work with tumors, you gotta see how they come out," he had said in his gruff voice. But in the operating theatre, he was a completely different person – quiet and graceful like a dancer.

He worked in silence, with a natural flow, and I understood then why neurosurgeons are so arrogant. To open the skull of another human being and dig around in there, with the confidence that person would be better, not worse, at the end of the day, was a triumph of human endeavor. I recognized the job must be enormously rewarding. Will could have basked in this glory for the rest of his career, but instead he chose to be a scientist as well. He elected to have an entire additional full-time job, with the luxury of having his ideas torn apart and criticized by invisible panels of decision-makers. He did it because he wanted something even greater than the everyday miracles he already performed. He did it to boost our understanding and he did it to aid the search for a cure.

So now I watched as Will listened to other people, valued their expertise, took on their criticism, and honed his ideas. The extensive discussions between him and Steve blossomed into experimental plans.

We decided to trigger tumor formation at multiple points across the lifespan and observe how age affected cancer progression.

I isolated neural stem cells from the brains of young adult and aged adult mice, as we had planned. Working with the post-doctoral researcher and the technician in Will's lab, we introduced three key genetic alterations into the cells to achieve oncogenic transformation – the switch from normal stem cells to cancerous cells. We then transplanted these cells into the mouse brain, as we had planned, but with the addition of multiple age groups.

The tumors that grew in the brains of these mice did look like real human gliomas. They were proliferative and invasive and they had all the right markers. We had accomplished our first goal, of making a better animal model of this cancer.

What's more, the cells originating from aged mice created more malignant tumors, regardless of whether they were transplanted into young or old mice. We had shown that age-associated malignancy was not a result of the aged brain environment, but of the originating cells themselves. We published that paper too.

The question then was: what happened to neural stem cells during normal aging to predispose them to malignancy?

To answer this, I studied the neural stem cells in their normal state, before they were transformed into cancer cells, watching them divide over and over under the microscope. I found there were fewer dividing cells in the cultures taken from the aged brain – most of the cells were quiescent, doing nothing – but the stem cells that remained in the aged brain divided faster. Around that time, another group found an astounding number of mutations in the neural stem cell population in later life. There it was, a mechanistic link between aging and cancer: the random accumulation of mutations in a dividing cell population over a lifetime, due to sporadic errors in DNA replication, causing cells to gain an increased potential for over-proliferation.

In other organs, like the liver or the lungs, exposure to carcinogens and toxins in the environment can contribute to an accumulation of mutations. But the brain is largely protected from the nasty contents of the bloodstream, and there is little evidence of environmental exposures lead to glioma. And there are not genetic predispositions linked to glioma formation either. It seems to be just a chance thing that happens sometimes – the terribly unlucky combination of a few bad mutations accumulating in the same neural stem cell, causing it to go rogue and form a tumor.

At the same time I was watching glowing cells divide under time-lapse imaging, to track how fast and how often they divided, I was studying their molecular biology too.

I wanted to learn what changed inside these cells. But I didn't want to go searching for a particular answer, I wanted the cells to tell me.

Luckily, next door there was someone who could do that. His name was Snoop. Steve encouraged me to talk to him. I asked Snoop if we might work together and he agreed.

Snoop had developed a method of identifying all the proteins in a cell culture and comparing the abundance of proteins between two cell cultures. Proteins are the critical elements that make up a cell – they are the gates and motors and switches and assembly lines and construction crews and cargo transporters that allow the cell to function. Proteins are encoded by genes, and they allow a cell to manufacture everything it needs to do its job – to secrete bile if it's a liver cell, to contract if it's a heart cell, to send electrical signals and chemical neurotransmitters if it's a neuron.

To identify all the proteins and compare their abundance between young and aged cells, we needed to take several steps. First, I fed the two different cell cultures with two different versions of arginine. The cells grew in a special broth, containing either the heavy isotope or the light isotope of arginine. Arginine is an amino acid, a molecular building block of proteins, and the version provided would integrate into every single protein that a cell made over the course of several weeks. Then I collected the cells and sent them to Snoop who would compare their mass. Since we know the amino acid sequence that makes up every protein, and we know the exact weight of every amino acid, the super-accurate mass measurements allowed us to identify every protein in the cell. Each protein had a distinctive signature on the spectrum, a double peak. Since arginine has six carbons, the heavy and light isotope of arginine were separated on the spectrum by exactly six units. We could compare the height of those twin peaks, to compare the abundance of each protein in our two cell cultures.

"So we'll just observe whatever's there?"

"That's right," Snoop confirmed.

"No hypothesis to prove or disprove?"

"That's right," Snoop agreed.

"And we can publish whatever data comes from this experiment? There's no right or wrong answer?"

"That's right," Steve said. "I promise."

Will nodded too.

After the experiment, I spent the spring doing data analysis. One-third of the proteins that changed in abundance with age had to do with energy metabolism.

"This is interesting," I told Steve when the results were in. "I think I should study how the cells make energy. It seems like the cells might be less able to make energy as they age."

"That seems like a pretty fundamental characteristic of aging cells."

"Yeah, I know, right?"

"Are you sure no one has done that yet?"

"Yeah, I checked. No one has published on the energy metabolism of neural stem cells at all."

"What are you going to do now?"

"Uh, I dunno. I guess I want to measure the enzymatic activity of cells, to track how much energy they're making."

"That's some serious chemistry you're getting yourself into. Are you sure you want to go down this route?" Steve asked.

"The cells are telling me what they do," I shrugged. "If I want to understand them, I have to learn their language. And their language is biochemistry."

He recommended a few people to speak to and meet with. The most helpful was Georgios, a post-doctoral research fellow who worked downstairs. He sat me down and told me everything he could about mitochondria. I got a taste of the complexity of the problem I was trying to tackle.

After that, I read and read. I found all the papers I could about mitochondria, the batteries of the cell, and how these compartments created energy from raw materials. I met with other people and worked to develop protocols for measuring mitochondrial content, mitochondrial genetic integrity and mitochondrial enzymatic capacity. I discovered how people track cellular oxygen consumption rates and metabolite production rates. I devoured information and read until I could read no more.

On Labor Day, I took a break. Andy was in town, and we drove out to the Cascade Mountains, for a romantic trip to some hidden hot springs.

That weekend, we decided to get back together, even if the relationship would be long-distance for a little while. I promised to wrap up my PhD in the next two years, by the end of 2010, and move to England to be with him. I would seek a relevant post-doctoral research position in Newcastle upon Tyne, where Andy was building his own lab. We were excited about the possibility of building a future together.

Back at the lab, I looked through the stack of papers I had been reading all summer. Many of the studies on mitochondrial genetics and enzymology were conducted in the lab of Professor Nick Armstrong, who happened to be in Newcastle upon Tyne.

I was not about to let a coincidence like that go. There were now several good reasons for me to move to England. And like any rational neural network, I would allow coincident events to remodel my systemic priorities and my behavior.

A year later, I was well underway with my study and I was growing more and more aware of how little I knew. I needed to learn from the masters. I flew to England for the winter holidays, having set up an interview with Professor Armstrong.

It was a perfect fit – I was looking to learn more about mitochondria, while he was looking to bring more stem cell expertise into his lab. He told me to come back when I finished my PhD, and he would be able to fund a post. Elated, I spent the first of many Christmases with Andy's family; we celebrated the new year by toasting our future.

Back in Seattle, my results had taken me in a new direction – identifying the metabolic fuel requirements of neural stem cells.

I initiated a collaboration with Professor Evan Salter

downstairs. He had devised a new method to measure the respiration rate of mitochondria in live cells, by measuring the amount of an oxygen-sensing dye. The first thing we did was set up an experiment to watch how the neural stem cells responded to changes in glucose concentration.

Neurons and other cells in the brain enjoy sugars like glucose, and they oxidize it to produce energy. Cancer cells notoriously break down glucose without using oxygen, in a biochemical process called glycolysis. So basically, if the normal neural stem cells use glucose like neurons, they should increase their respiration (their oxygen consumption rate) when they are given sugar. But instead, if the cells use glucose like cancer cells, they should decrease their respiration when they are given sugar (because they can make enough energy through glycolysis alone, without oxidative respiration). The hypothesis was: neural stem cells from the young adult brain would act like neurons, while those from the aged brain would act more like cancer cells. One would go up, the other would go down.

So we ran the experiment, and the cells did nothing. Absolutely nothing at all. After 45 minutes without glucose - nothing but salt water – they were still maintaining their aerobic respiration. This result was not just unexpected, it seemed impossible.

"Evan, what's going on?"

"I don't know, they must be using a different metabolic substrate."

"Like what?"

"I don't know, you're the brain person. What other substrates can brain cells use to make energy?"

"Luc Pellerin and Pierre Magistretti have found that neurons can use lactate to power metabolism." It was a neat finding: neurons essentially request nearby astrocytes to deliver fuel whenever they release neurotransmitter. The astrocytes have direct access to glucose in the bloodstream, and they provide it to neurons either as glucose or as lactate.

"Let's try lactate then." But again, nothing happened.

"Evan, what's going on?"

"I don't know, the neural stem cells must have a completely different fuel preference."

"Like what? What else could they be using to make energy?"

"Amino acids, maybe?"

There are 21 amino acids. We would have to run 21 separate experiments to find out whether any or all of them could be used as a fuel. I did not want to do this.

Also it would be inefficient for cancer cells to burn amino acids, the building blocks of their proteins, to make energy. Cancer cells are not known for being inefficient, so I thought this strategy was unlikely.

"Evan, is there anything else they could be using?"

"Well, fats, I suppose. Some cells run on fatty acids."

"OK, can we try feeding the cells a fatty acid?

It worked. There was an effect. Adding a fatty acid increased the cellular respiration rate, which meant the neural stem cells were oxidizing that substrate. Adding an inhibitor of fatty acid oxidation reduced the respiration rates. It was an incredible finding: neural stem cells had unique metabolic fuel requirements among brain cells.

There was a lot of work left to do, but the path from there was clear. I would go to Professor Armstrong's lab to determine how neural stem cells broke down fatty acids to produce energy.

There was only one time I got cold feet. At the annual meeting of the Society for Neuroscience, a man came up to me.

He was the deputy director of a large funding organization that supported research in aging and cancer.

"I want to fund your postdoc," he told me, after introducing himself.

"Do you support research in the UK?" I asked.

"No, why? Are you planning to do your postdoctoral research there?" he asked, appearing confused.

"Uh," I stammered, starting to wonder if I was making the right decision.

I did have some other options I had not followed up – a professor in California and a professor in New York had each floated the idea of a post-doc position. They were aware of my work and they were looking for energetic researchers to build up their neural stem cell labs. But I had not pursued a job with either professor. I wanted to learn more about biochemistry and mitochondrial energy metabolism, and Newcastle was the best place to go for that. Now I started to doubt myself – maybe I should be considering those labs instead. I called Andy.

He listened, disappointed and frustrated with my uncertainty. He told me that he loved me and that he wanted us to be together, but it would be difficult if I stayed in the United States.

A few days later I got a mixtape in the post. The last track was a song Andy had written and recorded himself. It was about how we had bonded on the bus all those years ago. It went:

From Bellevue Avenue/
To the university/
I fell in love with you/
On the 43.

Once again, I was smitten. Once again, I decided to follow my heart. I informed my supervisors I would be moving to England after defending my dissertation.

Chapter 9
Dissertation Defense

After years spent diligently working in the labs of Steve Heckler and Will Bromley, I began to wrap up my experiments and write my dissertation. Each of my projects would be a chapter in the book. In addition, I was scheduled to give a one-hour public lecture on my findings before defending my dissertation to the committee, who would question me relentlessly then decide if I would be awarded a PhD.

I was extraordinarily nervous, until I realized that I would have a captive audience forced to listen to me speak on my favorite subject for a whole hour. Suddenly the apprehension melted away and I began to look forward to the date.

My parents suggested they fly out for the event. My father wanted to celebrate with me, and also see in person how new facts were vetted through rigorous questioning by other scientists. My mother gave me an extensive list of requirements for hotel mattresses and amenities, as well as a list of restaurants she wanted to try and attractions she wanted to visit in Seattle.

"Mom, I have a lot on my mind. I cannot handle all of this information. If you're going to make the whole week about you, then you aren't invited."

"Oh!" she responded, and decided not to come. My father flew out on his own.

When the big day arrived, I had my talk prepared. I sat anxiously in the auditorium next to my father, waving at friends and colleagues as they entered the room and took their seats.

It is traditional, in these United States, for a supervisor to roast a PhD candidate before their talk, providing the audience with a funny anecdote that summarizes the student's time in the lab and often mocks the greenness of their early years. In the excitement of my preparations, I had completely forgotten about this custom.

As Steve stood up to introduce me, I realized what was about to happen, and I sunk down in my seat.

What would he talk about? I remembered our first meeting, on that long awful day of interviews, when he had informed me gravely about the importance of developing rodent models of neurological injury, to understand the physiological damage that occurred during car crashes, and for some reason I responded by telling him how I used to drive my pet hamster around in a remote-controlled jeep. He had paused before saying dryly, "That's not how we do it in the lab."

Oh no, was he going to tell that story now? Steve approached the podium, taking in the large audience. He waited for everyone to quiet down.

"It is traditional," he spoke in a booming voice, "for the supervisor to say a few words at this point about the candidate."

I slid further down in my seat. Steve looked around, savoring the moment. I thought of the time when I signed up awkward pairs of professors to sing duets when someone had made the mistake of bringing a karaoke machine to our annual departmental retreat. I hadn't thought people would go onstage, but as the names were called, each esteemed academic walked up to the mic and belted out a tune. Steve had gotten a Madonna song, which he handled well enough. This was years ago, but he could have his revenge now.

He chose another incident. Several years earlier, at another departmental retreat, there had been quite a lot of drinking on the last night and it was decided by certain members of my class – there were eight of us in total – that we would have a little fun with the posters that some labs had printed to summarize their research findings.

No, oh no, this was the most embarrassing story he could have chosen. But why me? I thought all of us had agreed to keep mum on who was most guilty that night. How did Steve –

And then it hit me. An extra face present that night, sitting calmly with a beer as the night progressed toward its destructive end, suddenly resolved itself in my mind. It was Steve. Steve was there that night. Oh no, this was bad.

He described how two of my classmates took down a poster from the wall and one of us – me, it was me – snorted and revved my foot before running full-blast and plunging through the poster, ripping it in half, like a bull running at the flag held by the matador.

I could not sink any lower in that seat. I didn't often get drunk and totally let loose, but my classmates were brilliant and fun and we did have a habit of egging each other on. In this case especially, I was definitely one of the guiltier ones. After all, I was the bull.

"Beth is, in fact, like the bull," Steve went on. Oh no, he was turning this whole dreadful scene into a metaphor. I like a metaphor as much as the next person, but this was torture.

He continued. "Once she catches sight of some goal, there is no stopping her from doing everything she can to chase it down. She truly has the persistence and tenacity of the bull."

I let out a sigh of relief. That was embarrassing, but it could have been worse.

For a moment I wished I could tell some mortifying story in return, but then I realized it wasn't appropriate and I didn't have the ammo anyway. No, the best thing to do was concentrate. I was getting a full hour to talk about my years of research to this big crowd of people and suddenly a huge wave of gratitude swept over me. I was so lucky that Steve and Will had taken me on-board, so lucky to have gotten that second chance to do graduate research in neuroscience.

I took a deep breath and began to speak. By the end of the day, I had been awarded my PhD, I was drinking champagne with the wonderful people who had supported me through it all, and Steve was doing his best impression of Yoda to offer congratulations.

Chapter 10
Moving to England to Pursue Post-Doctoral Research

After successfully defending my dissertation, I packed up my life in boxes and shipped everything across the pond, presented my research at the annual Society for Neuroscience meeting, and celebrated Thanksgiving with my family. Then I boarded a flight to England to start my life there.

As I fished a book from my tote bag, I exchanged pleasantries with the man sitting next to me on the plane. He was the pastor of a big church, and he was interested in the fact I did research.

"A scientist, really? Are you also a person of faith?"

"Faith in what?" I asked, pretending not to know where this conversation was going.

"Faith in God Almighty," the man said.

"No," I replied. "I tend to make decisions based on evidence. There's no evidence for this god."

"Jesus Christ was a living man, two thousand years ago."

"Yeah, I believe that part is true."

"He was also the Son of God."

"That's sort of where I lose you."

"You cannot live without God, without faith," the man

asserted. He was wrong. I could and I did.

Nevertheless, I sighed and closed the book on my lap. I wished I could explain that truth is my god, or at least serves that purpose in my life.

Truth is an invisible force that cannot be denied. Without truth, the universe would be unknowable and there would be no stable reality. Without acceptance of verifiable facts, a shared experience on the same plane of existence would be impossible for humankind. Absolute truth may never be completely knowable, but it must never be denied.

Every time I find out some new fact about the world – something that can be validated by myself and others – I grow closer to this sense of absolute truth, and I develop a bond of shared understanding with other people too. Learning is a pilgrimage, a journey undertaken with passion, that bestows a sense of wonder in this world.

Truth does not require worship. It did not create the world, but like us, exists within the world. Belief – or lack of it – on my part does not affect the truth at all. Truth does not require faith; truth is impervious to doubt. Testing, even disproving, received wisdom brings me closer to truth, while having faith that is not questioned leads me further away.

I looked at this man, and he looked at me. I could not see beauty in his faith. All I saw were threats of damnation used to bully other people into believing his claims to speak for an almighty god, a god with changeable whims who could never be fully appeased. Asserting there is some father figure always telling you that you're not good enough? This was not some higher truth – this god was human nature, through and through.

"I think I'll keep my skepticism," I said finally.

"A girl from our church once moved to England, just as

you're doing now," the man said conversationally. "She had insufficient faith. Instead of studying and going to church, she spent time with her friends, and one day she got an injury playing rugby. She had to fly back to the states for medical treatment, but the wound got infected and she had to have her foot removed."

"I'm really sorry to hear that."

"Her parents were distraught, so they asked me to make the medical decisions for her."

"That's nice that you were there for her and her family. It must have been a difficult time," I said.

"Well, after a few months the infection spread and gangrene went up her leg, so I had the doctors remove some more, to the knee."

I looked at the man, uncertainly.

"But afterwards the infection returned, and they had to remove most of her upper leg."

"It sounds like you and the doctors didn't make the best call," I mentioned. "I mean, I'm not a clinician, but it sounds like you should have taken a larger area to make sure the infection was completely removed in the first place."

He shrugged.

"How is she now?" I asked.

"She's been fine for several months."

"What if the infection comes back? It sounds like there's not much leg left to remove before the gangrene spreads to her abdomen."

He shrugged again. "We must have faith that it won't come back."

"Um, do you feel like you have any personal responsibility in this situation?"

"No, the problem here is the girl's insufficient faith."

"Yeah, I don't think that's the main problem here," I replied.

The man sniffed and turned to face the window. I opened my book. He spoke up again.

"Just be careful who you ally yourself with," the pastor counselled.

"Your congregation might benefit from that same advice," I remarked. He turned away and did not speak to me again. I shook my head and read my book.

Andy refers to England as "civilization" as if America is not. He loves his complicated country, which has an official state religion although most people are atheistic, as if that makes so much more sense than what we have. I suppose we have much higher rates of homicide, largely on account of gun ownership, which is common in the United States but banned in the United Kingdom. Despite that fact, England seems anything but civilized. The British are not prone to creature comforts, such as indoor heating or clothes dryers – you just have to put on a sweater and a stiff upper lip and hang your clothing up to dry. Andy's driving license at this time was a decades-old folded-up piece of paper with no photo, as if he were living in the 1930s. It was 2010.

When I arrived, the flat had a broken showerhead, a broken toilet seat, a broken TV, nothing in the fridge but a bottle of ketchup, and a car with windshield wipers that acted up and a battery that didn't. Apparently Andy thought that when I showed up, everything would get fixed, and so I set to work tending the bachelor pad I moved into and taming the bachelor beast I now lived with, wondering if my PhD was somewhat going to waste.

I learned how to count Her Majesty's change, developed a taste for warm, flat beer, oriented myself to being in a vehicle on the wrong side of the road, and resigned myself to the sort of reputation I would unwittingly accrue by living in Newcastle upon Tyne. I grew to appreciate the tense build-up in a game of snooker or darts, as pub games were officially considered sports here. I sustained a recurring dream in which I gathered with a group of strangers: we did not share names, but we spoke in a common dialect and brushed our teeth together with Crest.

I began to find my way around town, wandering past the statue of Earl Grey along the architectural marvel of Grey Street, past the New Castle – built in 1094 – which gave the town its name, to the Quayside, bustling with seagulls, until I reached the open-air terraces and underground music venues of Ouseburn, quiet in the daytime and covered with snow in December. Other days, I walked upriver along the waterfront path, past the fisherman and the seven bridges of the city.

I watched football games in the pub down the street, rooting for my new team, Newcastle United. The enemy was Sunderland, a town about twenty miles away, whose red-and-white striped shirts were banned on this side of the river. Our team, nicknamed the magpies for having black-and-white jerseys, was not doing well that season. At the annual derby, held in Sunderland, an actual magpie landed on the field and strutted about for two full minutes while the players cleared the field and the entire metro area of both towns screamed at the top of their lungs, in joy or anger, at the oblivious bird.

I bought tickets for us to watch the cricket, and immediately regretted it. Like baseball, cricket involves hitting a ball with a bat; the similarities end there. In cricket, the batsman bats until he is out, forcing others to stand in a queue for hours; in baseball, you get three chances and then someone else gets a turn. A fielder can catch the ball in mid-air for an "out" in both sports, but only the Americans have figured out they can improve their chances by wearing a giant mitt. Baseball is a three-hour affair, unless there is a tie, in which case the game goes into extra innings to settle the score; cricket is played for five days and can still end in a draw. Baseball has long, quiet moments of rising tension that can suddenly break; cricket has tea breaks at set times and strategy is often based on the weather. During post-season games, baseball fans of all ages jump up and down cheering; at cricket tournaments, old men hold battery-powered radios to hear the play-by-play, unwrapping their pork pies and washing down their beta-blockers with Talisker and Tetley in the thrilling anticipation of winning The Ashes.

We spent Christmas in London, strolling around the city in the darkening mid-winter afternoons. Andy attracted foreign tour groups by speaking loudly in his native London accent. Clusters of people straggled behind him, listening as he authoritatively misnamed all the buildings, including Buckingham Palace, and insisted we could not visit London Bridge because it had fallen down.

We visited the British Museum. Over the centuries, British archaeologists and pillaging colonizers purchased and stole great art from every other society on earth – the majestic Moai of Easter Island, golden statues of divinities from ancient Mayan temples, parts of the Parthenon, royal mummies from Egypt, and some of the earliest writings of the human species, including a tablet discussing beer rations and the Rosetta Stone. The history of the British Empire is tied into the history of the world, and it was all collected and contained in the British Museum. Awe was a natural reaction.

After Christmas, we returned to Newcastle. The holidays were over and the gloomy long winter set in. Andy went back to work. When he came home after his first day back, he popped open a local brew, then began uncorking a bottle of wine as I prepared dinner.

"Honey, it's not the holidays anymore. We're not still going to drink a bottle of wine every night, are we?" I said, laughing. I had begun looking forward to a break from over-indulgent feasting.

"This is what I do on a normal evening," he replied, looking me in the eye. I realized, over the past several years, we had only been together for vacations and holidays. I had always thought we were celebrating. I hadn't expected this level of drinking would happen on a regular basis.

"There are cultural differences," Andy explained. "British people drink more than Americans. This is normal here."

"OK, honey, but maybe you split the difference? It's not that weird to have a beer or a glass of wine when you come home most nights, but a beer *and* a bottle of wine, every night? It seems a bit much. Maybe it would be worth cutting down."

"I'm not going to cut down my alcohol intake for you." His face was serious. "Don't try to make that a requirement of our relationship."

"OK," I said, putting my hands up. The thought had not occurred to me.

Andy went back to opening the bottle. I shrugged. Most nights I had a glass too. But only rarely would I have more than that - I was nearly thirty, and my body had started telling me to take it easy. I figured that we all have our own limits and we know how to recognize them. Anyway, Andy was adamant that he would make his own decisions, so I let it go and focused on my own problems.

As time passed, I grew concerned that my visa was not coming through. The new conservative government, under the Home Secretary Theresa May, had cancelled immigration temporarily. Andy and Nick told me to be patient – the Home Office was just rejigging the system and visas would be issued shortly. But the months continued to pass.

"Andy, maybe I should just take a job in the states as I wait for things to work out here."

"You'll just get embroiled out there. And we don't want to be long-distance again."

"But I'm bored here." I had taken to making cheddar cheese by hand, measuring the temperature and pH in the sterilized pot as I separated the curds and whey, salting the curds and using the whey to make bread and fortified juices which Andy would not drink.

"I'll give you some money to keep going." It had been expensive to move, and I did not have enough money to go back to the states. Andy was certainly not about to lend me some cash to leave him. Pocket money was given to me regularly only on the promise that I would stay.

I headed north on the train to Edinburgh, and explored the gritty, pretty city in heavy snow. I visited labyrinth bookshops in York, watched a film at the Cinerama in Bradford, and cooked dinner for Andy every night in Newcastle when he returned from work. As the weather turned brighter, I bought a bicycle, departing for day-long jaunts east toward the seaside at Tynemouth, west toward the charming villages tucked into the hills around Corbridge, and south to the stunning medieval city of Durham.

I learned to respond to the greeting "Whey-aye, pet! Alreet?" with "Aye, ta."

I learned about Cockney Rhyming Slang, supposedly invented in East London by drug dealers trying to evade the police, but more likely invented by Oxbridge undergraduates studying English and trying to establish street cred. Using this phrasing, a friend is called "china" because mate rhymes with "china plate". "Trouble" – short for "trouble and strife" – refer to the wife. People who use this slang are called "muppets" because they're ridiculous.

But language isn't just dialect and vocabulary – it's also connotations and facts themselves, which vary across the country. For example: in answering the question "Who won the Battle of Trafalgar?" – a defining point in the Napoleonic Wars – southerners will say "Admiral Lord Nelson" and northerners will say "Admiral Lord Collingwood". In fact, Nelson was mortally wounded during the battle; his last words "Kiss me, Hardy!" were recorded by an obliging Captain Thomas Hardy as well as other witnesses present at the scene. Meanwhile, Collingwood rose to commander and finished the battle, losing not a single British ship and thus establishing British naval supremacy over the combined French and Spanish fleets. Today, a statue of Nelson stands in Trafalgar Square in London. In the history books and on the relevant Wikipedia page, the death of Nelson during the battle is described in great detail, with his heroic last words listed as "God and my country", while Collingwood, a Geordie hero, is mentioned only briefly. Consequently, the northerners hold a grudge against both the French and the southerners.

Despite being anti-French as a rule, the British readily appropriate French wording, especially in the kitchen. A zucchini is a courgette, an eggplant is an aubergine, a coffee maker is a cafétiere. In fact, everything food-related is called something different – corn starch is corn flour, French fries are called chips, chips are called crisps, and crisps are called clusters. A crepe is called a pancake, a pancake is called an American pancake, and if you ask for a flapjack you will be handed a granola bar. I stopped reading in the shops and learned to just look at pictures on packaging.

But that did not solve every linguistic problem. Wearing a skirt on a chilly evening, I mentioned that I wished I had worn pants, and people furtively checked if I was wearing any underwear. After that, I learned to call them trousers so no one would call me Britney Spears.

Even the government enjoyed an ironic turn of phrase. "Leave to stay" was both the permission stamped on my passport to visit for six months and the fact that I had to go back to the states to apply for a more permanent work visa. In mid-May, I did just that. I had no visa yet in sight.

I fell back into the arms of the city I loved, the city that loved me.

When I arrived in Seattle, I stayed with close friends for several weeks, until they told me I needed to find a more permanent situation. I could not formally rent an apartment, since I did not have a job and could not show income. I sought a sublet under the radar, and found two medical students who were abandoning their pad in the U-District for the summer. One of the guys was already gone, and the other handed over the keys to a three-month sublet in exchange for $600 in cash.

The next evening, after I had moved in, I sat in the open-plan living room while my new roommate puttered in the kitchen behind me.

"I thought you said you would be flying back to the Midwest today," I mentioned.

"I've decided to stay another week," he said.

"Oh, I see."

"Hey, I'm making some pasta for dinner, do you want some?" he asked. "I think I'm gonna open a bottle of wine too."

It sounded like this was turning into date night. I thought of all the other times I had unexpectedly found myself trapped in a place with a man I didn't know well, in a rapidly evolving situation. This would not necessarily end the same way, but I would not be able to sleep the night as long as he was there. The last thing I wanted right now was a he said-she said situation to deal with.

"No, thanks," I said, shutting my laptop. I packed a blanket and a change of clothing into a bag, and walked out the door into the evening air, heading west. At Gasworks Park, I found a little knot of trees tucked behind the building and slept there until first light. I watched as the sun rose over the Cascade Mountains, then advanced slowly over the city and the lakes. As the noise of traffic began to fill the air, I packed up my bag and walked through Wallingford, crossed the University Bridge, and headed down Eastlake Avenue to reach the South Lake Union complex where Steve and Will had their labs.

When we moved from Harborview Medical Center to South Lake Union in 2008, the city's wealthy benefactor Paul Allen had just begun renovating the neighborhood before providing the University of Washington and Amazon with 99-year leases on a number of stunning new glass buildings. When we arrived that year, the location was still a no-man's-land above Belltown. There were a few dingy pubs nearby and a trophy shop across the street which allowed us to recognize our friends and colleagues for their achievements. Within a year, there were luxury apartment buildings and a light rail system under construction on the surrounding blocks, with a Whole

Foods, several martini bars, and a Tesla dealership already open for business around the corner.

I arrived at the South Lake Union labs and went in search of Steve. He was in his corner office, accessible from the lab office, which itself was separate from the bench-space we used for experiments. The lab office contained a few desks with computers, some printers, and also a couch, which I had convinced Steve to buy so that I could nap while doing 72-hour thymidine analog labelling experiments on my cells. He had agreed, as the furniture completed the space well. One of the post-docs had brought plants in, and the office became a really nice place to work.

Now the reviewers of my paper had demanded that I repeat the 72-hour thymidine analog labelling in animals, not just in cells in a dish, to find out if the effect was true in the actual brain. It would be a massive effort that I expected to take most of the summer. I was glad the couch was still there, although I would only need it for the next week or so while I was conducting the experiment, not while I was analyzing the tissues and using the microscope. Hopefully my unexpected roommate would have left by then, and I could stay in the apartment I had paid for. It was a reasonable plan.

"Hi Steve, it's me. I'm back."

"Oh good."

"How are things over here?"

"Fine. How's England?"

"It was fine when I left."

"You're back here now?"

"Just for a couple months. Um, hey, can you buy me some mice?"

I explained what experiments I thought would address the concerns raised during peer review, practicing the argument I would present to the editor of the journal. "So in summary I think that two big animal experiments are necessary in order to publish the two papers. And I am prepared to do these experiments this summer."

"OK, sure." Steve did not seem at all surprised that I had returned to Seattle to finish the job.

"Great, so I can order some mice then?"

"Yep, that's fine."

"Cool. Also, Steve, can I sleep on this couch for a little while?"

"Yep, no problem."

"And... is there any chance you'll pay me to do this work?"

"Nope." He had somehow gotten the impression I was not in a strong negotiating position. I should have started the discussion by asking if he would pay me to do the experiments. In the end it had seemed like I was asking him for a favor, when in actuality it was a mutually beneficial situation. He was getting senior authorship on both papers.

"OK," I agreed anyway. At least I had a safe place to spend the night, and a chance to do something productive over the next few months.

Later that week, I met up with my friends Cynthia and Skye at the Redwood Tavern for some beer and burgers and catch-up time.

Skye had long curly blond hair and often wore double denim. Her job involved mapping lakes and rivers for an environmental consulting firm. Cynthia had long straight dark hair with blue streaks, and was prone to wearing t-shirts with curse words on them. She worked in IT and projected films at the local indie movie theater. They were both good company, especially when you were having a bad time of it.

My thirtieth birthday was in a few days. I groaned when they brought this up.

"You can't skip celebrating your thirtieth," Cynthia argued. Hers was coming up soon too, and we were helping her to mark the occasion by remaking her favorite birthday-themed movie, the John Hughes classic Sixteen Candles.

"I don't have anything to celebrate. I moved to another country for a man, which was stupid, and now I'm homeless, jobless, not sure where my life is going."

"Come on," Skye said. "You have to do something for your thirtieth."

We eventually agreed on a Sunday morning picnic in the park, with a small number of close friends.

When the day arrived, I realized that Rose and Lila, my old roommates, had never met my other group of friends. We just had separate spheres – I spent a lot of time with them, just the three of us, and the rest of my time with the big crowd. I enjoyed introducing them, finally.

We laughed and told stories over mimosas and cinnamon rolls and coffee and a Tupperware full of crispy American bacon. After the party, my friend Ryan asked for Rose's phone number. I had never imagined them together, but apparently the list of things they had in common was long and there was a little spark too.

When the two of them got married three years later, and I stood up to give a toast at their wedding, I decided it was for the best that my life fell apart and I ended up in Seattle that crazy summer. I had unfinished business there, introducing those two.

My work done, I dusted my hands, wrapped up my

experiments, and submitted my revised manuscripts for publication. A few days later, I finally received my visa in the mail, allowing me to return to England and my future husband.

I breathed a sigh of relief. Now I could really begin my life in the UK.

Chapter 11
Competition

Stupidly, on Steve's suggestion, I had written a grant proposal on 'Metabolic fuel requirements of adult neural stem cells' and submitted it to the National Institutes of Health under his name. Steve had told me it would be good practice for writing grants before I graduated, and it was. I wrote myself into the grant as a fully-funded Named Research Fellow, as a backup plan in case things did not work out in England.

Steve was awarded $347,000 for the grant proposal in 2011 but never told me it was funded. I found out later, through the public database maintained by the National Institutes of Health (NIH). The money arrived a month after I spent the summer working for free in his lab. I never saw a penny.

The following spring, not knowing my project proposal had already received significant funding from the NIH, I applied for a fellowship to support my post-doctoral research project. The virtually identical grant proposal was also entitled 'Metabolic fuel requirements of adult neural stem cells'. I was selected for interview by the European Molecular Biology Organization (EMBO). I flew to Zurich for an interview to visit Bentham Noeburger in his laboratory there.

Bentham had been a post-doc at the same time as

Steve, years ago, in the same large prestigious lab in California. They were buddies. I almost felt part of a network.

The interview went well. Bentham seemed very familiar with biochemistry, much more so than most other cellular biologists. He was even at home with fatty acid metabolism, the particular biochemical pathway I was investigating. He asked very good questions and I was pleased for the opportunity to elaborate on my theoretical framework and experimental design. The discussion built on itself, with the thrilling excitement that my interviewer understood that I was onto something.

I left the interview elated, knowing I had done my best. Later that evening, I met up with friends who were working in Zurich and nearby Basel, including my old classmate Jack Fadden. We had a barbeque and drank beers around the fire pit. Long after midnight, I walked back to my hotel in the city center, appreciating how the spring blossoms on the trees glistened pink under the moonlight.

After flying back to Newcastle, I learned that I had not received the fellowship.

Months later, I saw Bentham at a conference on neural stem cells in Bavaria. He had been awarded a new, more senior fellowship with that same organization, EMBO. He had also gained a few pounds. He was comfortable, and he looked it. I cornered him at the bar after the first day of talks. He didn't waste a second with small talk.

"I heard you didn't get that fellowship," he said, sipping his pint. "Must have been your other interviewer."

"I didn't have another interviewer," I replied. "It was just you."

He honestly looked surprised. "Really? I gave you the same review as the other guy I interviewed – strong scientist, great project."

"That can't have been the whole story," I said. "Are you sure there were no other factors?"

He tilted his head. "Well, I also mentioned that I wanted to pursue the research you proposed myself."

"Ah," I said. "You know, that might have had an effect on their decision. You were already funded by them, and they wanted you to be successful."

"Maybe," he said, pretending not to be interested in my point. "Anyway, I'm working in that area already."

"Yes, I saw your talk this afternoon," I said, seething now. "But you're working on how neural stem cells synthesize fatty acids, not how they break down fatty acids to make energy. You're on anabolism, I'm on catabolism. They're two entirely different stories."

"Yeah, and I want both of those stories." Bentham set down his drink and looked straight at me, his voice and his eyes hard, dropping all pretense of it being a friendly conversation. Our gaze held for a moment, but I looked away first, frustrated by his heartless cruelty. His fatty acid synthesis paper was under review at *Nature* and he had enormous resources at his disposal. But I had a head-start on the fatty acid breakdown study. I would continue my work.

It's like I bring out this ferocity in the men around me. In conversation, I draw out their aggressiveness into the open air like a tapeworm. I had figured out what Bentham was willing to do to get ahead, and he didn't care – he let me see his ruthlessness and ambition, he even reveled in showing it to me. I just shook my head and backed away.

I didn't go to any conferences for the next three years, except Society for Neuroscience - which is more of a reunion of old friends and classmates than anything else. Also, it's conveniently dated in November so that neuroscientists living across the globe can celebrate Thanksgiving with family and friends on the same trip to America.

So I kept my head down and worked for three more years. Then, in June of 2015, I booked myself into a neural regeneration conference in Dresden. My paper identifying the metabolic fuel requirements of neural stem cells – primarily fatty acid metabolism, indeed – was published days before the meeting. Four years of work before submitting that EMBO fellowship application, two years of work afterwards, and one year of submitting to journals, revising the text and proofing the manuscript. I had gotten my story out, and in a decent journal: Stem Cells. Upon arriving, I saw Bentham in the conference lobby.

"Hi Bentham."

"I saw your paper," he said right away, not wasting any time on chitter-chatter.

"What, do you have a google alert on me?" I asked, feeling saucy.

"Yeah, of course I do," he said matter-of-factly. "So I can find out when you scoop me."

My mouth dropped. "You didn't actually pursue that project, did you?"

"Yeah," he replied. "Of course I did. It's interesting, it's true, and it's potentially really important."

"You weren't a reviewer when I submitted it to Cell Metabolism and got rejected from that journal?" I asked, honestly not knowing if he wanted the story out there or he did only if he could tell it. "I'm sorry, I shouldn't have asked that," I said. Reviewers are supposed to remain anonymous.

"No, but I knew it was coming out."

"But you worked on it these past few years? You thought, because I didn't get that EMBO funding, that I wouldn't be able to pursue that project?" I was stunned.

He just looked at me. I continued. "Do you know how much funding Nick Armstrong has?! He has the financing to support an entire center for research on neural and neuromuscular aging. He covered my post-doc work for years because he has tons of money and he knows a good project when he sees one too. Just because he's not in your field, doesn't mean he wasn't able to support this work. Also, you could have asked Steve, my PhD supervisor, if I was likely to drop a study that I had already been pursuing for years."

I shook my head, honestly baffled at Bentham's bad decision. "You should have done your homework. Then you wouldn't have wasted your own time."

"My staff's time," Bentham said mildly.

"You put a post-doc on this?!"

"Yeah, and now they've been scooped."

I shook my head incredulously.

"It's okay," he declared, brightening up. "We're going in a different direction on it. You'll hear about it – I'm giving a talk this morning." He smiled. It was all in the past already.

I was intrigued, and I went to his talk. It was about palmitoylation, the process by which fatty acid molecules are attached to proteins to affect their localization, facilitating hydrophobic interactions, particularly with lipid membranes. It was good, there was a story there. It was early days though - there was so much novelty to the study that it was hard to even fathom all the potential directions it could go. There are just too many fatty acids, too many proteins, too many sites on those proteins that potentially could interact with fatty acids, so many implications for cellular function and disease, and to make it even more complicated, much redundancy in the system. My mind swirled. What an ambitious problem to have chosen, I thought. I'll stay away from this one. He's marked his territory.

During the next session, I sat next to Bentham in the lecture theatre.

"I liked your talk," I said. "Interesting direction you're taking."

"Yeah? Do you think it's a worthwhile problem?"

"Definitely, there's a lot to dig into there."

He smiled and leaned back in his chair.

Chapter 12
Marriage

After not being awarded the fellowship, I felt knocked down. My boss, Nick, had informed me that he would not renew my visa a third time, so with one year of post-doctoral research experience under my belt, I had just one year left before I would have to leave the country and seek another job. Nick was very supportive, but not unconditionally and forever.

I was devastated. I had grown to love Andy, and I wanted us to stay together.

We spent my birthday weekend in the Lake District, hiking along the fells and stopping for tea along the lakeside. I had come across a cookbook with recipes from each the local restaurants in the region, and Andy took me to dinner to one of my favorites. I thought maybe he would propose during the special meal; getting married was the only way I could stay in the country now.

He didn't.

At the end of the weekend, on the bank holiday Monday, we gathered our things together and packed them into the car, ready to drive back to Newcastle.

He wasn't going to propose.

In one year I would have to leave him and our life

together. And during the next few months, he would be angry that I was looking for jobs elsewhere – that I was getting ready to abandon him. I sat down on the sofa and cried.

"Why are you crying?" he asked.

"Because after everything we've been through, I'm going to have to leave you. I wish you would do something to help us stay together. I've done everything I can."

"What, you want us to get married?"

"I don't want to tell you what to do. I don't want this situation to be forced. I want you to know what to do."

"Well, I was going to talk about engagement this weekend, but there just wasn't the right moment. I planned a walk for today to do just that, but now you're crying."

"I thought we were about to leave. The car is already packed."

"No, I thought we'd go for a walk first."

"OK, then," I said hopefully.

We strolled along the low path that swung past Loughrigg Fell, crossing a field edged by a stream and following the water upriver, toward Rydal Falls. We sat down on the large stones alongside the cascading water. Andy took my hand.

"I would like us to get married," he said.

"OK," I said.

"The time will come, you just have to be patient."

"Andy, you need to step up if you want us to keep going. Otherwise I will have to leave. I just don't have a choice in this." My fingers played in the grass, picking the blades in nervousness and hope.

"You could just propose to me, you know."

"I could, honey, but I need something from you. My position is coerced, and so I wouldn't be asking out of pure love alone. You though – you are free. You can decide truly if you want to be single or if you want us to be together."

"OK," he agreed, and smiled. "One day we should get married."

"I hope so," I said.

When we arrived home, we settled into our pattern for the week, making our usual Sunday evening phone calls to our parents and my friends back home in Seattle.

Over dinner, Andy got upset.

"You didn't tell anyone we're engaged!"

"We're not engaged."

"Yes, we are. We had that talk."

"That was a conversation, not a proposal."

"No, it was a proposal. We're engaged."

"But honey, there's no ring on my finger. We're not engaged."

"What, you just want expensive jewelry now?"

"What?! You know I don't care about jewelry – all I wear is a watch, I don't even have pierced ears. This has nothing to do with expensive jewelry."

He stared at me doubtfully.

"You could have put a blade of grass around my finger," I stated. "I need something to show people back home. You announce an engagement with a photo of a ring, that's traditional. Every time one of our friends back home has gotten engaged, I have shown you that kind of photo."

"Well you should have explained this at the time, not gotten angry after the fact."

"OK, I'm sorry, I'll try to do better next time." I was feeling frustrated now, and not sure why I was apologizing.

We went back to work. It kept both of our minds busy. But every weekend, I woke up remembering that our life together would have to end soon, and I would sob in bed, unable to get up. The noise did not wake Andy – I slept in the loft bedroom now so that his snores at night would not wake me and my tears in the morning would not wake him. He refused to discuss either.

We had moved into a bigger place than the one-bedroom flat along the Quayside. It was a cute little house in a new subdivision, with a grass lawn in the back. We had planted flowers and shrubs around the edges, and allowed the grass covering the rest of the area to grow freely into wildflowers, only weeding away the dandelions that outcompeted other species. Our little prairie, with its neat hedges, exploded with color – azaleas, begonias, Puget Blue, red poppies, yellow buttercups, violet campanula. It was a collaboration, a mix of both English and American gardens. On Sundays, we worked in the garden, then sat in lawn chairs in the late afternoon sunshine, grinning at each other and the fruits of our labor.

One weekend that summer, there was an art installation at Bamburgh Castle, one of the marvelous twelfth-century ruins along the east coast of England and Scotland, so it was possible to take a night walk lit by lanterns. Andy suggested we go.

My hopes rose. It sounded so romantic.

We put on our jackets to brave the chilly English summer evening, but the car would not start. Andy tried several times, with no luck.

We sighed, got out of the car and trudged through the yard back toward the house. I stopped in the grass behind him as he reached the door.

"Andy, if there's something you need to do, you can do it right here," I said, gesturing to our beautiful yard, with its abundant vegetation, still living and vivid in the waning light.

He hesitated, his fingers no longer fiddling with the key.

After a moment, he spoke. "I'm not going to piss in the garden. I'll just use the toilet inside." He unlocked the door and stepped into the house.

I stood outside for a moment longer. There are a few seconds that linger in the shadow of words, a short moment when they can still be taken back. After that, everything changes forever and you would need to build a time machine to find your way back to a moment when there was still hope for the future.

I walked in the house, sat down on the sofa and cried. I cried most of the rest of the summer.

Early one Saturday morning, I crawled into bed with Andy.

"Don't you want us to stay together? Won't you do something to help us stay together?" I begged him.

He was angry to be woken up this way. He threw off the sheets, told me to stop complaining, then got up and went into the en-suite bathroom, slamming the door behind him. I put my head in my hands and wept harder.

He stormed out of the bathroom and out of the bedroom too. He returned a minute later, holding a small brown box with a gold trim along the edges.

"You think I don't have a ring?" he shouted. "I have a ring. I'm waiting for a damn weekend you're not crying to give it to you."

My eyes were wide with terror. This was not how I expected to receive news of an engagement ring.

"Don't open the box," I uttered. "Don't open the box now."

"Don't worry, I won't," he snarled. "You're too much of a bitch to ever deserve it anyway."

I couldn't breathe. The pain was agonizing. "Andy,

Andy," I called as he reached the frame of the bedroom door. He stopped and turned around.

"Andy, if you ever change your mind and you want to show me that ring in earnest," I spoke, the words flowing through my tears, "Please, please, promise me you'll put it into a different box. Please don't ever make me see that same brown box again."

"Fine," he shrugged, and walked away with the box.

Through the autumn, I grew resigned to the fact I would have to leave. Andy had made his position clear. I had just begun digging into my post-doctoral research and the studies were nowhere near complete. I would not be getting any papers out any time soon. I would have to start from scratch, calling these two years in England, plus my period of unemployment, a complete wash.

It was almost liberating. I decided to travel in Europe before leaving my post. After all, we got weeks of vacation time and there was no good reason to waste it. On the first weekend in December, six months after my birthday weekend and eight months before I would have to leave England, I booked myself a few days' trip to Prague. Then, when I arrived back in Newcastle after my short holiday, I would begin applying for jobs back in the states.

That week, Andy attended a conference in Munich. Afterwards, he took the train to meet me in Prague. He found me in my hotel room there, and suggested we dress up to go out for dinner. I could see what he was thinking. I had been cheerful over the past few weeks and months, feeling in charge of my future, and as a result he was much happier with our life together.

We strolled through the city toward the river. On Charles Bridge, Andy slowed to a stop under one of the baroque iron lampposts, knelt down on one knee, and took a box out of his jacket pocket.

The light was dim, but the thin gold trim around the edge of the small brown square was unmistakable. My heart stopped, but for the wrong reason.

He spoke words about building a life together. I did not hear them much, although they seemed to summarize all the right notions in the right order. There was no way to concentrate on what he was saying underneath the shrieking of that little brown box. It was open now, like a mouth, the tongue a soft cream color with a ring sitting snugly inside. The ring didn't move despite the shattering noise emanating from the box, except perhaps a small discernible tremor. I stared at this ring, hypnotized. It was perfectly round, and in its center it held a diamond that was perfectly round too.

It was as boring as such a thing could be – brand-new, with no history to give it heft; the stone clear, with no color inside it; the circular shape unbearably plain and anonymous, like the monochrome stock photo of a happy couple that comes with a new picture frame. This ring may have cost money, but it barely existed in the dimension I cared about.

I looked at it, and I looked at him. My Andy. He was so beautiful, his face so hopeful in that moment.

He was trying so hard. He just didn't care about symbolism, he never had. I had fallen in love with this literal man, knowing perfectly well that he had always been unembroidered by abstract notions of beauty – How could I fault him for that now? How could I fault him for picking such a boring engagement ring? And how could I, at a time like this, say something about the box it was in? Or the fact that diamonds were a product of slave labor, a signature of privilege built on the back of global inequality? Surely what mattered was our bond. That was the important thing.

Andy wanted us to set aside the past and all our differences. After all, once circumstances got easier, agreement would be easy between us. He was hoping for the best, and he wanted us to have a future together. He said all these things, and he looked at me. How could I say no?

"Yes," I said. What was I going to do, after all this time, leave him? Lose faith in us, right when he was ready to make things work? He rose to his feet, still looking in my eyes, and smiling harder than I'd ever seen him smile before.

My heart soared, seeing that smile. He kissed me, and people passing by stopped to clap and cheer. We parted lips, laughing, then kissed again and stumbled through the snowflakes to the other side of the bridge, holding hands through our winter gloves.

We spent Christmas with my family. I had been so scattered that year, I had skipped the annual Society for Neuroscience meeting followed by Thanksgiving in the United States, and instead had forced Andy's family to celebrate Thanksgiving in London. They were as flustered as I was.

"We're going to have a roast goose, a month before Christmas?" Andy's mother asked.

"Christmas won't be Christmas if we've already had a goose," Andy's father pointed out.

I had Andy explain to them we would be having a turkey and Christmas would still be Christmas. I thought that settled the discussion, but Andy had enjoyed the mild confusion, so he kept it going.

"Cranberry sauce? Are you sure you don't want mint sauce with the goose?" he asked as I stood by the stove.

"It's not a goose, honey, it's a turkey. And yes, I'm making cranberry sauce."

"We won't be able to find a turkey. But it's nearly Christmas, we might be able to find a goose."

"There are tons of American ex-pats in London, we can find a goose. I mean a turkey."

"Are you sure it has to be a turkey? A goose is lovely around the holidays."

"Yes, it has to be a turkey." As expected, we had no trouble finding a turkey. There was a whole range of options, including free-range and grass-fed birds, at the Waitrose shop in Hampstead. I picked out a massive turkey that would be big enough for the whole family, with more for leftovers.

Andy sat with his sister's children as I prepared the family meal in his parents' kitchen. The two boys were making drawings on the kitchen table. I had shown them how to trace their hands to make the outline of a turkey, and Andy was providing expert advice on the color of feathers.

"Do you know about Thanksgiving?" Andy asked his nephews, as they switched crayons.

"Yes, I do," replied Bobby, who was six.

"No, what is it?" Timmy asked. He was three.

"It's when the Americans killed all the native people so they could take their land," Bobby explained to his little brother. The boy was clearly receiving a thorough education at the expensive private school he attended in north London.

"Uh," I said. "It's more of a celebration of the one time we all tried to get along."

Timmy looked at me suspiciously.

"We should have kept doing that," I explained, "But Bobby's right, we hurt our friends instead."

"Are Americans bad people?" Timmy asked, still eyeing

me distrustfully.

"We're just like everyone else," I explained. "Sometimes we can be good, and sometimes we can be bad."

"Your holiday sounds perfectly dreadful," Timmy declared, in his baby-posh voice.

"It's supposed to be nice. It's supposed to be about sharing food with each other," I told him.

"Do we get presents?" he asked.

"No, but we'll have a nice meal together. And we can go around the table and each of us can say what we're thankful for this year."

"No presents?"

"No presents."

"Hmm," Timmy said. I could tell Thanksgiving was not catching on here. In future years, I promised myself, I would remember to go back to the states for this holiday. It would be better to be around Americans for Thanksgiving, then celebrate Christmas in London with the kids.

But this year was already mixed up. After our engagement, we flew to Chicagoland for Christmas. Andy mentioned the goose so many times that my mother went out and found one.

"Is this a goose or a duck?" Andy asked, holding it up.

"Duck, duck, goose," my father said helpfully.

"I don't know, I looked everywhere, I called everyone, and when I found this one, they said it was a goose," my mother replied anxiously.

"It's a bird that will produce more fat than a turkey or a chicken," I told Andy pointedly, through my teeth. "That is what you wanted."

"If it's not the right thing, we can call around some more places," my mother spoke quickly, purposefully ramping up the tension. "I called all the grocery stores in the north and west suburbs, and your father went to pick this one up. If it's not right, we can try to find something else. He can drive around until he finds the thing that you want. He can keep driving, you just need to explain what you want."

This was getting out of hand. "Andy, this bird is good enough, right?" I noticed my mother tearing up at the words 'good enough'. "Andy, this bird is great, right? It's perfect. It'll be delicious."

"As long as this bird produces fat that will make the roast potatoes and parsnips properly crisp in the oven, I will be happy," he announced, refusing to be kind to my mother when she was trying so hard to make us feel indebted for her efforts.

"I don't understand what you want, I'll just leave you to cook Christmas dinner," my mother said, the tension broken. I knew she was relieved not to have to be in the kitchen. Her preferred contribution was a store-bought plate of shrimp and carrot sticks and celery sticks and olives. My brother and my father were sensibly staying out of the kitchen.

As we prepared the holiday meal, my mother returned with a pile of folders.

"These are the plans for the wedding," she announced, plopping them down on the table. "See what you think." Andy and I looked at each other.

"Uh, hey Mom," I said as she walked out the door. "Hold up. What wedding?"

"Oh, I've reserved a private room at the Signature Lounge, on the 96th floor of the Hancock Building."

"Holy Christ, what?"

"Yes, it'll be on a Saturday in August, so there'll be fireworks over Lake Michigan." She turned and walked up the stairs.

I strode across the kitchen, my heart pounding with excitement, set the stereo to the Kanye song with those exact lyrics, and started dancing.

"What's going on?" Andy asked, peeling parsnips.

"Fireworks on Lake Michigan!" I sang, pointing at the stereo. "Our wedding!"

"When?" he yelled over the music.

"August!" I yelled back. Then I stopped dancing. I needed a visa before then.

I ran up the stairs. "Hey, Mom," I said, "We need to have a wedding in Newcastle before then."

"That's fine, but this'll be the real wedding. I need all of your efforts on this."

"Hey, Mom, we're gonna need to sort out things in Newcastle before June. Do you want to plan the party here?"

"No, we're going to work on this together. There's a lot to do and you need to put the work in."

"Well, Mom, that'll be hard to do from Newcastle, when we're planning a wedding there."

"You're having a wedding here."

"Mom, I have to get married in England this spring."

"I have nothing to do with that."

"Uh, do you want anything to do with that?"

"No, I'm planning my wedding in Chicago."

"You mean, my wedding?"

"Yes, your wedding. In Chicago."

"OK," I agreed, and slunk out of the room.

My mother's best friend Louella came over to visit. She sat in the dining room over dinner as my mother described the wedding she was planning, and then sat in the bedroom upstairs as my mother tried on various outfits she might wear. Louella listened and watched patiently. I sat next to her.

"I'm also having a wedding," I mentioned. "And I also have a dress. No one cares."

Louella gave me a dirty look. "Your mother is enjoying this, and that's okay."

I nodded – it was a fair point. Louella was a very wise woman.

I wished I was closer to her, actually. She was my godmother and my confirmation sponsor, but I had never really spoken to her about my childhood depression and resulting loss of faith. I knew my mother had talked to her about it though. At one point – years ago – I had tried to reach out by email, but Louella had not written back. I tried again now.

"You know, I was a sad little kid."

"I know, your mother told me."

"Yeah, I realize she told you a lot of things. Like when she found my journals as a teenager – all that stuff was about killing myself, but she thought I wanted to kill her."

"Don't put everyone through this again."

"I just want you to know. That stupid teenage angst poetry was about suicide, not about hurting my mother. She just assumes that everything I say and do is about her."

"Stop. Just stop putting everyone through this. It's in the past now."

"But the poems were called 'suicide' and 'desolation' and stuff like that. I never wanted to hurt her."

"Don't bring this up again."

"You know I had two best friends growing up? One of them threw herself in front of a train, and the other spent her entire life in and out of hospitals, with anorexia, trying to starve herself to death. My depression started when they both exited my life in the fourth grade."

"Stop dredging it all up," Louella snapped. "Stop

torturing everyone." I sighed and turned away, the sadness tightening like a vise around my heart.

The days that followed were filled with so much disagreement and confusion that it is difficult to remember exactly what happened. Only flickers of memories exist from that week.

I remember that, at some point, we decided it would be a good idea for Andy's and my parents to meet each other over skype, so we set up a video call. I set my parents in front of the computer, and Andy's sister set their parents in front of her iPad in London.

Andy and I stepped back as the connection was made, glancing at each other silently.

"Hello," the four parents greeted each other gingerly. Both fathers poked at the screen.

"How is your Christmas?" Andy's mother Mary asked, in her perfect Queen's English.

There was a pause.

"Are you wearing a hat to the wedding?" my mother responded. I breathed deeply in the background.

"No, I don't tend to wear hats," Mary replied.

"But maybe you should wear a hat," my mother tried again. "And we could coordinate." She unraveled a story which she had already chronicled several times that week, of how her mother and her mother-in-law had coordinated at her own wedding. Hats had been critical to the effort.

"That's nice," Mary said. "But I wish not to wear a hat."

"I don't wear hats either," said Pete, my future father-in-law.

"Oh, me neither. Don't wear hats," said my father, who had acquired a sort of Cockney accent. Andy and I opened a bottle of wine and poured ourselves each a glass.

"I don't normally wear hats in warm weather, but this does seem like the sort of occasion that requires it." My mother had chosen this battle and she was not done fighting it.

"Well, you should definitely wear a hat then," Mary encouraged her.

"Well, I'm not going to if you're not going to. But we really should. I think we should wear hats."

"I don't think I'll wear a hat," Mary said, as if it were the first time it had been brought up.

"You know who likes a hat?" my dad said.

"Who?" Mary and Pete asked, simultaneously.

"I don't know, I was asking you," my father said.

"No, no one really wears hats anymore do they," Mary and Pete tuttered. My mother looked crestfallen. She began to explain about the second wedding, or rather the lead-up to it, including each of the restaurants in Chicago she was booking in the week preceding the party.

"Oh, my, this is all quite overwhelming," Mary said. "We'll have to get back to you."

"No, the plans are all being made," my mother said. Andy and I poured another glass each. The wine was disappearing fast.

"Well, these two kids will plan their own wedding, I suppose," Pete said.

"No, they won't. Well, they can pick the flowers. At my florist. There will be roses and a spray. And they can pick the cake, but the caterers have already been chosen, they come with the venue."

"Well, the important thing is that our children are happy together," Mary said. "And I know Beth makes Andrew very happy."

"Who's Andrew?" my mother asked.

There was silence at the other end of the line. I was holding Andy as if he were a life preserver. I thought we might be within his parents' line of sight, so I tried to apologize with my face. Andy drank wine directly from the bottle. My dad walked out of the room.

"Who's Andrew?" my mother asked again.

"Andy, Mom," I said quietly behind her, holding onto my future husband as hard as I could.

"Oh, Andy!" she cried. "I thought you said Andrew." She paused. "Oh, Andrew! Right."

"Honestly, she's a brilliant woman," I told Andy later. "She just doesn't care about other people, or what they say, or their feelings."

He nodded wisely, patronizingly.

"Honey, I'm sorry," I told him.

He grinned at me, drunk.

By the end of the week, resentments had reached a boil. A key turning point, for Andy, was when my mother yelled at him for fixing the electronics in a heirloom Christmas music box while he was supposed to be doing wedding planning. No particular instructions had been issued, but it should have been obvious what the priorities were.

This was so far within my range of normal that I had trouble understanding his problem for a moment. Then I realized I had to say something to my mother.

"Mom, I'm really grateful you're planning this wedding."

"Yes, it's a nice thing. You'll have a beautiful wedding and lovely memories of it."

"But Mom, it sort of seems like you have a particular thing in mind. Are you sure you don't want to plan this party by yourself?"

"You're saying you're not going to help? You're just going to leave all this work to me?"

"Mom, I'm sorry, but I think this is a situation where there are too many cooks in the kitchen."

"I do all this for you, and this is what you do to me in return, leave me with all this work?"

"Mom, trust me, there's nothing I would like more than this wedding, but I just can't put the energy toward it right now. Maybe if you'd put it off for a bit longer, until we're done with the wedding in Newcastle –"

"You don't want this wedding in Chicago?"

"No, trust me, I do!" I thought of the Kanye song again. I really liked that tune. I wanted to hear it while actually watching fireworks over Lake Michigan. I could not imagine a more special wedding present. "I want it more than anything, Mom. I would love for my friends to watch me get married, and most of them won't be able to come to Newcastle, and they would love to come to Chicago. No one on the west coast has visited here, and it would be so wonderful to get everyone together –"

"Your friends aren't invited."

"Sorry, what?"

"This gathering is only for my friends. Your friends are not invited. This is going to be a classy party, and your friends are not classy."

I was baffled. My mother had only met a couple of my friends, and this description did not fit them. "Mom, what do you mean my friends aren't classy? That's not true, and not a nice thing to say."

She snorted in derision.

"Mom, if this party is for your friends, then it's your party."

"But you'll help me plan it."

"Mom, I can't do that, I have a lot of things to sort out in Newcastle."

"You're leaving all this work to me."

"Mom, if you want this party for your friends, you're going to have to plan it yourself. Andy and I may or may not come. But don't pretend it's about us, and don't involve us anymore."

It was settled. Andy and I would have our wedding in Newcastle. My mother changed her booking to the following April and used the party to celebrate her 40th wedding anniversary with my father. There were no fireworks and no hip-hop music, but other than that, it was a very nice gathering.

In the meantime, Andy and I had a wedding to plan in Newcastle. As soon as we returned to England after the holidays, we set to work.

Work, if you could call it that. I had never managed a project this fun or rewarding. We tried cakes at several bakeries, three-course meals at several venues, wine at the local distributers. We had our photo taken professionally in the park, put together a mixtape of our favorite songs for our guests, and sat in the florists surrounded by a harmony of sweet scents, all jumbled together like jazz notes.

Every single venue was booked every single weekend through the entire summer, except for 13 April 2013. We looked at each other and shrugged, figuring everyone else must be superstitious. We went ahead and booked the date, at a charming hotel right in the center of town. The venue had a stunning ballroom and a photo-perfect winding staircase in the foyer, a convenient location across the street from the main train station for our guests coming from elsewhere in the country, and a wedding package which totaled £5000 including the catering.

We set up a meeting at the registrar's office and arrived at the town hall on a weekday. People were getting married right then and there. I squeezed Andy's hand and smiled at him warmly. I was so glad that, even though we were rushed, we were going to get hitched properly, with a big party.

When our names were called, we went into a little office. The registrar welcomed us and explained her role: to ensure our marriage was real and to make sure we weren't blood-related.

"Gross," I whispered to Andy. He nodded. Upon questioning, I revealed my American citizenship, German heritage on my father's side and Irish heritage on my mother's side. Andy confirmed he was English as far back as he knew. We submitted our birth records.

"And I know your marriage is real," the woman said, nodding at our hands entangled on the armrest between our chairs. "I can tell just by looking at you too."

I felt a tiny pang of guilt then, and looked at Andy. "Well," I said, swallowing. "I am looking to get a spousal visa. We're doing this so we have stability in that regard."

"Yes, but I can tell you're in love," she said. "And that is something I am required to confirm."

"Yes," Andy and I said, smiling into each other's eyes. "Yes, we are in love."

"I can always tell," the woman said warmly. "An American and a Brit, you two, it's for sure."

We turned to look at her.

"An Indian and a Pakistani, now, that's a different story."

Our smiles faltered, and we looked at each other uncertainly.

"Or a Turk and a Greek, you know that's not real."

Andy shifted in his seat.

"Um," I whispered in a hoarse voice.

"These people just don't get along, so you know it's some kind of scam if they're pretending to want to get married."

"Um," I said again, swallowing. "Do you ever get, like, a Romeo and Juliet situation?"

The registrar stared at me from across the desk. "No," she said, with a hard stare.

"OK," I said.

"OK," Andy agreed.

"Let's get you two married then!" the woman grinned at us and stamped the paperwork.

We stood up and thanked her, took the paperwork and left the building as quickly as we could. Outside, we stopped and faced each other.

"I really hope she's not the registrar assigned to marry us on the day," Andy said. He was ruffled.

"Is that possible? What should we do?" I asked.

"Let's just make sure the ceremony is as nice as imaginable otherwise," Andy proposed.

"That's a good idea." I grinned. "I know, let's get a backup minister for the ceremony just in case."

My old classmate Jack, who had introduced the two of us shortly after I moved to Seattle, was just the guy. He had long ago acquired a license to marry people, and indeed had presided over the weddings of several couples in our group of friends over the years. He had gained the certification and the title of Reverend Fadden for ten dollars off the internet from the Church of Beer, which was registered in the state of Nevada. This arrangement was completely legal in the United

States of America. We doubted that Her Majesty's government of the United Kingdom of Great Britain and Northern Ireland would recognize this sacred institution, but the two of us certainly answered to no higher spiritual authority. We asked the Reverend Fadden to give a sermon at the wedding so as bind our hearts together, and he agreed.

Luckily, on the day, the registrar who showed up was not the racist Shakespearean neophyte we had previously encountered. She was a lovely woman who was happy to accommodate our own vows and a sermon from a dear friend as part of the ceremony, as well as waiting patiently during the inevitable ring mix-up and cheering with everyone else as we danced down the aisle at the end.

In the hallway outside, Andy and I kissed, thrilled to finally belong to each other. I recounted the feeling I had, seeing him waiting there at the front of the room, as I entered with the music. I had never seen anyone so handsome, and walking up to him I only became more suffused with joy.

"My brilliant, beautiful Andy. Now you're mine, you're mine, you're mine forever," I repeated, tears running down my face. "I love you so much, honey."

"You were so beautiful coming up the aisle, sweetie. And everything went so well. The ring mix-up was funny, and the way you hitched your voice during the vows, it was just perfect."

"Huh? My voice might have hitched because I was crying, honey."

"I know, but it was perfect timing. I could tell everyone in the audience felt that emotion, that tug at their heartstrings, like at the climax of a movie."

I looked at him funny. "Andy, you know that was real, right? I feel like I shouldn't have to say that."

"Oh, yeah. Yeah, of course, I know." He sort of winked.

"Honey," I spoke gently. "You know that's how people feel at special times, right?" Then I realized something. His voice hadn't hitched during our vows. In fact I'd never seen him anywhere near tears.

Before I could speak, our guests streamed out of the chapel. Waiters swarmed, handing out glasses of champagne as we received hugs and kisses, greeting babies with little warm nudges on their cheeks and hands. We could see our parents in the next room, receiving congratulations too. Friends and colleagues and cousins and toddlers from both sides mingled, and the room took on the atmosphere of a party.

My mother-in-law Mary had recited a sonnet – beautifully and from memory – during the ceremony, and now my dad gave a toast. Then Andy stood to thank each person in turn who had helped with our planning, especially his groomsmen and my bridesmaids and our parents. I stood up next, not one to be quiet while my husband spoke for the both of us. I took a deep breath.

"I especially want to thank our parents, both Andy's and mine," I announced, looking around the room as I spoke into the mic, my gaze coming to rest on the family table.

"I have watched you, Mary and Pete, for years. And I have watched you, Mom and Dad, all my life. I have watched how you treat each other and I have watched your love stay strong and grow. You have shown us, through your words and actions, what it takes to stay married for many decades, through thick and thin. Your love inspires us, and it teaches us how to love each other too." I choked up and could not continue. I just ran over to their table and hugged all four parents in turn, my heart overflowing with happiness.

The DJ started playing the first dance, and everyone

cheered as Andy and I took the floor. Andy made a bit of a show at the end, dipping me low until I laughed, and when the next song began, everyone got up and joined us on the dancefloor. We had one heck of a party.

The next morning, I woke up and slipped out of bed, stepping up to the large window of our hotel suite that overlooked the nineteenth-century stone façade of the train station, the Literary & Philosophical Society, the castle and the cathedral just beyond. The morning air was crisp and fresh.

I looked down. On the street below, thousands and thousands of red-and-white striped jerseys were pouring out of the central metro station. They began to chant, loudly, and the noise filled the air.

"Andy," I murmured. I heard no response and I turned from the window. "Andy, is it the derby this weekend?"

"What?" he mumbled, rubbing his eyes. "What about the football?"

"Andy, did we ever find out why no one else is getting married this weekend?"

"It's the thirteenth," he smiled, his eyes still half-closed. "But it was fine. It was all fine."

"Honey, I think it might be the annual derby today. The Newcastle-Sunderland game. Come here."

Andy joined me at the window, pulling his hair as he stood looking down at the stream of singing Sunderland fans emerging into the streets of our city.

"Oh my god," he said softly. We put our clothes on and went downstairs to the ballroom. There were jackets and camera equipment everywhere. We found some leftover cake and ate it.

"Whose stuff is this?" we asked the staff.

"The local news teams," they answered. "The hotel is a

convenient place to leave their things while they're covering the riot."

"Are you sure there's going to be a riot today?" I asked.

"Seems like it," they shrugged.

Newcastle was always peculiar this way – like the city contained a hive mind. You could always tell when it was going to be a big night out on the town – a buzzing, energizing feeling filled the air in the late afternoon when the whole town was preparing to hit the razz on the Bigg Market.

Andy and I headed downstairs to the hotel café for some beverages to go with our cake. The café and the attached bar were crowded for a Sunday. The game was showing on several screens.

We found the bridesmaids and groomsmen sitting together on a few couches and joined them. The bridesmaids and I drank coffee. The guys sipped pints of draught beer.

Sunderland was up 1-0 when the two of us arrived, a few minutes into the second half. I looked around, sensing the tension, and wondered if the rumors of a riot were right. The sky outside was dark and ominous; thunder rumbled in the distance as if the heavens over the River Tyne were murmuring in sympathy with the apprehension on the ground.

Newcastle scored, but the flag went up. Celebrations collapsed into a maddened fury – everyone had seen Cissé, the striker, onside and they let the referees know. The momentum picked up, and so did the disappointment. Two more chances for Newcastle United – one after the other – came to nothing. Sunderland scored again. They were now two goals ahead, and the roar from the stadium shook the building, mixing with claps of thunder and the noise of helicopters now circling overhead. The air crackled. Men standing in the bar shifted their feet. A swelling fury pervaded the atmosphere.

Within minutes, Sunderland scored again. They were up 3-0. I stood, grabbing Andy by the arm.

"Find your parents. We need to get out of town."

The bridesmaids and groomsmen stood up too. Those who were planning to head back to London that day opted to do so immediately, and the longer-term guests headed back to their hotel rooms. We all hugged quick goodbyes.

Andy and I turned around, ready to move. Mary and Pete were already standing behind us.

"We came downstairs after hearing the hullaballoo," Pete declared.

"We were watching the game in the room, and we decided it would be a good idea to find you," added Mary.

"We thought it might be refreshing to take a drive to the coast this afternoon, have tea, instead of hanging around town," I offered casually, pretending not to notice all the squad cars pulling up outside.

"Yes, that does sound nice." Mary and Pete nodded and smiled politely.

"OK, great. Pete, could you pull your car around? I'll go grab my parents."

"Will do," said Pete.

"I think I'd like to take the metro out to the coast," I heard Mary mentioning to Andy, as I bustled my parents downstairs. They were still pulling their sweaters on, asking what the hurry was. The police had begun to form a barricade around the metro station, just outside the hotel.

I looked at Andy. It would be difficult to fit all six of us in the car. His mother was the oldest and most frail of the parents, but the only one interested in public transport even under normal conditions. My mother would only travel by car, my father would not separate from my mother, I was not about to leave the four parents alone in a vehicle together in an unfamiliar city rapidly descending into chaos, Andy was not going to leave his mother on her own, and Pete would not let anyone else drive his car.

After a few seconds of thought, we looked at each other and shrugged. Andy took his mother's arm and headed toward the nearly-barricaded metro station, and I packed my parents into Pete's car before hauling myself in too.

"Hello dear," Pete leered at my bridesmaid Cynthia as he adjusted the rearview mirror. She had gotten into the backseat right behind me.

"I heard something about tea. Thought I'd join the trip to the coast." She grinned at me. I smiled too and put my arm around her, glad she was there.

My father, sitting to my left in the backseat, leaned over to examine the tattoos that covered Cynthia's arms, then sat back again.

My mother, in the front seat, chattered about the wedding, ignoring the police cordons going up around us in the streets. We got onto the coast road and the tension of town fell away.

Half an hour later, we arrived at the Grand Hotel, a paean of faded seaside glamour overlooking a long white-sand beach just south of Whitley Bay. When Andy and his mother arrived, they recounted a harrowing journey with the sensible folks trying to get out of town before the metro was shut down.

"Hello, dear," Mary smiled, noticing Cynthia.

"Hello, Mary. I'm a big fan," Cynthia said, introducing herself. Mary shook her hand, and warmly asked Cynthia about her interests.

As trash can fires burned across our city and police barricaded the bridges, shut down train stations, and arrested fans for damaging property, my whole family was miles away, eating sandwiches with the crusts cut off and drinking tea from porcelain cups.

When we returned to Newcastle, anyone who was going to punch a police horse that day had been arrested, everyone who had been drinking since the morning was now sleeping it off, and the streets were quiet.

Andy and I looked at each other and breathed a sigh of relief. We were married. Now all we had to do was get that damn visa.

Finally, after a few trips to Scotland – attempts rejected on the grounds of insufficient paperwork not placed on the record – I held my new spousal visa in my hand. Now I had the freedom to look for a job anywhere in the country. Andy and I could decide our lives together.

Relaxed at last, we went on honeymoon in a place of sea and sand.

Laying on the beach, Andy turned to me. "See, that wasn't all so bad."

I laughed. "No, I guess not."

Chapter 13
Honeymoon

It was my idea to go to Israel for our honeymoon. I wanted to go somewhere off the beaten path. Andy had been invited to speak at a conference in Be'er Sheva on a date shortly after our wedding, so I planned a trip around this external constraint. It was the best way to get Andy to do what I wanted – he couldn't very well opt out of both our honeymoon and a work commitment, especially when they were tied together.

We arrived early on a Saturday – Shabbat – and no hotel room was available until sundown. My new husband and I disembarked at Ben-Gurion Airport at dawn, caught a sherut to Jerusalem, stashed our luggage, and set off on foot. In the gardens below the Old City, we sat down to rest and fell asleep under a grove of olive trees. Hours later, we woke up not so much to the gentle sounds of birds and traffic but to the overpowering scent of hibiscus flowers in the increasing heat.

We entered the Old City through the Jaffa Gate. Thousands of people stood in a snaking queue to attend Orthodox Easter Mass at the Church of the Holy Sepulchre. Bypassing the throngs in search of breakfast, we found a little Arabic café offering shakshuka. After serving us, the waiter set up a chair and a hookah in the doorway of the restaurant. A small parade materialized around the corner, led by a marching band. We joined the waiter by the door.

"But we came here to escape the bagpipes," Andy murmured, disappointedly watching the kilts parading past. Then he added, as if realizing for the first time, "Colonialism was a bad idea."

The waiter laughed. "It's really unusual for the rival bagpipers from Jerusalem and Bethlehem to join together, but it is after all a special day." Then, for our benefit, he explained the traditions of the Orthodox Easter Mass. Each bishop of the city – Greek, Coptic, Armenian – would go into their own distinct holy section of the church and come out with highly symbolic candles lit. Still keeping an eye on the parade, our storyteller gleefully recounted tales of stolen candles and inter-church punch-ups of years past.

"Nobody gets along in this town, nobody," he concluded, laughing. Another patron crowded behind us to cheer on the marching band, whooping excitedly when a man with an identical face and an identical grin to his own came past, banging a drum. Despite the multitudes of pilgrims a few blocks away, Jerusalem felt like a small town.

After breakfast, Andy and I ventured along the road toward the Citadel of David. The fortress, having borne witness to millennia of invasions and occupations, had been converted into a museum cataloguing historical events – a bloody story of oppression and resilience and revenge, a story seemingly without beginning or end. No one could remember exactly how all the fighting had started. Human nature dictated that recent memory held stronger on both sides.

The sun beating down, we ambled along the ramparts of the city with a view across the sea of white buildings, then returned to the ground level to explore the markets, overflowing with pottery and rugs and souvenirs. We watched athletic-looking twenty-year-olds in military uniform, with machine guns slung around their shoulders, licking popsicles. We wandered through the stalls of Mahane Yehuda, buying olives and honey pastries and rice wrapped in vine leaves. We glimpsed the golden shape of the Dome on the Rock through an archway but were not allowed to go closer.

At sunset, dehydrated and tired after a very long day, we sat in the declining light and still-strong heat. "I'm going to soak up this beer like an aubergine soaks up olive oil," Andy declared. Overnight, Israeli planes bombed a truckload of missiles in Syria bound for Hezbollah in Lebanon. Over breakfast, we read that retaliation was expected to ensue.

It's hard to stop fighting once you've started.

A few days later Andy and I found ourselves en route to Be'er Sheva. We had to change buses, and so we stopped in a desolate area with wild camels grazing in the hills above Arad. An ibex came down from the dry mountain to join us at the bus stop. There was only one other person standing there, a little old woman. For a moment, the four of us stood together quietly. Then the woman explained in Russian that this was the last ibex in this part of the country and his name was Bruno.

I looked at her, then leaned over further to observe the majestic creature standing beside her. I hadn't realized I could still understand Russian. I turned to Andy, who shrugged. I was not certain what had just happened. The woman had spoken words, and this strange information had appeared in my head, like magic.

The past can hold onto the brain in certain ways. Connections, once molded into place, can remain in place for years, untouched and nearly forgotten.

To travel between cities, we had waited in a queue to pass through a metal detector. Every single person in front of us was a teenage soldier in uniform holding a rifle. One by one, the youths stepped through the scanner, beeping. When we passed and did not beep, we were stopped and subjected to an additional weapons inspection. Onboard, the young people chatted and Andy shifted uncomfortably whenever a rifle was inadvertently pointed at him. I didn't like it either, but I certainly felt at home with this side of human nature.

The next morning Andy left for his conference early and I went wandering through the city. Overhead, power lines intertwined with treetops bearing purple blossoms. I ambled toward Be'er Sheva's town center, past a deep well that legends say belonged to Abraham, the father of Isaac.

As I was walking along the street, enjoying the early morning flurry of activity, a man stopped me.

"I've passed you twice now, I can tell you're a tourist. Come help me open my shop. If you give me a hand, I'll make you some tea and tell you about the history of this town."

"OK," I agreed. I followed him to his store and he handed me a display of remote controls to position outside the shop. Afterwards I sat at the front counter next to a fan while he made tea.

"So what's the history of this town?" I called toward him in the next room.

He poked his head around the corner. "Oh, there's no history, it was built in the 1950s."

"Then why'd you say you would tell me stories?"

"Oh, I just wanted to practice my English."

"Your English is fine. It's as good as mine. What's the deal?"

"OK," he said, returning to the register and handing me a cup of tea. "I need someone to help with a few things."

"Sure, happy to," I shrugged. I had nothing else to do that day. The man set me up soldering connections in a partially-operational amplifier. We chattered as customers came and went.

"So what brought you to Israel?" he asked.

"I'm on my honeymoon," I replied.

"Where's your husband?" he asked.

"Working," I replied.

He looked at me funny.

"We agreed on this beforehand. He won't be working the entire time."

"But you, aren't you bored?"

"It's fine, I like electronics," I explained, testing each of the channels of the amplifier with a meter. "And I don't really find anything boring."

"OK," he said, doubtfully. "But you really ought to see the city today."

"Alright," I agreed. I handed him the repaired equipment and he gave me directions to a market on the outskirts of the town, suggesting I find myself a local souvenir.

Surrounded by the emptiness of the desert, Be'er Sheva had long been a neutral meeting place for rival Bedouin tribes before it was a town. The marketplace harkened back to those days. It comprised mostly family fruit stands and vendors selling fashionable burqas. I bought some strawberries and ate them on the roadside, watching cars and camels lumbering past. Then I walked back toward town, stopping to haggle with a grumpy man selling antiques on the sidewalk. Both of us only grew crankier during our interaction, but I did come away with a silver teapot as a souvenir.

"How was your day, honey?" I asked Andy later. He told me about the latest philosophical and scientific advancements in transhumanism, the practice of using neural interfacing technology to overcome our natural biological limitations.

"And what did you do today?" he asked, after we had finished that discussion.

"I worked at an electronics store. I ate strawberries. And I got into a fight with a man over a teapot."

My husband drew me in and kissed my forehead.

A few nights later, Andy and I were eating dinner at a resort hotel on the Dead Sea. We ordered wine from Golan Heights, and the waiter accidentally spilled it on my plate as he was opening the bottle. Maybe a little bit splashed onto me, but not enough to make a fuss.

"It's alright, no worries at all," I said, smiling politely at the waiter as I brushed my chest lightly with my napkin.

The woman at the next table turned to me and spoke sharply.

"It's not alright. It's not alright at all. You do not deserve that."

I was stunned. No one had ever said words like that to me before. It was completely irrelevant, but my mind flashed back to the day I finally told my mother, years after the incident, about the time in college when a man had broken into my house and attempted to rape me.

"Could you repeat that?" she had said, crunching potato chips loudly into the telephone receiver. "The whole story. Your dad walked away while you were talking, but I'll get him back here."

"Wait, Mom – "

"George! George, come back here! OK, I've put you on speakerphone."

"Mom, just hold on," I had said. "Wait. What do you have to say about this whole thing? What should I have done?"

"Oh, I don't know. You did the right thing to compromise with him."

This had been the source of my pain, that I had decided to negotiate with this man when I found him in the middle of the night on top of me, in my bed, in my home. He had broken into my house, jigging the lock on a weekend my roommate was away. When I woke up, he was naked on top of me and I had little time to think in that sudden moment of danger. Even though it protected me from a greater physical trauma, my own hands had later felt like the enemies of my soul.

"I did the right thing?" I asked. I guess he did agree to leave afterward.

"Yeah, the nuns always told us to compromise in that sort of situation."

Oh my god, did she seriously say that. "What, Mom, the nuns actually talked about this?"

"Well, that was part of educating a young lady." Holy Lord Jesus Christ. I tried to imagine the nuns who taught me saying such a thing. But I never heard anyone speak about sex until I went to high school, and then it was not very informative – some people saying you should do it and other people saying you shouldn't do it, a lot of secretive whispering about who was doing it with no clear message about what it actually was. Throughout my childhood, sex had just been something you thought about for 9 of every 10 hours in the day and never discussed aloud. It was just a feeling you had, with no words to describe it and no idea how it fit into your life. When I got my first period, I assumed I was dying for several days, until a friend's mom noticed I was bleeding and took me aside.

I had thought I had received a horribly inadequate education, but suddenly I was glad my mother didn't teach me everything she knew. But maybe she did pass it on somehow – after all, I followed the advice she would have given me.

"Mom, did you – did anything like that ever happen to you?"

"No, of course not! I never got myself into situations like that."

Well that made me feel like a pile of nothing. As if it was my fault the guy broke into my house.

Thinking about that conversation all those years ago, I stared at this woman in the restaurant and wondered what she would have said to me if she were my mother. She wouldn't have stayed there listening to my story on the phone, eating potato chips and saying it was perfectly okay to be scarred for life like that. This woman here would have vowed justice. An eye for an eye? Hell no, she would have found that guy and gouged out both his eyes, then strung him up by the balls in the center of town as an example to others. What is proportional justice when you have forever taken away someone's feeling of security and her belief in the goodness of this world?

It was an interesting question, and it captured my mind. What is the cost of that damage and what is the proper price to pay, I wondered. Not just for the physical injury of a rape, but the psychological damage of all actual and attempted sexual assaults. The time lost, of staying up all night, every night, for months, after someone has broken into your house? The time lost, wondering if your body was really your own, after someone had grabbed you on the street and felt your breasts? The time lost, worried about your safety and staying away from situations where it could not be assured? The time lost, alone and scared of your own friends, after one of them slid his flesh into yours while you were kissing together at a party and the others did not believe you when you spoke about it afterwards?

I was upset, and Andy could tell. He harangued me until I shared what I was thinking, and he got angry when I finally confessed.

"We're on our honeymoon!" he exclaimed. "How can you bring this up now? You're with me. That stuff is all in the past."

"I can't help it," I tried to explain, crying. "It's nothing to do with you. It's just my history, sitting in a corner of my brain. It just got woken up a little bit tonight."

"Why is everything tinged with sadness with you? You find negativity everywhere."

"I'm sorry, I don't mean to be negative. It just came over me for a moment, that's all." I wiped away my tears.

He looked doubtful. I wanted to comfort him.

"You're right, honey, it's over," I said, taking a deep breath. "I'll try to forget the past. After all, we have our future to look forward to."

Chapter 14
Developing a Gene Therapy to Treat Epilepsy

Although I had received a spousal visa which allowed me to stay in the country, I still needed a job. Without that fellowship, my current post would not last much longer. And I would not go back to making cheese and asking for pocket money.

So Andy and I devised a scheme to win ten million pounds sterling to develop a new treatment for neurological disease that involved both a gene therapy and an implantable biomedical device. The plan hatched, as plans do, from an entirely different conversation.

One evening, as we were walking home from work, I was telling Andy about my current experiment, which involved making a viral vector-based gene therapy that forced a cell to increase its mitochondrial content. The idea was that, if neural stem cells could make more energy, they could produce more new neurons.

The experiment had worked. My gene therapy had increased the regenerative capacity of the aged brain. But I worried that the stem cells would grow too much, so now I was working to reduce their energy metabolism instead, as a way to slow the growth of brain tumors.

I was excited. Andy was quiet.

"Wait a second," he stopped walking. "You can make viral vectors that deliver gene therapies?"

"Yes, Husband, were you listening to me?"

"Yes, I was listening," he replied testily. "Does that mean you could make a viral vector that would deliver a gene for optogenetics?"

Optogenetics was the biggest new thing in neuroscience. Normally, when neurons send messages to each other, a neurotransmitter binds to a receptor on the receiving cell's surface. That protein reconfigures its shape to open a channel, allowing positively-charged ions to flood into the cell. The positively-charged ions cause a change in voltage somewhere in that enormous arbor of dendrites on the receiving cell. If a neuron receives several of these signals at once, on different branches within the arbor, the voltage adds up and the neuron is triggered to send a message forward. The circuitry of the brain operates by computing coincidences, assuming they are not coincidences at all.

But optogenetics avoids coincidence altogether. Optogenetics employs a naturally-occurring gene in algae, which encodes a type of channel that opens when hit by a photon of light. The algae use this channel to help them move around a bit when the sun is shining. But in a neuron, the artificially light-stimulated flood of positively-charged ions forces the target cell to send an electrochemical signal. There were a variety of related genes, some of them allowing negatively-charged ions into the cell to keep it quiet, even when other inputs were telling the cell to go, go, go.

The only thing stopping Andy and others in the department from doing all sorts of cool experiments with this technology was the fact they didn't have the gene therapy.

That's why Andy was asking whether I could make a viral vector that would allow him to do optogenetics.

"Sure," I responded. "I can order those genes off the internet and subclone them into my plasmid."

"Um, does that mean yes?"

"Yes."

"Then they'd have to give you a job in the institute!"

"Yes! And I could work on my brain tumor studies alongside!"

"Then we can do optogenetics," Andy murmured, stars in his eyes. "Nathan's gonna love this."

Nathan Cook was Andy's mentor in the department. We saw him the next day. He liked the idea.

"So what's this virus?" he asked.

"Well," I explained, "It's not really a true virus. It's just the part of the virus that delivers the genetic material into the cell. We actually call it a viral vector, because it's just a delivery vehicle."

"So how do you make it, with the gene we want inside?"

"We know what genes encode the proteins that make up the viral shell and we know what genes encode the protein machinery that helps the virus to replicate, kill the host cell, escape and infect other cells. So we just leave all those genes out. We just make the viral shell, with your gene inside."

"And where did this viral shell come from?"

"Well, over the past few decades a lot of funding has gone into infectious disease research. So now we know a lot about viruses that get into human cells effectively. For some viruses, we know every single gene and what it does. Someone clever took the useful ones that make the viral shell and just put them together as a vehicle to deliver other genes. So basically, we took the scourges of previous centuries, tamed them, and are now using them to cure other diseases."

"This is fantastic." Nathan had stars in his eyes now too.

We went and found Colin, the director of the Institute of Neuroscience. We needed someone in a position of power to lend his support. He agreed to act as lead for the project — after all, he knew all of us and line-managed most of us anyway.

We got together everyone who was interested in the project to decide the best disease to treat with optogenetic technology. Right away, we decided against schizophrenia, since those patients would almost certainly not want their neural tissue genetically modified to allow scientists to control their brainwaves. We decided instead on epilepsy.

Epilepsy is a condition with abnormal brain activity. Neurons seem to fire all together, and the normal chaos of neurons chattering to each other at different frequencies is lost underneath this large, synchronized signal. One research group in London was trying to use optogenetics to inhibit excitatory neurons; one research group in California was trying to use optogenetics to excite inhibitory neurons. We thought both interventions would just dull neuronal activity across the brain; we wanted to develop a millisecond-precise pattern of stimulation that would cancel out the high-amplitude, highly-synchronous signal while leaving all the other healthy brain activity intact.

We had to get the two epilepsy experts in the department on board: Gavin and Oliver. That would be tricky. They didn't get along, and they had recently had a fistfight with each other in the hallway. Gavin thought Oliver was a dim-witted parasite who could not come up with his own ideas, and Oliver thought Gavin was an arrogant jerk who did not value the work of others. Gavin had the distinctive appearance, scowling expression, precise dialect and unsettling intonation of a Bond villain. Oliver had an affable Irish charm. It was difficult to tell which one would be more dangerous. We had to convince the two of them to work together.

The prospect of money proved sufficiently useful motivation for them to put aside their differences. The team came together. Gavin would test the viral vectors carrying the gene therapy in cells in a dish to evaluate the physiological effects of each construct; Oliver would test the viral vectors in human tissue resected from epilepsy patients; Nathan would develop the algorithm and the prototype processer box that would deliver it; Mattias would narrow down the possible patterns of stimulation that would calm the overexcitability of the epileptic brain; Andy would eventually test the best combinations in the monkey brain. Dominic would engineer the part of the device that would be inserted into the brain, containing the recording sites that would track neural activity and micro light-emitting diodes that would flash light to control the neural activity; Logan would make the processor to be mounted within the body; Tony would link the parts of the device; Vincent would ensure the whole thing, including the battery pack, was well-insulated so that it could survive the environment of the body; Roger was the clinician who would identify the epilepsy patient for the first human trial and work with the neurosurgery team to implant the combined product.

My role was to design and make the gene therapy. It had to target the best cell type to reset abnormal brain activity and it had to contain the optimal gene to handle the pattern of light stimulation needed for the therapy to work. These two traits would be contained in the genetic sequence. My task involved not only doing a lot of molecular biology but also ensuring that everything was linked up – that the device the engineers made would activate the gene therapy we made, that the cells the neurophysiologists wanted to control were the ones we were targeting, that the patterns of light stimulation would lie within the physiological parameters defined by the channel kinetics of our genes. Because I had manufactured and validated viral vectors, built neural recording equipment, surgically implanted electrode headstages, and conducted electrophysiology in awake animals, I was well-placed to ease communication among the groups.

No one had any idea how we would translate our lab work to a biomedical device and a gene therapy that was actually safe enough to go into a person, but we figured we'd find that out along the way. No one had really done it before anyway.

Andy was writing the grant outline. One day he called me excitedly.

"You've gotta come over here," he said. I found him working amidst a colossal pile of papers.

"What's going on?" I asked, intrigued.

"I've come up with a name for the project," Andy announced, sitting back in his chair. "It's called CANDO: Controlling Abnormal Network Dynamics using Optogenetics."

"That's brilliant, honey!"

"It's funny," Andy explained, "because the whole thing is crazy and there's no chance it'll work."

"If we get ten million quid, we'll damn well make it work."

"That's the CANDO spirit," he replied, with a grin.

Andy and the others had asked for a special power, the ability to control the activity of neurons on demand. So I gave them what they wanted. I cast a spell of transformation, and within it, a spell of breakage and repair.

In the little pot they went: polymerase from *T. aquaticus*, from the deepest hottest springs of California, to build the coding sequence; a restriction endonuclease, to recognize and cut a palindromic structure held in common with both parts; the parts themselves - an algae gene, involved in phototaxis, and the obligatory circle, a plasmid containing all the necessary genes to build the viral shell; alkalinic phosphatase and enterophage ligase, to bind the parts together. I combined these with coliform bacteria from the stomach of a calf, by introducing sudden heat, then sudden cold, then sudden heat again, to achieve the transformation. The bacteria would then hold the final product, all the genetic sequences joined up together. I mixed the contents with warm broth – just a few drops upon a plate, no more – and left it overnight, upside down. I crossed my fingers and voiced an incantation.

Just kidding – I had already optimized the protocol, so there was no need for that last step.

In the morning, there I had it, in my hands – the ability to awaken a neuron with a flash of light, to make it send an electrical signal on demand. I isolated the newly encased genetic material from the bacterium and built it into a viral vector, just the shell of a virus really. I did this by tricking weary mammalian cells in a petri dish to manufacture loads of viral particles containing the precious cargo. The viral particles, once collected, would act as a delivery vehicle for the genetic material.

I brought the final product, in a little tube, to Gavin. He treated fresh neurons with it, to test whether the stuff served its intended purpose. The cells began to glow with the green fluorescent protein marker I had included as well, a good sign. A few days later, Andy and I sat with Gavin in his lab while he flashed light – not the full spectrum, only blue light with a wavelength of 470nm, and not a full blast either, only a tiny sliver of a second. It worked. The target cell that was being measured changed voltage, indicating a charge was moving through it. We tested more cells, containing genes with different modifications. Each gene acted as we had expected; the red-light-activated ones responded only to wavelengths that were around 590nm while the on-off constructs started firing electrical signals when a blue light was flashed and stopped when a red light was flashed.

We had shown we could make the tools, now the engineers needed to go to work to build a head-mounted gadget that could record the ongoing signals, detect an oncoming seizure, and send the appropriate light signal back into the brain to calm the abnormal electrical over-excitability. And the neurophysiologists needed to create models of epilepsy to test the combination of the gene therapy and the gadget. The funding, if awarded, would allow me to start a lab, with two staff members and a regulatory manager, who would develop new tools, help with the preclinical testing, and find out how to get the gene therapy safely into people.

Our fearless leader, Colin, traveled to London for an interview with The Trust, a large funding organization for science and engineering. He presented thirty slides, explaining the need for a new treatment for epilepsy and how our combined gene therapy and implantable biomedical device was the way forward.

The rest of us were in Newcastle. I was in the basement,

doing mouse surgeries with Gavin for another project. Late in the afternoon, an email pinged through. We had been awarded the grant.

"Check if it's for real," I said, refusing to get excited yet. It was too good to be true.

Gavin texted Colin back, since I was trying to remain sterile.

"Yep, it's for real," he reported. "You can have babies now."

My split second of excitement fell flat. "What?" I asked.

"You have a stable position now. You can take maternity leave and have babies."

The thought had never occurred to me. All this time I was getting excited about the prospect of developing new treatments for epilepsy and brain tumors, everyone thought I was just biding time before having kids?

"Uh, I'm not planning on having kids."

"You should have kids. I have kids, they're fun."

"Can we just talk about science please."

"Sure, suit yourself."

When Colin arrived back in town, we all went out and celebrated, then got back to work planning the start of the project. Colin and I had meetings in his office too, both of us excited about the prospects for my research program in my new home institute – the Institute of Neuroscience. My job was now secure.

As the weather began to turn, Andy and I purchased a house in the leafy neighborhood of Jesmond. We built a wardrobe for the bedroom, cooked dinner together in the kitchen, sat chatting over meals in the dining room, and curled up by the fireplace at night, reading to each other or watching television. We started to build patterns into our days and weeks, started to feel the steadiness and security of a comfortable life.

One Monday morning in December, we received an email ordering everyone in the institute to arrive at 9am sharp for a meeting. Andy groaned.

"They're probably going to tell us that we dropped a few places in some league table and we're in big trouble unless we publish more papers." The Research Assessment Framework was coming up, and the higher-ups in the faculty were taking it quite seriously.

We arrived in the main meeting room. Professor Anna Harvey-Dent, the deputy director of the institute, was sitting at the front of the room – impeccably dressed as always, but with an unsettled look on her face. The other chair was empty.

Andy and I looked at each other. This was not good.

At 9am, Anna stood up and told us that Colin had had a heart attack and passed away the day before. He was 53, and he was leaving behind a wife and three teenage children.

Tears streamed down my face. Colin was our leader, both of the institute and of the CANDO project. He loved us, he encouraged us – he was like a father figure to us too. I looked around. No one else was crying.

Later that week, we had a meeting about CANDO. The whole group sat in a big circle, in the same meeting room where Anna had broken the news. We were there to decide who would spearhead the project in Colin's absence. The Trust would not provide the funding unless there was clear leadership.

The vote was unanimous. Everyone thought Nathan Cook should lead the project. Like Andy, he was a neurophysiologist who worked closely with engineers to develop new neural interfacing technology. But he was much more senior in the faculty than Andy was.

Nathan shook his head. "No," he said. "I'm not taking this on." Instead, he would spend the following year capturing wild baboons in Kenya to conduct brain surgeries on them, an activity he then had to justify to the newspapers, the courts, his funding agency, and everyone else in the country.

Next we approached Anna, since she was our new institute director. She was a brilliant scientist, and a viscountess as well, having married a banker from a noble family.

"No. No way. Absolutely not," she said. "I'll help you, as a senior member of the faculty, to get back on track, but I am not taking the lead on this project. It should be someone in that area of expertise."

The next choice was Andy. He was only a senior lecturer, but he had other funding support from The Trust and they were satisfied to give him an opportunity to grow into a leadership role. His skillset was otherwise perfect for the job. His lab was central to the neuroscience research, he had strong working relationships with the engineers, and of course he would get daily updates on the gene therapy side of the project from me.

Tony would take the lead on the engineering, Andy on the neuroscience, and Roger on the clinical side of the project – moving the therapy into patients. The gene therapy – my team – was folded into the neuroscience part of the project, along with Gavin and Oliver.

I mentioned – to Andy, to Anna, to Gavin and Oliver who would be my new mentors in the department – that this arrangement essentially made Andy my boss.

"It'll be fine," they said. "You might even get favors out of the situation."

"I don't want favors," I replied. "I just want my career

to progress as a result of the work I put in."

They assured me this would happen. I just had to build my research program, and I would be in line for a tenure-track position within a few years.

As planned by Colin before he died, I was awarded an open contract by Newcastle University, with half of my time dedicated to CANDO and half of my time dedicated to studying the importance of fatty acid metabolism in brain tumors. I was thrilled to be pushing forward these twin projects, each with the goal of devising a new therapy for patients.

Meanwhile, Andy dug into his new role as leader of CANDO. Every night, he'd share the doings of everyone on the project and we'd discuss the next steps forward.

"Dominic says he wants to build a golden trench for the virus to seep out slowly."

"Does he even know how biological materials work? They degrade over time. We'll obviously inject the virus directly and then place the device in the same needle track during the same surgical procedure."

"Yeah, that does sound like a better idea," Andy agreed. "He really wants a golden trench though."

"I'll put a golden trench in his head," I said sarcastically. Andy snickered.

"Dominic has budgeted 100,000 quid per micro-LED," Andy mentioned a few days later.

"You can get those things for one quid each from the electronics catalog," I pointed out.

"Yep," Andy said. "He just really wants to buy them from this Irish company Trindell."

"How are you going to keep him from using one-sixth of our entire budget on overpriced electronics?"

"I think I'll propose he compare them against another

brand, then we make a decision as a team."

After months of work by the engineering team, it was apparent the competitor micro-LEDs were not only 100,000 times cheaper, but also brighter, longer-lasting, and produced less heat.

"You saved the project 1,599,984 quid, that's like two million dollars!" I calculated.

"Dominic still wants the LEDs from Trindell."

"Ugh, he clearly has shares in this company. You can veto that decision, right?"

"Yeah, I can and I will."

"You're doing a great job of leading this project, honey."

"Thanks, sweetie."

In 2014, we officially started the project. New staff were hired. I found a technician and a post-doctoral researcher, both with strong skills in molecular biology, to join my team. We also hired a project manager, Luke.

The first thing Luke did was meet each member of the team for coffee, to get to know the person and their role on the project. The two of us had a nice chat.

Explaining the rationale of the project, I reminisced about how it all got started. "For me, the whole point of applying for CANDO was to provide support for my lab, so I can develop a new treatment for brain tumors," I told Luke.

"Really?" he asked. "This project seems complicated enough as it is."

"Yeah, it sounds crazy, but it's just a delivery vehicle for this other thing."

He looked at me doubtfully, and asked Andy later.

"Yeah," Andy nodded. "It's true. The whole reason we started CANDO was so Beth could continue working here, so she can develop this new treatment for brain tumors. That's the real goal. Everyone knows this other thing will never work."

Chapter 15
Running a Blinded, Placebo-Controlled Preclinical Trial for a New Cancer Drug

"Well, this one's a no-brainer," declared the head of the panel, a blond woman in a sharp gray suit. She closed the folder and looked up at me. "This is exactly the sort of project the Translational Research Fund is looking to support – novel drug target, excellent animal model, and a disease indication crying out for new therapeutic options."

I kept holding my breath. There were a dozen other people on the panel. They had each spoken in turn during the question-and-answer session, but now they were silent.

The blond woman looked around the table, making eye contact with the others, who nodded.

"You'll be awarded the funding for your brain tumor study, to develop a new treatment for glioma," she announced. "Good luck, and report back how things go."

"I will," I promised, a feeling of elation sweeping over me. "Thank you."

I left the room and walked quickly back to the lab. When I got there, I threw the door open.

"Sophie!" I hollered. Sophie looked up from a row of tubes, saw my grin, and set down her pipette.

"Looks like it went well." A grin was spreading across her face too. "Do we get to do the drug testing study?"

"Yeah, we sure do." The two of us high-fived each other. Sophie was my technician. She had only been working with me a couple weeks, but we felt like a team already.

"I also just received news that a master's student has chosen this project, so we'll have an extra hand this year too," I added. "We'll need it."

"This is fantastic, everything's coming together so well!" Sophie exclaimed.

"It sure is."

The master's student came over to discuss the project. Her name was Xi. She was a tiny and extremely nervous twenty-one year-old. I tried to put her at ease, asking about her studies and her interests. She began to smile and make eye contact. She showed interest in the project, so I told her how far I'd gotten with it.

I explained how normal neural stem cells can acquire mutations, occasionally going rogue and forming malignant brain tumors called gliomas. I also described how I had discovered these cells break apart fat molecules to produce energy. Then I explained the hypothesis that, since the normal and malignant cell types were related, the tumor cells might be using fats to make energy too.

"Do you have any evidence so far?" Xi asked.

"That's a good question," I replied. She smiled. "First I looked for the relevant enzymes in brain tumor samples that had been removed from patients. And I found that all patients had the enzymes required to break down fatty acids – at least in some of their tumor cells. And when I looked closer I found that some of the nastiest cells in the tumors were the ones that tended to have the enzymes."

"So malignant glioma cells are equipped to break down fatty acids," Xi verified, writing this down. "Does it matter how much of each enzyme they have?"

"That's a good question too," I remarked. "I did evaluate the levels of those enzymes. I found that, if a given tumor sample had lower levels of these enzymes, the patient was likely to survive longer."

"Wow," Xi said, looking up from her notepad. "What next?"

"Now we try to experimentally lower rates of fatty acid metabolism in glioma cells and measure whether that intervention slows the growth of the tumor."

"How do we do that?" Xi asked.

"Well, there's a drug called etomoxir. It specifically and irreversibly blocks a key enzyme in that energy production pathway. When treated, cells cannot break apart fat molecules to make energy."

"Cool," Xi said.

"The best part is, etomoxir has already been evaluated in people. It's been through Phase I and II clinical trials before, for moderate congestive heart disease. 2% of people taking the drug had high liver enzyme levels, so they stopped that trial. But the balance of risk and benefit would be really different for patients with a highly fatal brain tumor. A lot of people with cancer choose to take rough chemotherapy drugs, to get a few more months or years."

"So how do you test this drug for glioma?" Xi asked.

"So far, I've only tested it in cell cultures," I said. "I found the drug slows the rate of cell division without killing the cancer cells."

"Is that good enough?" she asked. Then she covered her mouth, alarmed. "Sorry!" she cried.

"No, that's okay," I assured her. "It's a really good question."

Xi looked relieved.

"Seriously, that is an important question. If the cells survive, they could switch how they make energy and recover."

Now Xi looked slightly overwhelmed.

"But one, it might buy the patient time. And two, any other strategy a cell could use to make energy would be far less efficient. So the cells might not be able to make enough energy to divide, even if they do adapt."

Xi looked somewhat encouraged now.

"Fatty acids provide a lot of energy for a cell. Even if we can't kill the cancer cells, it might be really useful to stop them making energy this way."

"That's really cool. So what do we do now?"

"Right, this is where you come in." I grinned, and Xi did too.

"We have to give mice tumors." Our grins faded with this glum reality. "But we'd be doing so to find a way for them – and people with brain tumors – to survive longer."

Xi took a deep breath. "OK," she said. "I'm in."

Her confidence and composure were gaining already. Over the next couple of years, I would watch her grow into a self-assured young woman, still terrifically sensitive toward people and animals, but no longer prone to reflexive apology after making an astute criticism.

Our team was growing.

Shortly after that conversation, I received an email. The funding was coming through, but there was a catch. I needed to talk to the university's business development office.

"Ugh," I thought. Everything had to be monetized nowadays. But I went over to the business development office as directed.

A Scottish woman with a PhD in biochemistry and a low level of patience greeted me with a clipboard. "Marie," she said quickly. "I'm gonna cut to the chase."

I didn't say anything. My lack of interest was evident.

"You need to have a corporate partnership for this study," Marie explained. "A biochemist has developed a slightly different formulation of the generic drug, and he has been awarded a patent for it. His company is aiming to find a use for this drug."

"That's their problem." I replied. "They can find a use for their drug if they want to make money on it. As far as I'm concerned, there's a generic formulation and I plan to use it."

"That's not how things work," Marie said coldly.

"I feel pretty strongly about this," I said. "After years of publicly-funded research, someone should not be able to swoop in and make a profit of this work."

"It's a partnership," Marie explained. "They would be making a contribution from an early stage."

"I don't want a partnership, I just want to conduct the study with a generic drug."

"But if your mouse study is successful, the drug should go to clinical trial. And for that, you need a corporate partner."

"Why, if there's a generic drug?" I asked.

"Because, clinical trials are really expensive. Funders expect a company to provide the drug as well as all the pharmacology and toxicology data on it. Then everyone shares the profit."

I sighed. "But surely the generic drug —" I stopped. The generic drug still cost a lot of money, and it would be difficult to get those costs covered if investors had no chance of making a profit. I could not work around the logic of capitalism. The only way around this problem would be to nationalize the entire drug industry, so that all research & development costs and all profits were shared by taxpayers. That seemed unlikely. "I just want to use the generic drug," I said stubbornly.

"Well, you don't get the funding unless you agree to the corporate partnership," Marie said, setting her clipboard aside and meeting my eyes.

"Can I think about it?" I asked sadly.

"Fine," she said. "Come back soon."

Xi and I were already in the midst of a pilot study to establish the mouse model. We had only a few animals in each drug group, since we didn't have our big funding yet. But the important thing was, we got the tumors growing and verified as gliomas – a pathologist at the hospital next door who spent his days looking at human brain tumors had agreed to examine the mouse brains. He carefully documented each feature, pointing out characteristics only a person with years of training would spot. I was thrilled to my bones when he looked up from the microscope after several hours and announced the tumors to be high-grade anaplastic astrocytomas. Real gliomas. We had a great animal model of the disease, now we could use it as a platform for testing new drugs. I emailed my Ph.D co-supervisor Will the great news – our work together had taken on new life in England.

The results from that initial study suggested the drug might have an effect, but we couldn't say for sure. We had to run the study with a big group of mice, half receiving the drug and half receiving a placebo. All the animals would go through the same procedures, but only half of them would have the drug in their bloodstream. And we, the experimenters, would be blinded – we could not know which mice were receiving treatment and which were not, in case we would assess them differently. It was a challenging, time-consuming and expensive undertaking. We needed support. So I went back to Marie in the business development office.

"Is there any benefit of this corporate drug over the generic version, other than the fact someone can make money off it?" I asked.

"Yep," Marie said, with her biochemistry training. "Better pharmacology. The new formulation should last longer in the body and get into the brain more easily."

"Alright, I'll go along with the corporate partnership," I told her.

"You're making the right decision," she said.

But later I groaned and complained about it to Sophie.

"I don't know, it sounds like this is just how people do things," she said. "Take the advice. Get the drug from the company. Make use of the funding and the support."

I nodded. Nick and Steve had always told me to listen to advice too. It just sounded wrong – I was pretty sure I could do everything on my own.

"Partnerships can be a good thing," Sophie said. "Just accept it."

Wise woman, wise words. Still, there were ways it could go wrong.

The drug arrived – five grams of white powder in a tube with a scribbled label, sent in an envelope through the regular post. The secretaries in the institute office were unnerved. They had also received a delivery of cockroaches that day, and they were considering quitting their jobs.

I tried to cheer them up by explaining how useful insects were to neuroscience – elegant in their simplicity, with three-neuron circuits generating a flawless coordination of sensory perception and advantageous movement. But no one seemed to care about the neural networks underlying central pattern generators. I took my white powder and went back to the lab.

Sophie, Xi, and I spent the following three days trying to get the drug into solution. The generic formulation went into water or saline well, but the new version had a feisty little hydrophobic bond. The feature which improved the availability of the drug in the bloodstream was the same feature that made it so difficult to work with. We tried to get the white powder to dissolve in ethanol, methanol, dimethyl sulfoxide, cyclodextrin, beta cyclodextrin, anything. But nothing worked.

I emailed the company, asking what to do.

"It's a hydrophobic molecule. It mixes well in oil, not water," the lead biochemist responded.

"I get that," I responded. "But oil is too thick to be released from the little pumps implanted in the mice that deliver the drug continuously for thirty days."

"Hmm," the man responded. "Try glycerol."

I checked the label. The pumps had no specific instructions against glycerol-based solutions.

I went back into the lab and made up the drug with glycerol. It worked like a charm. The three of us filled the pumps with the solution and implanted them in the mice over the following days. We were glad to be on track with the project.

We spent the following months checking the animals every day, weighing them and looking for signs of illness — scrunched eyes, flattened ears, hunched posture, lethargy, or seizures. Just like people with brain tumors, the animals were fine, fine, fine, and then suddenly one day very sick. Each day, we carried out a health evaluation for each mouse, using a customized scoresheet, reached an agreement about the prognosis, and euthanized each animal once he grew ill with the tumor burden, about two months after the cells had been implanted. None of us knew what treatment each mouse had – two of my other students and the post-doc Georgiana had systematically coded the drugs and each of them held a copy of the codes. But the three of us conducting the study had no idea.

The study ended and I completed the data analysis, with a formal unveiling of the codes at lab meeting. We held our breath, but there was absolutely no effect – the two groups were identical.

Xi put her face in her hands. Sophie tilted her head.

"Are you sure there's no technical reason we could have gotten a null result?" she asked.

"Everything went perfectly smoothly. It was a well-planned and well-conducted study."

"Nothing could have gone wrong?" Sophie asked.

"Only if the drug was not delivered for some reason," I replied.

"Are we sure it was delivered?" Sophie asked.

"Huh," I said, suddenly realizing that glycerol has the exact same viscosity as oil. A feeling of dread set in.

"Uh, should we do another experiment?"

"Yep," Sophie said, pushing her chair away from the table.

We went back to the lab and put on our white coats. We made two solutions – one that was nine parts saline and one part blue dye, one that was nine parts glycerol and one part blue dye. Then we loaded the pumps and placed them in tubes of saline to mimic the environment of the body. After one week, the pump with saline was surrounded by a blue liquid and the pump with glycerol was surrounded by a clear liquid.

"Oh crap," I said, holding up the tubes.

"All that work," Xi moaned. "All those mice."

Sophie shrugged. "This means there's no real negative data. Let's just repeat the study."

"Alright," I said. "This time, let's make sure the drug actually gets delivered."

There was only one problem: we were out of money. I went back to the funders. They encouraged me to reapply, although the fund was being reorganized. Instead of a panel of people evaluating the grant applications, it would be a single person: the head of cancer drug discovery at the university.

It was perfect. A local professor, dedicated to drug development in oncology - he was bound to value my project and consider it worthwhile. I applied right away and was granted an interview.

As soon as I walked into the room, I sensed tension. The man with my fate in his hands, Professor Harold Norwich, sat across the table from me with a scowl on his face. As I sat down, I smiled politely and nodded to him, ready for a fair argument.

The fact that brain tumor cells used fats, not sugars, to make energy was a ground-breaking assertion. It overturned seventy years of dogma in the cancer field. Extraordinary claims require extraordinary evidence – I understood that, and I was prepared to meet the skepticism of the scientific community with data.

Harold questioned me at length, his secretary taking notes. I addressed all of his queries, until I got stuck on one.

"The pharmacology and toxicology dataset for this drug," he stated. "You don't have this?"

Suddenly I was relieved to have that corporate partner. "The company can provide that," I said.

"Why don't you come back when you have that

information," he said.

I emailed him a few days later, after the company had sent me dozens of pages of documentation, with permission to share the data within the university community. Harold agreed to meet again. Again I found him in the conference room with a scowl on his face. I sighed.

"These pharmacology data are insufficient," he said.

"OK," I replied slowly. "Should I ask for more funds to build a more complete pharmacology dataset, alongside the study I have proposed?"

He did pharmacology studies himself, so I wondered if he wanted to collaborate on the project. Tentatively, I suggested this option.

"Yeah, I could help you collect those data," he offered. I nodded, understanding how things worked now. "You don't have the 24 hour timepoint, see."

"Oh, actually we do," I affirmed, helpfully pointing to these data in the documents.

He snorted and slammed the folder shut. "There's nothing we can do then," he snarled.

I was taken aback. I had thought I had everything in hand, but suddenly it was not going well.

"Sorry, but that means we have all the pharmacology data, right?" I asked, confused. "So now, it makes sense to run the study evaluating if the drug slows tumor growth."

"No," he said.

"But why?" I asked, wishing I was in front of the huge panel instead. I remembered their previous assessment of the study, and I repeated their words now. "It's a novel drug target, an excellent animal model, and a disease indication crying out for new therapeutic options."

Harold's face twisted into an ugly scowl. "You think you

can just show up and discover a new treatment for cancer, when other people have been working on this for decades?"

My jaw dropped. "I've been working on this drug target for seven years," I said helplessly. "I didn't just show up. I've been working on this for a long while."

He shook his head firmly. "I'm not funding this study," he declared. His secretary noted that down, then looked up at me with a nasty smile.

"But why?" I asked. "What's the problem with the study?"

"There's no problem with the study," he replied. "I just don't like you."

I looked around, as if there was anyone watching who could validate how weird this was. The secretary continued to leer, as if enjoying the view of someone being eaten by a shark.

"Is there anything I can do to change your mind?" I asked.

"Nope," Harold said. "You can go now."

I walked out of the room in a daze and headed to Andy's office. I explained the situation to him, and he leaned back in his chair.

"I've got loads of extra money," he said. "I'll fund your study."

"Wow, thank you. Thank you so much," I said, shocked that my problem could be solved this easily. "But honey, it'll be around twenty grand, without any staffing costs."

"That's fine," he replied. "Just keep track of the budget as you order things."

I was stunned. How lucky was I, to have a husband who supported me like this?

I went back to my lab and prepared to redo the study. This time, I would skip the corporate drug, and just use the generic formulation that went so easily into saline solution.

We repeated the study, and the results were significant. The animals treated with etomoxir lived 17% longer than placebo-treated mice, similar to the benefits of current chemotherapy treatment in people.

It was useful to know the animals lived longer, with similar tumor size at the end of their lives. But it would also be useful to know whether the tumors actually grew more slowly.

I emailed Professor Ethan Constantine, who ran the high-resolution MRI machine to visualize tumors growing in mice. He invited me over and offered to track tumor growth in a few mice with and without treatment.

"Um," I said. "Why are you offering me thousands of dollars of free MRI time?"

Ethan shrugged. "No one else around here has a good animal model of cancer. You've put in the effort to get things right. Also I'm sick of sarcomas, and these brain tumors sound interesting."

I could not believe my luck. For weeks, Ethan and I watched the tumors grow, saving the images. When the study was over, we revealed the codes and found the animal with etomoxir treatment was the one whose tumor had shown up long after the other animal died. Those two animals happened to be perfectly representative of their respective groups. We grinned and high-fived each other. Ethan was on the team now. We applied to get a PhD student onboard, to continue the study.

In the meantime, we published the initial work, showing that gliomas relied on fats to make energy and demonstrating the generic drug actually slowed the growth of these brain tumors.

Sophie hugged me. "You know I don't stay here

because people are friendly and the pay is nice. It's because I'm really proud of what we're doing, what we've built here."

"I know, Sophie," I said. "Me too."

We congratulated Xi, who was listed as an author on the study and had used her training to win a coveted post as a technician in a big lab.

When the paper was published, the university issued a press release and the media took notice. For days, the lab was occupied with massive television cameras. I did a live radio interview on the local BBC Radio 1 morning show, a few recorded radio interviews for national stations, and held several calls with print media too. Most news organizations just reprinted the university press release, but others actually contacted me for details.

The university press office gave me training in the days leading up to the publication, as we wrote the press release. Lisa, the press officer, coached me thoroughly.

"Remember to stay focused," she said. "Just stick to the science."

"OK," I said, and I did as I was told for once.

My mother was diagnosed with breast cancer as I was trying to get the paper published. I flew home to Chicagoland to see her.

In Deerfield, we paged through her medical records. A lot of the data was breast-specific, and I had no idea what to look for in radiographic images of breasts. But the pathology was something I could dig into. Even though breast tissue looked very different from brain tissue, the markers used to identify cancer and estimate malignancy were the same. We talked about the radiography and the pathology, about the doctors and what they said, about the cancer diagnosis and the suggested treatment.

"Mom, you should really consider a full resection."

"I'm not getting a mastectomy!" my mother cried. She loved her breasts, I knew this.

"Mom, people do this pre-emptively. It's not a bad idea to do it now."

"I'm not doing it."

I tried one more time. "Mom, when people have tumors, the best thing they can do is get as much removed as possible. One of the reasons it sucks to get a brain tumor is because the whole thing cannot be removed. With breast tissue, you can take a lot with no negative side effects."

"OK," she conceded. "I'll get a large area removed but I'm not getting a mastectomy."

I sighed. My mother had huge breasts, and after the surgery there was no noticeable change whatsoever. She always complained about her weight and back pain, and so I was baffled as to why she would not take this opportunity to get a massive reduction.

But she loved her breasts. And that took priority over other things.

After the surgery, the doctors were optimistic about the prognosis but could not confirm they had removed all of the cancer cells. They recommended radiation or hormone therapy.

My mother was adamant. "I'm not taking drugs," she said. "I feel healthier than ever."

"Mom," I sighed. "You should take the doctors' advice."

"Your father didn't need radiation or chemo or any other drugs after his prostate cancer. And he's been clear for ten years now."

"I know, Mom," I said. "But he got a full resection and the doctors called him clear."

"Well, I feel clear," my mother declared. There was nothing I could do to convince her.

Back in Newcastle, Ethan and I were awarded the PhD studentship. I would be the primary supervisor, since I had written the grant proposal. 24 people applied for the combined job and degree program.

The prospectives were decent, but many of them – even those with master's degrees in related fields – seemed at sea, unsure of themselves or the details of the project. After a long day of interviews, we were growing weary. We called in the last candidate.

Renata introduced herself and took a seat across from us. We eased into the interview with some chit-chat, then launched into some discussion of the project.

"Are you familiar with cancer cell metabolism?" I asked.

"Well, supposedly all cancer cells burn sugars," Renata replied.

I loved that 'supposedly'. "Where do you get that from?" I asked.

She expounded on the work of early twentieth-century biochemist Otto Warburg, who had established this dogma. He had worked in Germany during a golden age of biochemistry, but also during a difficult period of life for both himself and his country. He was half-Jewish, and basically imprisoned in his lab for the duration of the Third Reich. During that time, he methodically isolated enzymes involved in sugar fermentation, from both yeast cells and human cancer cells.

"So then why did you say 'supposedly' before?" I asked.

"Well, that can't be the whole story," Renata explained. "The fermentation of sugar does not provide much energy. And cancer cells must need a lot of energy."

She paused. "Go on," I encouraged her.

"Well, I did some histopathology work during my master's degree, and I noticed that cancer cells – especially those in malignant brain tumors – they have giant lipid droplets inside."

"Uh huh," I said, grinning.

"Well, what are they storing those fats for, unless they are using them for energy?"

I looked at Ethan. He looked back at me with a wry expression. Over the past few years, we had run into dozens of highly-regarded oncologists, neuropathologists and neuroradiologists who had acknowledged the large amount of fat in malignant brain tumor cells – evident through tissue staining or metabolite analysis. None of them had ever made this leap.

We chatted for a while longer then wrapped up the interview. When I called Renata later that day, she was ecstatic to hear she had won the position.

In autumn of 2016, she started work in my lab. She received training on cell culture from me, training on magnetic resonance imaging from Ethan, and training on the ethical use of animals in research from an accredited university course.

We ran a pilot study again, with a small number of animals. The mice would grow tumors so we could try out the patented corporate formulation of the drug and watch the cancer grow using MRI.

We could not deliver the drug systemically through osmotic pumps because of the physical limitations of oil and glycerol, we were not legally allowed to inject the drug into the mice every day for the entire length of the study, and the Home Office would not let us force the mixture down the animals' throats either. We had to come up with another solution.

"We should definitely try oral dosing," Sophie said. "That's how patients would get the drug."

"That's true," I agreed. "The drug availability changes with the route of delivery, so we should make the study as relevant to human patients as possible."

"Maybe we could trick the mice into licking oil containing the drug," Renata said. We tried that one afternoon, but it didn't work.

The following morning, I arrived at the lab with a grocery bag from Waitrose.

"Ooh, you've been shopping somewhere fancy," Sophie announced.

"Yep," I said, pulling out a cannister of expensive organic coconut oil. It was the only kind Waitrose had.

Renata slapped her forehead. "Of course!" she called out. We melted the coconut oil until it was clear, dissolved the drug easily into solution, then quickly pipetted out exact milliliter amounts into spots on a sheet of wax paper. The spots solidified at room temperature, so we had little pellets to feed the mice.

The next step was to find out if the mice would eat the pellets. They had as much food and water as they wanted, so we weren't sure if they would go for the treats. We dropped a pellet in each cage and stood back to watch. Each mouse ran over, picked up the pellet, and gobbled it up in seconds, then licked his paws.

I turned around and looked at my team. Renata and Sophie were grinning, just like I was.

We got to work. The plan was to run the imaging study

with a few animals in each treatment group first, then follow with the large, blinded preclinical trial to evaluate the median survival of the mice with and without treatment.

Ethan was onboard – he wanted to identify the chemical composition of the tumors as well as imaging them. Renata and I prepared sixteen mice for the study, four in each treatment group.

"Why do they like me?" Renata asked a few weeks later, holding her hand still as one of the mice nuzzled against her fingers. "I'm slowly killing him with a brain tumor."

I watched the small creature in her hand. I knew only one other person who could pacify an animal like this, and it was Xi. My students were so calm and tender. "Your gentleness matters more than what you do," I explained.

"But both things should matter," Renata pointed out.

"I agree, but that's not how people or mice work. We'll put up with a lot, as long as we're treated kindly."

Every day we gave the mice coconut pellets and every day they scarfed them down, licking their paws. The tumors never grew in the drug-treated animals, even a month after the placebo-treated animals had died with massive tumor burdens three months into the study.

We knew the drug extended life, but we didn't know for how long. We had to end the study early; the Home Office had instituted severe penalties for anyone caught with a suffering animal and the enforcement was tightening. Although we had tried to care for the mice as best we could, we could not continue running the risk of fines and jail time. We euthanized the remaining animals, although they were healthy and showed no signs of tumor.

There was only one thing left to do: run the preclinical trial to test etomoxir in mice, with sufficient statistical power to assess the effect of the drug on total survival time. It was the same setup as before, but now we needed to evaluate oral dosing, with the patented formulation of the drug, not just for thirty days but for as long as possible, with and without clinically-relevant doses of the standard-of-care chemotherapy drug used for human glioma patients.

This study would provide a go/no-go decision point for moving into clinical trial. But we had to stop. A number of factors converged to make it impossible for me to continue working in England.

Chapter 16
In Laws

"Mum used to sing dirty show tunes while Dudley Moore played the piano."

"Is that true, Mary?"

"They weren't that dirty." She sang a few bars to *Anything Goes*.

"You see?" Andy said pointedly. "Scandalous."

"Do you not know that song? It's like a Broadway standard!" My husband was a philistine when it came to certain things, despite his Oxbridge education. "You're obviously exaggerating your mother's penchant for vulgarity. Mary, did you really know that crowd?"

"Oh, everyone knew everyone back then," my mother-in-law waved her hand dismissively.

"And when Mum moved to London after university, she lived next door to Sir Humphrey Appleby."

"You mean the guy who played Sir Humphrey Appleby on tv? Sir Nigel Hawthorne?"

"He wasn't knighted back then," Mary said. "He was just a working actor. And he didn't have his own shower, so he used ours."

I giggled. Andy egged her on. Hearing these old stories

was one of the best things about visiting Hampstead. The game was as traditional as the neighborhood pubs with their cask ales and dark wooden tables, or the horse-drawn carriages trotting down the street on snowy winter mornings. It felt like a connection to the ungentrified, original north London, before it was populated with bankers and lawyers and 'yummy mummies' as my father-in-law Pete disgustingly called them.

"Mum also lived next door to Christine Keeler and Mandy Rice-Davies during the Profumo Affair."

"We shared a wall, but we didn't go to the same parties."

"I bet you did go to the same parties, and you just didn't tell me," Pete said, with obvious jealousy.

"We weren't married back then," Mary said. "I didn't even know you yet." That hedge made it sound like maybe she had gone to those parties.

Pete sighed. Mary had nearly ten years on him, and he suspected her of having too much life experience. She was nearly eighty now, with a hunched posture, one glass eye, and stories hidden like gemstones. Pete glowered for a bit, then enthusiastically brought up his years in Canada, working as an engineer in the mountains and tar sands of Alberta, because no one knew about his life there and the mysterious things he may or may not have done.

From there, we got onto the subject of travel, ranging from Pete's upcoming ski holiday in the Alps, Mary's upcoming painting holiday in Lanzarote, our upcoming spring break with friends exploring the vineyards of Piedmont. Then we went back to reminiscing about previous trips. Their family had travelled a lot.

When I was a kid, my family drove to Wisconsin for a long weekend once a year, in summertime – the main highlights being the hotel pool and the mini-golf course. But my husband's family had more exciting stories – kayaking and camping adventures in the Scottish wilderness, climbing Mount Snowden and hiking the peaks of the English Lake District, all kinds of countryside vacations and urban expeditions. The conversation brought up Andy's memories of a family trip to Berlin in 1990.

"That's a bold move, to take your young family to East Germany right after the wall came down," I remarked to Mary. "But it sounds like you knew people there. Had you been there before?"

"Oh sure," she said, commencing a tale from the seventies, of ending up on the wrong side of the concrete-and-barbed-wire barrier after dark, how she charmed her way back to the west, and the people she met along the way.

Then I recalled a story she had previously told on occasion, regarding a long trip she took by road and rail through former Yugoslavia. The highlight of that trip, for Andy and Pete, was how, when she reached Greece, she could read the letters of the town names at each of the train stations because of her training in mathematics. They laughed again, retelling the story themselves and spelling Thebes aloud, in a sing-song voice, as if to a baby.

I ignored them. "So you travelled around Yugoslavia by yourself?" I asked.

"Oh no," Mary said. "I had a different boyfriend then." She glanced at Pete, who let it go. He was still laughing aloud about her possibly being able to read Greek.

"Have you ever been to Russia?" I asked, hoping to hear more and maybe share notes.

"Yes, well, I went to St Petersburg," she said carefully.

"I didn't know that," Andy said with sharp voice,

suddenly taking notice.

"Sure, that's the trip where I met the young guys on the ferryboat to Finland on my way back," Mary said. "You thought it was funny that I ended up hitting on twenty year-olds."

"Oh, right!" Andy and Pete hooted, relaxing back into comfortable mockery.

I looked at Mary. "What did you do there? In St Petersburg?"

"Oh, it was an art tour, we looked at paintings in the museums." Andy and Pete rolled their eyes.

"Did you go to the Hermitage?"

"Yes, of course," she smiled.

"Did you go to Moscow as well, to the Tretyakov Gallery? Or maybe it wasn't open to the public then?"

"Yes, I did go to Moscow as well."

"What? You never told us that," Andy barked, his attention pricking up once again.

"Did you see art there too?" I asked.

"Well, I think we may have gone to Tretyakov. I don't quite remember. Anyway we didn't really hear much about the art," Mary said. "The guide, Svetlana, wasn't very interested or well-informed on that subject."

"Huh. That's strange, it being her job to guide the art tour," Andy noted.

"Where did you stay?" I asked. On a road trip through the Baltics the previous year, Andy and I had visited an abandoned KGB outpost on the top floor of a swinging 60s-era hotel in Tallinn that had attracted westerners travelling across the Iron Curtain. There, we had learned that tourist hotels in the Soviet Union were all bugged.

"Well, the Russian tourist agency had set us up at a nice hotel in the center of Moscow, but there was a double-booking, so Svetlana had us stay in a rundown building on the outskirts of town," Mary explained. "A right dump, that place was."

"Huh," I nodded slowly. "So you didn't stay at the tourist hotel."

"Did you bring Svetlana any gifts, on instruction from anyone back home?" Andy joked.

"Yes, I did," Mary said, almost absentmindedly. "The person who organized the tour suggested we bring our guide a present. I brought a nice art book, but like I said, she just wasn't interested."

Andy and I looked at each other. "Um, who organized this tour, Mary?"

"Oh, it was my friend Jim Riordan."

I could see Andy tapping on his smartphone. I looked over his shoulder.

"Is that James Riordan, 'The Spy Who Played for Spartak'?" I asked when the page loaded.

"Oh yes," Mary said. "He did play football when he lived in Moscow. But he wasn't living there when I knew him. In fact I think he wasn't allowed back there."

"Yeah, no kidding," Andy said, reading the bio.

"How well did you know Jim, Mary?" I asked.

"So-so," she replied, keeping an eye on Pete.

"Um, do you think there were other gifts, along with what you and your fellow art enthusiasts brought over?"

"Oh, sure, the gifts all went in a big pile and they only searched some of them," Mary said. Then, changing the subject, she added, "Anyway it was a long time ago and Jim is probably dead now."

We checked Wikipedia. "Yeah, he is."

Mary looked into the middle distance. "Well, it was a long time ago."

After a moment, I stood up and cleared the dishes and loaded the dishwasher. Andy and Pete finished an earlier argument and a second bottle of wine. Then we all went upstairs to watch Match of the Day, the only show Mary watched on television and one she almost never missed.

Mary often sketched on walks near the family cottage in the Lake District, then used these drawings to make etchings. She deeply admired the artists and poets who had been inspired by the rivers and lakes and mountains and hillsides in this part of England, especially Turner and Coleridge. Sometimes I would leave Andy and his father to walk up Hellvelyn or Blencathra while I joined Mary in visiting art museums and galleries in the nearby towns of Grasmere and Ambleside.

One day the two of us visited the home of William Wordsworth, where the poet lived with his sister and his wife. Much of the nineteenth-century home was preserved to show their lifestyle; the rest was used to showcase the efforts of living artists currently working in the Lake District.

Later that night, the four of us briefed each other about our day, outdoors and indoors respectively.

"You know, William didn't actually write those poems," Mary mentioned.

"What do you mean?" I asked. Pete and Andy groaned.

"You know, the one about the daffodils," she said, and began to recite.

I wandered lonely as a cloud/
That floats on high o'er vales and hills/
When all at once I saw a crowd/

A host, of golden daffodils/
Beside the lake, beneath the trees/
Fluttering and dancing in the breeze.

I have always been enamored of people who can recite poetry, and Mary did it so well. I listened, smiling, until she finished the verse.

"But you're saying he didn't write it?" We had learned about that poem in school. It was one of the most famous poems in the English language. I was surprised the authorship was in doubt.

"Well, the people who inherited the estate found his sister Dorothy's diary. It has a whole thing about those daffodils, years before he published it. He not only pretended he wrote the thing, but also that he was alone on that walk."

"Really?" I was intrigued by this domestic melodrama.

"Sure," Mary replied. She went to the bookcase and came back with a book of Lake District lore.

"Look, here's the diary entry." A number of lines were similar, and the rest was pure beauty:

> "When we were in the woods beyond Gowbarrow Park we saw a few daffodils close to the water side, we fancied that the lake had floated the seed ashore and that the little colony had so sprung up – But as we went along there were more and yet more and at last under the boughs of the trees, we saw that there was a long belt of them along the shore, about the breadth of a country turnpike road. I never saw daffodils so beautiful they grew among the mossy stones about and about them, some rested their heads

upon these stones as on a pillow for weariness and the rest tossed and reeled and danced and seemed as if they verily laughed with the wind that blew upon them over the Lake, they looked so gay ever glancing ever changing."

"Wow," I said, putting down the book.

"William eventually admitted that he was inspired by conversations with his sister," Mary explained. "And that his two best lines in that poem were actually written by his wife. The ones that go:

> They flash upon that inward eye/
> Which is the bliss of solitude.

"Huh," I said. "It's funny we never knew that."

"Sometimes people don't always get the credit they deserve," Mary said, putting the book away.

"You're not a feminist, are you?" Pete asked me loudly.

"Of course! Aren't we all?" I laughed lightly, wondering where that was coming from. I was proud to be part of a family with such brilliant, dynamic women. I wasn't sure I could keep up, but I was proud to be in that kind of company.

On another occasion, Andy and I drove to visit Mary and Pete in the Lake District for a holiday weekend in early summer. On Friday evening, after a long week of work, we made the long drive from Newcastle, across nearly the entire width of the country – along Hadrian's Wall, over the hills, past the lakes, and finally around Red Bank, the bracken-covered fell that links Grasmere and Chapel Stile. As we arrived at the cottage in the approaching darkness, we saw Pete loading huge tubes of material into the recycling bin. I got out of the car and asked what he was up to.

"Just clearing the house, getting rid of all the old crap that we don't need." I saw what he was disposing of more clearly up close. The tubes of material were rolled-up canvases and large sheets of thick etching paper. It was the entire remainder of Mary's art that Pete had not already used to pad underneath the floorboards in their two houses in London. At seventy, he was too old to be re-laying floors, so he was just openly throwing out her work.

I was crestfallen and spent the dinner plotting to reverse this appalling decision. Mary refused to act upset about it, merely agreeing with Pete that the house needed tidying. The men used her dull reaction to argue that nothing of value was being lost. All the same, after the meal I went outside into the dim light behind the house, opened the bin, and started digging.

"Whatcha doing?" Pete asked, startling me. I hadn't noticed him out there, but there he was, standing against the side of the house in the dark, smoking a pipe and watching me.

I felt a little nervous, although I had announced my intentions to rescue the art over dessert and I hadn't met any opposition. "I'd really like to see these pieces before they're thrown away," I mumbled.

Pete was silent. I forced a light chuckle and took a self-deprecating stance. "I'm just intrigued with Mary's artwork, and I couldn't resist a bit of light dumpster-diving on my holiday weekend."

He sneered at the revealing of my low-class American instincts. "I'll allow it," he said, overturning his pipe and following me up the stairs to the main level, the etchings and paintings piled in my arms.

In the hours that followed, Andy and Pete sat silently in armchairs as Mary and I nestled on the couch, her regaling me with the story behind each series of pieces.

"Ah, here are some chalk drawings of Geordie fisherman, from your neck of the woods. I used to spend a lot of time in the northeast when I was on the Coal Board, in the mining communities. I think I did these near Wylam, or the other direction along the River Tyne, near Hebburn."

"Ah! And these are pencil drawings from a trip to Venice in the Sixties. My friend Veronica came with me, but she disappeared with an Italian man the first afternoon of our trip, so I spent the rest of the holiday sketching on my own."

"And these are some of my first screenprints." Mary pulled out a huge pile of ink productions made from pressings on metal plates. I looked at the mixture and could not believe they were all made by the same hand. Some were simple monocolor outlines of sailboats, and others were black-and-white prints of dense foliage with Gauguin-like complexity and beauty.

"Do we have to throw these away?" I asked as the clock approached midnight and we finished going through every single piece of artwork. "Can I take these sketches and prints with me?"

"We can't take all of it," Andy said. "It's not like we have room at our house either." His father snorted in derision with the idea that we would want things he had deemed junk.

I picked out some of my favorites – samples from each of the eras and places and styles, mostly Mary's own art but also some pieces from her teachers – and rolled them into a single lean roll of canvases.

I looked at each of them - Andy, Pete and Mary - and

asked, "Can I have these ones?"

All three of them nodded. I carefully rolled what I had rescued, and Andy returned the rest of the art to the bin behind the house. I'm so grateful for the precious pieces I have – a sample testifying to the life-work of a talented and dearly loved artist – but I wish more than anything I could have taken it all.

I loved spending time with Mary one-on-one. She maintained a certain dottiness when her husband and children were around, but she dropped it like a hot potato whenever they were out of earshot. She had a different voice when it was just the two of us together, and instead of shrugging off the importance of things, she delved into conversations passionately and eloquently. Alone, she seemed so much more awake and aware and complete.

But even in their gentle mockery, I could sense the pride her children had in her. My husband and his sister are both highly accomplished in their own fields, and enjoyed being in the presence of other capable people. They always pretended their mother was just a silly old woman and their father was a brilliant but underappreciated amateur inventor, but the truth was intact underneath and it came poking out. After spending several years with the family, I found out that Pete had stopped working for a big engineering firm after he punched his boss and walked out of his job. He tinkered with meters in the basement for a couple decades after that, but the home business never really took off. Although he worked at the house, he did not cook or care for the kids when they came home from school, as he considered that women's work. Andy and his sister made dinner themselves or waited for their mother to come home.

As for Mary, I was never really sure how much was true and how much was legend – the development of machine-learning algorithms, the early application of spreadsheets, the teaching of financial modelling to generations of students, and other contributions to the London Business School. I know she wrote a best-selling book called 'Who Owns the Blue Chips?' and several other useful texts on business, finance, economics, and expert systems. I know the royalties from those books paid the bills in the house. I know she spent years serving as a faculty member at the LBS – there was a photo upstairs of her during that time, meeting with the Queen. I know that earlier in her career she was on the Coal Board deciding national policy on natural resources, until the Thatcher government gave up on those industries and let them die. It's hard to fathom, though, how this person became the butt of jokes in her household. Her husband especially mocked her relentlessly, mostly for being an absentee mother. She always brushed it off, although I could tell it hurt.

In 2016, Mary's cancer came back. With the cancer came chemo, and with chemo came infection, like the one that had taken her left eye ten years previously. This new infection was systemic, and it caused an alarming delirium. Mary thought she was in an art gallery, when in fact she was situated in the women's hospital ward at University College Hospital.

This wasn't a pretend dottiness, like I had witnessed so many times before. It wasn't the use of a feigned absentmindedness to attain privacy in her thoughts. Mary really thought we were in the National Portrait Gallery. I wasn't sure if she saw us as the portraits or if she saw portraits behind us, but either way it was clear she was hallucinating.

Andy, normally impervious, trembled beside me.

Mary herself remained quiet, occasionally sitting up to

get a better look around at the imaginary portraits. Andy leaned forward in his chair, wringing his hands.

"Do you want to tell us where else you've been today?" I asked, to break the silence.

"No," Andy said, under his breath. "Don't do this."

"But right now she's isolated in this confusion," I whispered. "Let's reach out. Let her talk about what she's going through."

"I'm not sure how I got here," Mary said. "We had lunch at the library earlier, didn't we?"

We had indeed had lunch at the café attached to the British Library a couple days previously, right before she fell ill. "Yes, we did, Mary," I said, looking pointedly at Andy. He looked relieved.

"And yesterday I went with Pete to University College London," she stated.

"That's right, Mum. University College Hospital," Andy prompted. "That's where we are now."

"No, we're in the portrait gallery," Mary corrected. Andy's shoulders dropped.

"Anyway the other day Pete and I went to University College London," she went on. "For the machine-learning conference." Andy looked distraught.

"Did you learn anything interesting there?" I asked.

"Yes, I did," Mary replied. "And I presented my own work on coding too."

"That's fantastic," I murmured. I could tell Andy was growing angry at me for indulging the delirium. But his mother seemed so cheerful, engaged in conversation.

"Last night was quite a palaver, though," Mary said.

"What happened last night?" I asked. Andy seethed beside me.

"Well, all of us women had to stay in the bomb shelter," Mary said, gesturing to the other patients on the ward. "The one underneath King's Cross."

"Uh huh," I nodded, worried that childhood memories of the blitz would take this new hallucination on a disturbing turn. Andy gave me a dirty look. I wondered how to talk us back into a quieter part of London, during a quieter time in history. Maybe she would like to imagine sharing a pint with us at the pub, just around the corner from her house in Hampstead.

"But then we stormed the gates at Pimlico!" Mary exclaimed suddenly, lifting her frail arms into the air, hands clenched in fists.

"I think that's from a movie," Andy murmured softly.

"The police tried to barricade us all night, but we pushed forward and crossed the Tower Bridge," she continued, recounting the adventure.

"Damn it all," Andy muttered angrily.

"And now we're here," Mary finished, leaning back on the hospital bed. "In the National Portrait Gallery."

Andy put his head in his hands.

"Your mother is awesome," I whispered to him.

Two days later, the antibiotics had kicked in and the systemic infection had begun to clear. Mary's delirium passed, as the doctors had promised it would. But Pete would never trust her sanity again.

"You said some crazy things these past few days," he announced.

"Did I?" Mary said, laughing nervously. "No big secrets, I hope."

Chapter 17
Troubles

"The content of thought doesn't matter."

"What the hell are you talking about?"

"The stuff of thought," Andy explained. "It doesn't matter. Existing neural networks can input information and make complex, tailored, intelligent outputs when machine-learning algorithms are employed. There's no need to have a conscious perception of understanding at all."

"I guess that's possible," I replied doubtfully. We were sitting on an airplane, on our way to my parents' house for Thanksgiving Dinner after attending a thought-provoking Society for Neuroscience meeting. I shoved my bag under the seat and considered his point. "Maybe consciousness is just a side effect, a strange emergent but useless property that sometimes comes into existence in highly recurrent neural networks. But maybe consciousness always and inevitably manifests in sufficiently complex systems. Just because we don't recognize it, doesn't mean it's not there."

"I think we would recognize it if it was there," Andy argued further. "Humanity has now created problem-solving automatons that do not demonstrate or need consciousness. The experience of thought has proved unnecessary. The problem-solver does not require consciousness or even a sense of self to do its job."

I hated Google Brain right then. Assuming it was indeed unconscious, its existence did not invalidate my own, and I wished my husband of all people would appreciate that.

I sighed. "But we do have consciousness, Andy. We do have the feeling of self, we do process thoughts between sensory input and behavioral output, and we don't know for sure that problem-solving can occur without that experience of thought."

"But just because it can happen doesn't mean it's necessary," he argued provocatively.

"You in particular should appreciate the existence of top-down control," I told my husband. "You literally study how thought turns into action, how the mind exerts its will over the physical world."

"No," he corrected. "I study how neural signals encode force and direction to create movement in a natural or robotic limb. The work proves that a purely physical system can achieve goal-directed action. Thought may only exist as a perceptual experience, without being a necessary part of the sensory-motor loop."

"Excuse me," said the man sitting next to me, in the aisle seat. "Can I join your argument?"

"Depends," I said. "Which side are you on?"

"Oh, I'm definitely on your side," he replied.

I turned to Andy and gave him a smug grin.

"I'm a psychiatrist," the man explained, leaning over so he could speak to both of us. "I do a lot of talking therapy with patients."

Andy groaned.

The man continued, undeterred. "It really helps

people," he argued. "Somehow our discussions, which just alter the content of thought, really affect how people feel and act and treat other people afterward."

Andy groaned again, but he didn't offer the man any response.

"I think we won," I whispered loudly. The man gave me a high-five.

"You know," I mentioned, "I wish we had a psychiatrist specializing in the theory of mind present at every single one of our marital spats."

"Everyone could use that," he replied, settling back into his seat. "Anyway, it seems like you two have an interesting marriage."

"You have no idea," I told him, as my husband chuckled quietly beside me.

Andy and I were working too much. We took the train down to London, to meet with representatives of the European Medicines Agency who would be responsible for approving our proposed treatment for epilepsy. Our main query was whether the gene therapy and implantable biomedical device would be considered as two separate medicines, or a combination therapy.

A senior academic in the faculty of genetics was invited along, to lend the appearance of seriousness to the genetics side of the project. This professor had no background in neuroscience or production of our proposed gene therapy, but he was involved in the genetics field and he looked the part of wise older professor. His graduate students emailed me at times for advice and protocols, but I had never met him before. Everyone on the team was happy to have him along with us.

The esteemed professor fell asleep during the meeting with the regulatory agency, snoring gently. When he woke up, he asserted that our gene therapy should not be approved for use in humans. I jumped in.

"What we're trying to say is, are there any specific genetic sequences that would be prohibited?"

The Agency representatives explained that a burden of proof was on us to provide sufficient safety data for our medicine, in collaboration with our contract manufacturing partner. Nothing was actually prohibited. "Is there any particular sequence you would have difficulty justifying?" they asked.

This was a reasonable question. I explained the necessity of the genes making up the viral shell and the usefulness of the genes we wished to include as the therapy itself. The green fluorescent protein that allowed the cells to glow was useful in lab experiments but may not be sufficiently necessary at later stages to justify its inclusion in the human gene therapy.

They nodded, and asked more questions about the manufacturing process, which I answered. Then we talked a little bit about precedents in the field. Things were moving fast. I had spoken with the head of gene therapy at Glaxo Smith Kline and the technology development manager there too. They had a team of forty people developing new gene therapies, while I had only three people working with me. I was counting on others to make progress; it would help us to develop our case too. After all, there were only so many platforms – we were all converging on the same contracting manufacturing partners, although there were always new players popping up. In general, it was a small field, everyone knew each other, and people were more collaborative than competitive.

No one on the CANDO management team cared I was in the loop though. When I was invited to give talks at conferences, these events were not included on the project website. When I produced a massive document detailing the specifications for the clinical-grade gene therapy, the team shrugged. And then they invited a senior male professor who knew less than me to speak about the gene therapy to the regulators.

"Are you glad you invited Yorick along then?" I could not help asking the others on the train ride back to Newcastle from London.

Andy, Tony and Roger sighed and looked away.

"Yeah, he was not helpful at all," said Luke, the project manager. "What was that about? He almost imploded our whole project. You really saved the day there, Beth."

I smiled. Andy, Tony and Roger frowned.

I expected better from Andy – it would have been easy for him to play up my strengths at this point in the project, but he was more interested in getting senior faculty members on side. Tony, the engineering lead, was difficult to read – he had a friendly voice and an easy smile, but he was always serious. Roger was a clinician – he had soft brown eyes and a genial face, but I wondered what was behind that harmless-seeming appearance.

Back in Newcastle, we decided to call our first visit to the regulatory agency a success, and we got back to work on the project. Roger sent an email round to everyone which announced Yorick as CANDO's gene therapy lead.

"Andy, send out a correction," I said. "I'm the one leading on the gene therapy."

"I'm not going to do that," Andy said.

"Why?" I asked.

"I just don't want to get involved."

"But you're the head of the project."

He shrugged.

I sent an email to Roger myself, cc'ing the members of the project management team, to set the record straight.

"You're making the classic mistake of giving a man credit for thousands of hours of work done by a woman," I wrote, in a matter-of-fact way.

"You're a psycho bitch," Andy told me later that day.

"That's unhelpful, Andy," I replied. "I wish you would have stuck up for me."

I ran into Roger in the hallway a few days later. He shoved me up against the wall. "Don't you ever give me lip again," he snarled, his face close to mine.

"I won't, as long as you give me proper credit for my work," I replied, pushing him off and straightening my dress. He backed away, giving me a dirty look.

Despite incidents like that, I was incredibly proud of what I was building and how I was contributing to the institute. I converted a small lab into a state-of-the-art cell culture facility and a larger lab into a fully-equipped molecular biology suite. Sophie and I cleaned out the multi-user freezer room, removing old broken equipment, hooking critical freezers to backup power and alarm systems, and setting up liquid nitrogen storage tanks. Together the two of us installed a quarter million pounds sterling worth of brand-new and rescued equipment. My officemate was undertaking to set up a shared histology lab, and I gave him a hand moving chemicals and ensuring the fume hoods were set up safely. I printed out protocols and ethics approvals to share my expertise and licensing for human tissue processing, small animal surgery and viral-mediated genetic modification. Then I found another small lab filled with unused and broken equipment, and I acquired permission to make this room into a shared cryosectioning suite for processing brain tissues. I sourced one cryostat from a lab that was shutting down and wrote a grant with other members of the institute to get a twin piece of equipment. I ordered a boombox with an ipod dock from Amazon, out of pocket, and set two undergraduates to work in parallel, sectioning the brain tissue from the mouse tumor studies.

One day, I had lunch with Andy and gave him the update. Things were getting rolling, my team was coming together, and I was excited about the possibilities from here.

Andy shrugged.

"You know," I said. "I don't often speak openly about my hopes and dreams and future plans. I tend to just get going. But I wish you would appreciate how much this means to me. I'm starting to feel really happy and productive here, finally."

He shrugged again.

"Do you care, honey?"

He sighed. "If you have a histology lab, then you can process all the monkey brains for CANDO."

"Andy, I have never worked on monkeys. I do not even know how to section brains that large."

"Well, this work needs to be done. If you have a histology lab, you should do it."

"Honey, it's a shared histology lab I set up for the institute. Anyone can use it. There should be someone dedicated on the project to do monkey brain work. I'm not the expert on this. Surely someone in your lab or Nathan's lab should be leading on it."

Andy threw his napkin on his plate and stood up. I followed him out. We walked up the road back to the institute in silence. When we got to the door, he turned and laid into me.

"You don't care about CANDO," he yelled, as colleagues walked past, staring at us. "You need to be helping out more on this project. You may think you're helping the institute but you're just helping yourself. You're being selfish. The damn least you can do at this point is the monkey brain histology."

Andy's post-doc Sam and his wife, Laura, who was our CANDO regulatory manager, started to say hello, then froze and stared at us. I realized in that moment that Sam had the job dedicated to monkey brain work. Andy knew this, he had written the staff roles into the grant.

"I think you might have things confused –"

"I don't have anything confused," Andy roared. "You're the one who needs to be set straight."

He continued to scream at me. Our colleagues continued to stare. We were all frozen on the spot. Finally Andy stormed off and I trudged back to my office. I put off other work that afternoon to send a precise email detailing the process for training a person to analyze tissue – first they learn to use the cryosectioning equipment (from the institute technical manager), then they receive training on the neuroanatomy of the particular tissue (by me for mice, by Nathan for monkeys), and then, once the tissue sections are cut, they receive training on staining procedures (by me) and cell-specific labelling advice (from the neuron identification expert down the hall), and finally they learn to use the deconvolution or confocal microscopes (by the microscopy core facility manager). The things I don't do, I explained, are just the things I'm not qualified to do.

I copied in Andy's post-doc Sam, because the information was relevant to him and he might like to know how to go about things if there were monkey tissues he wanted to analyze. I did not mention the scene outside, and I did not tell him what to do. I merely stated that, if one wanted to be trained on histology, here is how one would do it.

Andy did not speak to me for days, saying only that I 'crossed a line' by involving his post-doc. But he had involved our colleagues to begin with, by yelling at me in front of Sam and Laura. They both quit the project shortly afterwards.

The weekend after our spat Andy and I took the train to London to visit his parents. He was silent.

"Andy, you're wrong – I had no intention of shirking CANDO work, I was just explaining that I was not the best person to deal with monkey brain tissue."

"I don't want to talk about it."

"But honey, we have to talk about this. We need to resolve the work issue and the fact you humiliated me in public."

"I'm not talking about it."

"Andy, we need to communicate in order to get through our disagreements. You need to confront the hurtful things you have done to me."

"Look, do you want to get a divorce?"

"What?!" I was taken aback. "What?!"

"I said, do you want a divorce?"

"No! What? No!"

"Then stop complaining."

I didn't even know how to speak. When we arrived at King's Cross, Andy bought more time for me to get myself together by stopping at a pub, but tears were still rolling down my face when we arrived at his parents' house in Hampstead later that evening. His mother Mary sat with me on the sofa upstairs, holding my hand. I could not complain to her. I just cried until I was able to stop.

On our return journey a couple days later, I brought up

our troubles again.

"Andy, you need to apologize for your hurtful words and actions."

"No, you need to stop bringing up the past."

"But Andy, the past does not just go away."

"Yeah, because you keep bringing it up."

"I think we have a number of issues that need to be resolved."

"Like what? What's the problem?"

"Well, you went to a work event on the evening of my birthday instead of –"

"That was ages ago! Jesus Christ."

"Well, you never apologized for it, and –"

"I'm not about to apologize now if I didn't before."

"Well, how are we going to get through this?"

"Get through what?"

"I don't know, maybe we should just focus on the more recent stuff."

"Like what."

"Well, you yelled at me in front of our colleagues the other day," I explained, once again.

"You wouldn't do your job."

"One, that was not my job you were asking me to do, and two, that's still no reason to yell at me."

"What do you want?"

"I would like an apology, please."

"I'll apologize to you if you apologize to me for all your nagging."

"Honey, that's not how this works."

"Oh, I have to apologize but you don't?"

"What? If I have hurt you, I will apologize. Of course I will."

"Well, you've hurt me, and now I'm waiting for my apology."

"You're kidding me." I stared at him.

He looked straight ahead. He was giving me nothing.

"Look, all I want to do is redefine our narrative. I want us to start over, establish new patterns that do not constantly trigger memories of bad things that happened in the past."

He was silent.

"Do you want to start over with me?"

"How?" he asked.

"Tell me a story. Tell me a story of our engagement, a different one than what really happened. Tell me how you would have liked to have done it that summer."

"What the hell is this? No. That's messed up."

"Honey, it'll help me. I want to overwrite our history with a different story. Please. I need you to join me in making peace with the past, so we can build a happy future."

"I don't even know what you're asking for or why you're asking for it."

"Honey, please try to understand. Try to be here with me."

"This is messed up. You're still nagging me."

"Honey, I don't know what else to do."

Andy was invited to apply for a professorship at University College London, with the opportunity to direct the primate neuroscience center there. His PhD supervisor was retiring, and the university was looking to hire a well-regarded scientist in the same field to replace him.

Another primate researcher at Newcastle had already applied for the post, then used his offer as leverage locally to get one million pounds sterling in lab equipment and a professorship for his wife, in return for staying up north. The whole thing was crazy – this woman was a talented neuroscientist herself, and she would have met the objective criteria for full tenure by earning just one more grant over the next couple of years. But she chose this route.

"Andy, you'll apply for that position, right?" I asked him one morning, as we made coffee in the kitchen before going to work.

"No, I don't want to leave Newcastle," he responded.

"What are you talking about? This is a fantastic opportunity for you!"

"I'm working to get my professorship at Newcastle. I should meet the criteria this year or next."

"But this would be a much more prestigious post."

"If I leave Newcastle, then I leave CANDO. And if I abandon such a large project, I'll never be able to get funding from The Trust again."

"Well, you could talk to them about it. Maybe you could continue to lead through a transition stage. You've never liked spending your time on CANDO anyway – this way, you could ease out of it and spend more time on your other projects."

"I don't want to do that."

"Andy, don't you want to live in London? We'd be near your parents and your sister and her kids. We could have kids ourselves – we'd have the support network down there, and the cousins could grow up together."

"I thought you didn't want kids."

"Well, you do and I'm trying to find a way to make it possible. We're just too alone up here."

"It's expensive to live in London, and you don't want to have to ride the tube every day."

"Public transport is not that big of a deal, honey. This would be a fantastic opportunity for you – for us. You should really explore it."

"I'm not going to," he replied, in a flat voice. "Anyway, how would you find a job?"

"I could apply for a lecturer position at University College London. Build a lab there too."

"The only way you'd get a post is through spousal hire," he said dismissively.

That stung. Months earlier, I had been invited to give a talk at UCL about my brain tumor work. Afterward, several of the clinical researchers had encouraged me to apply for a faculty post there. They had made me feel welcome, an asset to the neuro-oncology community.

"Andy, I don't think that's true."

"Yes, it is. You could never get a faculty post on your own."

I nodded silently, without the strength to argue. I felt like someone had just thrown shit in my face.

It was spring and the days were getting longer, but darkness still set over the university in early evening.

I leaned back in my chair. It was 6 o'clock and I decided not to get embroiled in anything else for the day. After all, it was Friday, time to wrap it up for the week. It would be nice to just go home and have dinner, sit on the couch and watch tv, settle in for the weekend.

It had been a disappointing day. I had received notice that my paper was rejected – the one describing our efforts to identify the metabolic fuel requirements of brain tumor cells and establish a potential drug target for slowing cancer progression. I was sad and tired, and I wanted sympathy.

I trudged over to Andy's office. He agreed to leave and gathered his things – standing up tall, smiling, throwing on his wool winter jacket.

Walking out of the building, I broke the news. I was already formulating a plan to submit the study to a journal that would be a better fit, although I was still disappointed with my first effort.

"You probably submitted the paper incorrectly."

"No, I didn't. The editors sent it out for review."

"But the reviewers brushed off the study."

"No, they engaged in a useful discussion. They just didn't accept it in the end."

"That's too bad."

"I wonder if I should argue."

"Not worth it," Andy said. "Maybe you'll find another journal that will think it worthwhile."

"Well, I know the study is worthwhile," I said, smiling proudly.

"Of course you do, sweetie," he said.

"Uh, you're being kind of patronizing here," I said, stopping.

"I'm sorry, sweetie," Andy said. He stopped too and turned to look at me.

"Thank you for saying that. I mean it," I said. We started walking again.

"OK. Do you want to hear about my day?" he asked.

"Yes, of course," I replied. He told me what was going on in his lab – updates on people, monkeys, and methods for data analysis.

"Also, Nathan has found some potential benefactors to the institute. It's a notable family up here, and they might be interested in supporting brain tumor work."

"Oh, that's great!" Then I hesitated. "I hope they don't have some personal reason for wanting to support that research."

"Yeah, I think one of their family members has a brain tumor."

"Oh no! That's sad."

"I think you're going to have to get used to people having tragic stories about brain tumors."

"I guess so," I said. We walked along for a little while in silence.

"Hey, does the institute still do fundraising for science-related art projects? I could show them my microscopy images that look like seascapes."

Andy snorted. "People might give you money to keep your art to yourself."

My heart broke. I wanted, more than anything, to create something – a scientific paper that reveals some truth or a piece of art that reveals some hidden beauty – and for someone to understand it. That has always been my dearest dream and my reason for living. I suddenly realized I had been in this place for five years and had not really connected with anyone on anything.

"Andy," I said softly. "Please apologize again."

"I'm not going to keep apologizing to you. Can't you take a joke?"

"In what way was that a joke? What you just said?"

"I don't have to explain everything to you. You're trying to make a big deal out of this."

"Honey, I need to you to be nicer to me. And I don't think I should have to ask."

"Nag, nag, nag, that's all you do."

We arrived home. Andy slammed cabinets and doors as he got out pots and pans to prepare dinner. I stood in the kitchen, not sure what to do.

"You're making my life miserable, you know that?" Andy shouted, waving the knife around in the air as he chopped vegetables. "I can't stand your constant criticism, your constant negativity."

"How do we stop this pattern then?" I asked. "I've tried to stop expecting so much, and I've tried to stop caring when you say hurtful things, but I just can't. I do expect a lot, and I do care about being kind to one another."

"Well, you forget that you're not being kind to me. You criticize me all the time. You never stop."

"You're the one who criticized me! This is crazy."

"Well, you're the one who won't let things go. God, we can't even get through Friday night without you starting a fight."

I didn't know what to do. I just went upstairs and went to bed. When we woke up the next morning, Andy was silent. He read the newspaper and drank coffee without speaking.

I packed a suitcase and went to a hotel. I couldn't continue to live like that.

I went to work, same as usual, but in the evenings, I went back to the hotel and wrote in a journal for hours. My thoughts cleared, and I started to feel stronger and more certain of myself. After a week, I returned to the house.

"Andy, I need you to treat me better."

"Well, I need you to treat me better."

"Can we just agree to treat each other better?"

"If you are willing to do so, then I will too."

Why was everything always conditional with him? Why did he always need me to give more, and give in first?

"Fine," I agreed, sighing.

During that week away, I had contacted a woman I knew at the university who was separate from our institute, from CANDO, from cancer research, just a lovely person who also knew about the challenges of academia. As a bonus, she was American, having grown up in Arizona. Her name was Clara. She was a botanist, filled with an understanding of how plants grew and how insect life was interwoven into the fabric of ecology.

Clara made dinner at her house. Her dining room was filled with plants and flowers, fossils, stones, pinecones, petrified tree-trunks, and all kinds of geological marvels. I felt encased by nature and our efforts to comprehend it. Clara listened to me explain what had happened between me and Andy. She stood up, left the room, then returned, handing me a spare key to her house.

"If you ever need to leave again, you come stay with me," she said.

"But he's gonna start listening. He's gonna change."

"Well, you have the key if you need it," Clara said.

"Andy, do you think it would be a good idea to visit a doctor about your snoring?" I asked one day. He had started to show signs of apnea, and I found it impossible to sleep at night when I suddenly sensed my spouse not breathing next to me.

"No, I'm not going to see a doctor."

"But honey, you've got to do something about this. It's not just for my convenience now, so I would be able to sleep through the night. It's for your own health."

"No."

"But honey –"

"I said no."

"But honey, you can't go on like this. It's not healthy."

He got in my face. "You know what they do? They'd do surgery. They'd pull down my face to poke around my sinuses. You want that? You want them to take apart my face?"

"Honey, no. No, of course not," I said, backing away from him. "But I don't think that's the first thing they'd do. They would talk to you, come up with other solutions." They would probably tell him to stop smoking, and we both knew it.

"You just want to cause me pain and trouble, sending me to a doctor."

"No, honey, that's not it at all. I just want you to be healthy."

I purchased a digeridoo online, because published medical research had shown that breathing into this slender wooden instrument for fifteen minutes per day significantly reduced snoring. A package arrived in the post from Australia and Andy excitedly unwrapped it. He had loved learning to play the guitar, the bongos, and the accordion, and he would enjoy learning this musical instrument too.

On days he played, he didn't snore. I could go to sleep with him, wake up next to him, and then wake him up gently by touching him. We had previously switched off cooking dinner, one of us preparing the meal and one of us entertaining the chef, but I offered to cook more so that he could play music in the evenings. After a while, he grew bored of the digeridoo and switched to the guitar.

"Andy, do you want to play the digeridoo tonight?"

"No, I prefer playing the guitar."

"Maybe play the digeridoo for a bit, then switch to the guitar?"

"I'll play what I want to play."

The snoring returned, and I went back to sleeping in the loft bedroom. I felt like I was turning into the crazy old woman who lived upstairs from Jane Eyre. I lay awake at night missing America, my wide sargasso sea.

"Honey, are you sure you don't want to try more, for us? So we can sleep together again?"

"Jesus, you've become such a nag!"

I had indeed become a nag. A nag is a woman with a husband who won't listen.

As time passed, I tried to get Andy engaged in our life together, but it was difficult.

"Honey, did you get that email I sent?"

"Yeah, but I didn't read it."

"Do you want to talk about it?"

"Not really, it's not something that interests me."

"Hey, will you help me weed the flowerbeds?"

"No, I'm just going to sit outside with a beer and read a book. You go ahead."

"Would you like to play a board game later?"

"No, I don't like board games."

"It's nice out. Would you like to have a squirt-gun fight in the park this afternoon?"

"No, that would be childish."

"Would you prefer to play croquet in the park, wearing a top hat and a monocle?"

"No, now you're being ridiculous."

"Hey, can we do something fun this weekend? Anything?"

"We can go to the pub and watch rugby. Six Nations is on and England is playing France this Saturday."

"Alright, but can we do something I prefer next weekend?"

"You can do whatever you want next weekend, I'm going down to London."

"Can we go camping in the Scottish Highlands?"

"No. I've already been there, and you wouldn't like it."

"But there's an owl who lives there, in a bird sanctuary along Loch Lomond. His name is Smudge. I would like to meet Smudge."

"Maybe later. I'm busy the next few weekends."

"Smudge is waiting. He wants visitors."

"Smudge can keep waiting. I'm trying to get some papers out."

"You don't understand. Smudge is a very sweet owl, and he lets you scratch his head. I read all about him on his website. He's out there every day, trying to raise money for other birds."

"I told you, I'm busy."

"You're always busy."

"Yes I am. Now leave me alone, I've got work to do."

For some reason Andy purchased our friend Evelyne a vibrator for her birthday.

She was delighted. I walked home from the party silent, as Andy chattered.

"What's your problem?" he asked. "It was a fun night."

"What's my problem? You bought another woman a sex toy."

"It was just a joke."

"Well it's not funny. You can't buy other women sex toys."

"Are you jealous? Of Evelyne?"

"This is not about me. This is about your behavior, which is inappropriate."

"Evelyne and I are friends. We were friends before you moved here."

"Are you trying to make me jealous?"

"No, I'm just pointing out a fact."

"OK, so what?"

"We have a silly relationship. It sometimes involves buying penis-shaped objects for each other."

"This is crazy. I shouldn't have to explain this, but it's not okay for you to flirt with other women."

"I don't flirt with Evelyne!"

"You two were laughing and taking photos of each other's crotches the last time we hung out!" Evelyne's boyfriend and I had exchanged looks, sighed, and looked the other way.

"It does sound like you're jealous."

"This is insane. Do you understand that your behavior is hurtful and inappropriate?"

"OK, I won't buy Evelyne any more sex toys."

"Jesus, I can't believe that had to be so difficult. I'm glad we sorted it out though."

But the next day, I found him at the pub telling a group of people about the birthday gift.

"I thought you were gonna let that go," I mentioned.

"I told you, I won't buy sex toys for other women."

"Great, stop telling the story about it as well."

"Fine."

But then I caught him telling the story again, a week later, at another evening out.

"Andy," I said, taking him aside later in the evening.

"Stop telling this story. It is humiliating when you talk about having interactions of a sexual nature with other women. Stop doing this to me."

"Fine," he said again. A week later, I put my head in my hands as he launched into the story again.

"Andy, it's not even that interesting of a story. The only reason you're telling it is to humiliate me."

"I don't know what you're talking about," he said, an innocent look on his face.

We went to our therapist, Sue.

"What seems to be the problem?" she asked. "It's been a while since you've been here."

I recounted how Andy had mocked my artistic efforts, yelled at me in front of our colleagues, and refused to stand up for me when I was being undermined at work.

"But I say nice words to you all the time," Andy said. "I love your art, and I always support you at work. You only remember the few negatives in between all the positives."

"Why are you feeling so negative?" Sue asked, tilting her head.

"I'm not sure that's a helpful thing to focus on here," I pointed out. "Isn't the problem here that he says hurtful things?"

"Are you going to let that ruin your relationship?" Sue asked.

"You know, a little bit of toxin can poison a well," I pointed out.

"Maybe it would be useful if you could ignore some of this stuff, or move past it," Sue proposed.

"I just want to say for the record, I do not say hurtful things," Andy stated. He turned to face me, gazing into my eyes. "I love you, and I think you're great. I would never say anything to hurt you."

I turned to the therapist, panicked.

"But he called me a bitch," I explained.

Andy looked down and shook his head sadly.

Sue watched us silently.

"What the hell is going on here?" I exclaimed.

"She just gets riled up and emotional so easily," Andy said. "Maybe she doesn't remember what actually happened."

"Oh my god, what is going on here?" I asked, panicking.

"See?" Andy said. "She's out of it."

"Sometimes people do say hurtful words in the heat of the moment," said Sue. "But you have to remember to look for the love that's underneath that."

I looked at Andy. He was gazing at me adoringly.

"This is fake right here," I pointed out.

"No," Andy spoke earnestly. "This is your husband trying to make things work. I wish you would appreciate that."

I sighed. "Maybe your effort is just coming as a surprise. It just seems a sudden turnaround from your previous behavior."

"What are you referring to?" Sue asked.

"Well, he bought our friend a vibrator, which I think is inappropriate, and he keeps telling people about it, which I find humiliating."

"Is this storytelling something that happens when he's drunk?" Sue asked.

"Uh, yeah. I guess," I said, confused. Did that make it okay?

"Well, you can recognize when he's starting to tell these stories, right?" Sue asked.

"Uh, yeah? I guess?" Now I was really confused.

"So when that happens," she continued, "Why don't

you calmly, without upsetting him, try to change the subject."

My jaw dropped. "You can't put the onus on me to prevent my own humiliation. Surely you could advise Andy not to humiliate me instead."

Sue watched silently as I grew upset.

"This therapy will not work if everything is being put on me," I said, my voice rising. "Andy needs to stop humiliating me. Simple as that. It's his behavior that is the problem here."

Sue just shrugged.

"I will not tiptoe around his anger," I stated, loudly and decisively. Both of them watched me silently.

"Are you sure you're not the one who's angry all the time?" Andy asked.

"I'm sorry, if no one is taking this seriously, I'm going to have to leave," I said.

I stood up and exited the room. Andy came and found me a couple minutes later, putting my jacket on in the lobby.

"I can't believe you left our therapy session. You're not even trying. You're just giving up on us."

"Andy, I'm not giving up on us. I'm just not putting up with your bullshit."

"Oh, you think my love for you is bullshit now?"

"Stop, that's not what I meant," I said helplessly.

"What did you mean then?" Andy demanded.

"I would like us to share a greater love."

"You're saying that my love for you is not good enough?"

"No, that's not it," I explained. "I just wish you would try harder."

"But you're the one who walked out of our therapy session. You're the one giving up on us!"

"You would not admit the hurtful things you've done.

You pretended everything was fine."

"You're trying to tear us down, always focusing on the negative. You're trying to tear me down."

"No," I said. I was walking fast, toward our house. I just wanted to be at home right now. "No. I believe, 100%, the job of a spouse is to build the other person up. I *always* strive to do so, even when I'm angry. I would *never* tell you that you're not good enough. I wouldn't have married you if I didn't think you are amazing and capable of anything. I just want you to make me feel amazing too."

"God, you are so selfish. You know I feel like crap right now? And you want to feel amazing?"

"You seem to hear something awful every time I speak, but you have to believe me when I say my intentions are good here. I just want to fix our marriage."

"You don't. You walked out of therapy."

"Look, I know you have a lot of distrust. But so do I. I do not trust that you know how to treat me with respect."

"You don't love me."

I stopped and turned to him. "Of course I love you. You're my husband. You are brilliant and beautiful, and above all, charmed. You go through life with this incredible charisma, and other people look to you with admiration, just like I do."

He sighed. I could tell those words had eased his tension, if only a little bit.

"You inspire respect, Andy," I continued. "You make a natural leader. I can see why you're so successful. It all comes so easily to you."

"No, it's not easy," Andy scowled. "You think my life is easy? I work really hard, you know that."

"Yes, you do. Of course you do," I said soothingly, my hand on his arm. "And you are really successful because of that.

But I work hard too. I work just as hard as you do. But I feel like I'm running in place. And you don't seem to understand – I've just been trying to stay afloat, ever since I moved here."

He looked at me blankly.

"You need to help me out here. You need to give a little bit more. Not just pretending to do so in front of the therapist, but for real. You need to be kinder, you need to help out more at the house, you need to be there for me, without keeping score."

"I do all of this stuff," Andy argued. "I am there for you."

"You hurt me when you called me a bitch. And you have never fully apologized for that."

"That's in the past."

"But the past repeats itself if it's not put to rest."

"You just keep bringing up the same old damage. It's over."

"Well the damage remains for a long time. Two of my toenails fell out that summer, and it took forever for them to regrow."

"Look, I don't get what your problem is. I proposed to you, I married you, and I went to Scotland with you three times to help you get your visas."

"Honey, that's not a favor to me. That's us trying to build a life together."

Andy sighed, turned away, and punched the wall.

"No," I said, grabbing his wrist. "Let's clear this up. Now calm your anger, apologize for your words. Help us to start over."

He walked away.

"Andy, stop. Don't give up on us. Swallow your pride and do something to make things better."

"You're just gonna keep asking for more."

I stopped. He sensed it and he stopped too. "Yeah, I probably will," I agreed. "I will ask for more and more from you, as time goes on and we build our lives together. Just as I expect you to ask me."

He turned around and looked at me.

"Is that a problem, Andy?" I asked.

"You're so angry," he stated.

"Yeah, what if I am?" I asked, tears rolling down my cheeks. "What if I am angry that you said such hurtful things? And angry that you refuse to apologize? You're damn right, I'm angry. And I do wish you'd just damn apologize."

"Why do you need to see me feel remorse? Why do you need this so much?"

I paused. "I need to know we're on the same page, regarding the way we treat each other and the way we expect to be treated. Acknowledging that we've fallen short or hurt each other is necessary for keeping our standards up. Otherwise, that hurtful behavior becomes our new norm."

"I think you need to think about why you're demanding I apologize," he said. "Seriously, take a moment to think about why that is so important to you. Do you think that making me feel worse will make you feel any better?"

"Honey, I don't want you to feel bad. I'm not trying to hurt you."

"Well, what is it that you're trying to accomplish here?"

"I don't know," I said sadly. It had all seemed to make sense a moment ago, but it didn't anymore.

During the next few weeks, my big toenail fell out again. And my hair started falling out in clumps.

I called Lila and tried to explain what was going on.

"I'm beginning to wonder if the relationship is abusive," I ventured.

"Has he hit you?" she asked.

"No, but there's been a lot of yelling, sometimes in front of people, and he mocks me all the time. It would be fine if it balanced out with more positive stuff, but we don't have a lot going on other than work."

"You should plan more activities outside of work."

"Well, I'd like to, but it never seems to happen."

"You need to put more effort into doing what you want to do."

"I'm not sure you understand. I don't really have a lot of freedom – I don't have much money, and I can't drive over here. Andy often doesn't want to do things on the weekend, but he only decides that after getting up late on a Saturday, so it's difficult to switch plans by then. We end up cancelling a lot of things, or just not showing up. I feel really alone and isolated over here."

"You should make more friends."

I sighed, remembering Andy showing up at the pub when I met up with colleagues last month. Everyone had gotten uncomfortable and left shortly afterwards. I couldn't remember why though.

It was all so difficult to explain. I tried again. "Sometimes I feel so unsure of myself. I'm not certain that Andy is treating me as well as he should. But then he acted differently than usual in front of our therapist, so she doesn't think there's a problem. Or she thinks that I'm the problem."

"I don't know," Lila replied. "Relationships aren't easy."

"So you don't think this stuff sounds like a major issue?"

"Maybe you guys just speak different languages. Like, he shows his love in different ways than you."

I sighed. "I guess so."

"Just keep trying," Lila said. "I know Andy loves you."

But soon Andy's anger came back and my sadness came back intensely too. One morning he just walked out the door without saying anything when I asked for his help with the errands. The next day I couldn't bring myself to get out of bed or go to work. I felt exhausted, foggy, lost.

The following Saturday, I woke up and began cleaning the house. Andy sat reading the paper while I scrubbed the dishes in the sink. I laid everything out to dry, then one by one, picked up the items and rubbed them with a towel as I walked to the cabinet.

In my fatigue, I dropped a wine glass on the floor. Andy watched as I slowly leaned over to pick up the pieces, in my dazed state. Suddenly he stood up, ran over, and pushed me out of the way. Startled, I stood in the dining room while he picked up the broken glass.

"I didn't know what you were going to do there," Andy said, his face twisted with worry.

I shook my head and went upstairs to sit in the bath.

"You have a problem," Andy told me as I dried my hair. "You won't admit it, but you're depressed."

"Maybe," I said.

"I'm calling the doctor. I'm gonna get you help."

"What? No! Don't call the doctor on me."

"You're refusing to get help."

"This is the first time it's come up. Give me time to process this, and let me decide what to do."

"You're not doing anything about it. I'm calling the doctor."

"No, wait." I had thought of a compromise solution. My officemate was a medical doctor and a good friend. "Will you call Barry over? It would be nice to see him. And he knows me, he can say if I should get therapy or get medication or whatever."

Andy disregarded me and went downstairs. I heard him calling to make an appointment at a clinic.

He hadn't listened. I had made a reasonable suggestion, and he ignored it. Instead he was doing something to me that I had not agreed to.

The thought appeared in my head that he might try to commit me. Being trapped in England was bad enough, but as my husband, he would trap me even further. I suddenly did not trust him at all.

I thought quickly, panicking. He would have to prove he was legally my spouse in order to commit me. I ran upstairs and found our marriage certificate. One copy was tucked away with my visa documentation, but I found the other one and ran back downstairs.

I stood in front of Andy, who was still on the telephone. He paused speaking and looked at me. I held up the document, signed by both of us on our wedding day, and ripped it down the middle.

"If you don't have this, you can't prove that you have legal powers over me," I stated with firmness.

"I have to go," Andy said, and hung up the phone. He looked at me, his face rigid.

"What have you done now?" he asked tightly, watching as I ripped the paper into smaller and smaller pieces. I was shaking, terrified.

"Andy, I'm so scared. I don't want you to do something that will make me feel trapped."

It began to dawn on me that I should have just hid the document instead, but the paper was already gone. Well, one half was thoroughly ripped up. I looked at the untouched other half, and I could not bear to rip it up too. I was so glad there was another copy, also signed on our wedding day, in a folder safe with my visa documents. Why hadn't I just put this copy there too? I had simply panicked. Now I felt awful.

"I'm so sorry, Andy," I burst into tears. "It was impulsive, I just needed to protect myself."

He shook his head. "This is not okay."

"Andy, Andy, I'm so sorry." I fell on the ground. "Please, Andy, please. Please don't hate me for this. I was just so scared."

"I don't know that we can ever turn around now," he shook his head sadly.

"I'm so sorry, Andy. I was just so scared." But I could tell he would never forgive me for this. It was too big. He was right, there was probably no way we could turn around now.

In the weeks after that incident, I went to work like usual, but when I came home I often stayed in the loft. I didn't feel I could talk to Andy, I felt so ashamed of what I had done.

When my birthday approached, Andy suggested we drive to his parents' cottage in the Lake District for the weekend. That cheered me up, and I grew the idea that our lives might return to normal.

That week, I found a new spring in my step. Andy was looking forward to the special weekend too – he suggested we leave work early on Friday so we could have dinner at a restaurant in the next village over the hill from the cottage. Then, on Saturday, we'd meet up with his friends who would be staying at the lakes that weekend too.

But on Thursday evening, Andy announced that we would have to work on CANDO the whole weekend instead. He cancelled our plans to go to the lakes. I cried a bit, like a child. Our lives were just so empty, and I had been looking forward to a break.

Then, after work on Friday, when we arrived home, Andy proposed we have dinner that night at a nice restaurant in the center of town. I smiled, tired but hopeful, and agreed to dress up for the occasion.

Before we left the house, he gave me a birthday gift. I sat down at our dining room table and unwrapped the box. Inside was a silver-plated razor blade, to be tied around my wrist with black leather. I sat there stunned, hypnotized by the shape of it.

"Andy," I spoke slowly. "Why did you pick out this bracelet?"

He shifted in his seat. "I don't know, it reminded me of you."

Terror enveloped me. All I could think of was slicing my wrists, and the blood that would pour out. I had real razorblades at work to open boxes; I had a bathtub at home I could fill with warm water. It was so simple. The bracelet told me it would even be beautiful. By the time I would feel cold, I would be gone. It would be fine. I sneaked a look at Andy again. He appeared to be expecting a reaction.

"It's perfect, honey," I said, giving him a big smile. "I think I'll wear it to dinner this evening."

Chapter 18
Things Fall Apart

A couple weeks later, on the night of the referendum that would decide whether Britain would remain in the European Union or be the first nation ever to leave, Andy and I scooped ourselves each a large bowl of ice cream and settled under some blankets in the living room to watch the results come in. The first announcement was from Sunderland – a slight majority in favor of Brexit. Andy and I looked at each other.

"It's going to be okay," Andy told me.

He had said those words so many times over the years – when the Home Office briefly stopped issuing visas, or I had to return to my home country to wait for a visa, or when the anti-immigrant sentiment ramped up dangerously over recent months. I had always believed him, but now I was ready to stop.

"I don't think it is going to be okay, Andy."

"Don't be so negative. Just wait." The results from Newcastle arrived next, a slight majority in favor of Remain. Andy smiled and sat back in his seat, feeling reassured. He thought his city was the bellwether of the nation. There was no way that job belonged to Sunderland.

His smile faded over the course of the night. By the time

we went to bed on that late June evening, the future of his country was decided.

The following evening, we tuned into the BBC nightly news again and watched as the Prime Minister made a speech resigning his post. He had called the referendum to settle the question of European integration for a generation and the whole thing had backfired, leaving everyone unsure what laws we would subscribe to or what alliances we would retain. Unbelievably, the man whistled as he turned from the podium and entered Number 10 Downing Street. I was sitting beside myself in fear, for what all this meant for myself and the country I had adopted myself into. In a parallel universe, I watched David Cameron make the same speech, with the same stupid expression on his face, but literally striking a match and throwing it onto the country as he turned away, whistling.

"Andy? Is it still going to be okay?"

"I don't know."

My grandfather passed away, my father's father. He was 104. My other grandparents had died before I was born. My Opa was the only one of them I had known, and then I barely knew him really. My father had stopped speaking to him in 1981, the year I was born, and only started again, reluctantly, when I went to college and I asked him how it would feel if I never spoke to *him* again. My father saw my point and handed over three international phone numbers. After that, we kept in touch with his father and kept in better contact with his three cousins.

The funeral was held in Bremen. The family gathered there – the cousins coming from Bremen, Berlin and Cologne, while I arrived from England and my parents flew over from the

United States.

My father had moved to America in the 1960s, in love with our country since GIs liberated his hometown in Germany in May 1945, at the end of the second world war. The Americans gave this little five-year-old boy chocolate candy bars and freedom, and that was all it took. As soon as he was old enough, my father moved to New York City and applied for US citizenship. A few years later, he switched jobs, moved to Chicago, met my mother, got married and started a family.

The memories of my father's early life were difficult, and he dreaded going back to his homeland. My brother and I had made him do so on two previous occasions, so we could meet our kin and learn our family history. Both times, he had grudgingly agreed.

I met my grandfather, then, when he was in his nineties. He had a puppy named Pretzel, who would run alongside his bicycle each day as he rode through town. My Opa lived in a small village up north, and sometimes took trips to the seaside in summertime. He seemed like an agreeable person, and it was hard to tell what happened so long ago to cause such lifelong bitterness in the family.

A hundred years ago, the family lived on a potato farm in Eastern Prussia. They built their life in a village called Kallningken – later named Herdenau during the Third Reich, and afterwards incorporated into Kaliningrad Oblast, a small additional part of Russia on the European mainland, nestled between Lithuania and Poland.

My father's grandparents were ethnically German, but far from home. They had twelve children, eight of whom survived into adulthood and three of whom had children of their own – my father and his cousins. When the Soviets rolled into the region in 1945, the elders were killed and buried in a tank ditch along the Curonian Lagoon, now a Russian beach resort. Most of their daughters escaped through German-occupied Poland to Germany, settling in Bremen. They took with them a few pieces of cloudy amber jewelry (called Baltic Gold), which now belong to me.

Their brother, my grandfather, was fighting in the war – first on the eastern front, then on the western front, where he was captured by the allies and held on an Irish farm until his release in the 1950s. I think his brothers were drafted into the German Army as well, but I do not know for sure.

As the tanks arrived and chaos ensued, the youngest daughter of the family, Frieda, did not escape to Germany with her sisters. She was instead captured by the Soviet Army. She was unmarried but had a little son, Karl, who was seized alongside her. During the years in captivity, Frieda began to fall apart at the seams. Karl tried his best to keep the two of them alive and safe, although he was very young. He worked in a Siberian labor camp and was not allowed to attend school. When Karl was finally released, in the 1950s, his mother had died and he was a grown man of eighteen. Illiterate but free, he moved to Germany and became a carpenter.

Karl was the one who had put me in touch with my grandfather when I turned eighteen, since he was the only person who had kept in contact. The once-fatherless boy took care of my grandfather during his last years, with simmering resentments pervading the rest of the family. Before the funeral, I had never met Karl in person, but there he was, radiating calm and warmth, assuming his role as the new patriarch of the family – the eldest child of the next generation, now that the last member of the previous generation was gone.

We held the funeral informally, with no priest, each of us reading solemn words over the grave in the cemetery in

Bremen. German cemeteries are not like American cemeteries, with those crewcut lawns; they are not like English cemeteries, which are overgrown and haunted, or French cemeteries, which are overgrown and filled with cats; they are not like Italian cemeteries, lined with cold stone, or Latvian cemeteries, hidden among the forests, or Bosnian cemeteries, spread out clean and fresh across the sprawling hillsides. In a modern German cemetery, each grave is a well-kept little garden, evenly-spaced from the others around it, planted with a unique combination of blossoms and shrubs as a memento of the matchless personality of the human contained within. We placed a bouquet of flowers and a candle on the fresh grave. It was windy and rainy, and the candle went out.

The entire week, my father was out of sorts, a disorganized wreck, completely unlike himself; my mother spent every waking moment interrupting stories I had waited my whole life to hear with non-sequiturs about her friends back home; the tension got so high at one point our taxi crashed into a tree. My cousin Maria was her usual hugging, smiling, laughing, loving self. My cousin Gerhart, normally rather sedate, let loose on the evening of the funeral and started dropping truth-bombs.

As we finished the bottle of wine and switched to whiskey to honor my grandfather, tongues loosened. The truth, Gerhart explained to me – finally, after all those years – was that no one liked my Opa because he was a Nazi. He hadn't been drafted in the war – he had signed up. And he never shut up about it. He never showed that side of himself to me, but he showed it to everyone else.

I returned to Newcastle in a state of stunned bewilderment. You thought you knew a person.

A few months later, $25,000 appeared in my bank

account. I was not about to refuse the gift, despite knowing where it came from. I was not my grandfather, and I was determined this money would be used for good. I didn't know exactly how, but I felt sure I would come up with something.

Over the following weeks, I found the money cheered me up enormously. I had never had savings before, and suddenly it felt nice to have options.

A few weeks later, one Saturday morning, I found myself singing along with the radio while I did the dishes and the laundry. I was much more happy than usual, thinking about the money, and the chores seemed to do themselves. After a couple hours, Andy came downstairs.

"Morning, honey!" I called, putting on a fresh pot of coffee.

"Good morning," Andy mumbled, slumping in a chair and picking up the newspaper.

"Guess what – I've got a plan!" I announced, sliding into the dining room dramatically in my socks.

"What is it?" Andy grumbled. He had been in a terrible mood lately.

"You know how I always said we should get the kitchen remodeled?" I asked.

"Oh god. Not this again."

"Come on, you want to have kids. And I say, if we want kids, we need a washer *and* a dryer, and it would be nice to have them right here in the kitchen. And we could have a freezer right here in the kitchen too. No hanging up clothing, no need to slice veggies fresh every time."

"We have a shed. There's extra space in the shed."

"Yes, we do have a spider-filled shed with rotting

foundations. That does not make my life easier."

"You've always been against the shed."

"I've always been against that shed in particular. Anyway we can have a nice space in the expanded kitchen to put storage items and, most importantly, the proposed appliances."

"That's not the same as a shed."

"It sounds like you'd prefer the shed."

"I want to keep the shed. That doesn't mean I don't want to have kids."

"Right, but there are certain requirements for having kids. You don't want to be washing and drying clothes by hand."

"I'm not planning to," Andy said.

"Someone will have to," I pointed out.

He was quiet.

"Hmm, it sounds like you're not stuck on having kids, really."

"Sure I am."

"Well, until we decide, I'm just going to keep this money I inherited in the states."

"You could put it into the mortgage."

"I thought about that, but then I realized that's not the best option. Our mortgage debt is quite sustainable, because of these historically low interest rates. And long-term, we're on schedule to pay off the loan just fine with our salaries."

"Huh," said Andy.

"And the thing is, I can't open an investment account here, because UK banks will not deal with US capital gains tax reporting requirements. So if I stay here and keep making a salary, I'll have nowhere decent to put the money *except* the mortgage."

"Huh," said Andy.

"So I think it might be best to keep the rest of the money in the states for now, especially considering the uncertainty around the value of the pound. You never know what might happen, with Brexit."

"Huh," said Andy.

"Honey, is everything alright? You seem off."

"Look, I said you should put the money into the mortgage."

"Andy, I gave you a number of reasons why that doesn't make sense. Do you disagree with my logic?"

He didn't say anything.

"Honey, I really think it might be better to keep the money in the states for now, unless we're itching to remodel the place. Is there something I'm missing here?"

"I think you should bring the money over and put it into the mortgage."

"Andy, we visit the states regularly to see friends and family and colleagues. Since our wages are in a rapidly-declining currency, it makes sense to keep a bank account in America to keep these visits affordable. This is not a weird idea."

Andy stormed out of the house, slamming the back door as he went. I followed him into the garden. The August sun was warm on my shoulders.

"Andy, what's going on? What's the problem?"

"You want to know? I've been angry these past few weeks because of this money thing."

I was stunned. "But you agreed it was my decision, what to do with it."

"Look, I can either be silent and hold my anger inside or I can share with you the reasons why."

"Andy, share it with me. Let's talk it out."

"Frankly I'm not going to stop being angry until you

bring the money over. I've put money into the house and you can put your money in too."

"But you have a bunch of savings accounts. You've put a fraction of your savings into the house, and now you're asking me to put in everything I have."

"I'm asking you to put in something!"

"Honey, I have put everything I have into our life together. And every month I put my entire salary into the groceries and mortgage. I do not have any other savings like you do. You are asking me to put in 100% of everything I have, when you are not doing the same."

"You're clearly not committed to us."

"Where is this coming from? This money came as a surprise, and I'm just trying to decide how best to use it, for both of us and our future together."

"You aren't contributing as much as me," he replied, his eyes glaring and bloodshot.

I didn't know what to say. "Andy –"

"I'm not speaking to you until you bring that money over."

"Andy, do you really want to make this a condition of our –"

"I'm done with this conversation."

I felt stunned as I walked back into the house. I just could not envision how this argument could be resolved, except for me being bullied into putting my entire savings into the house.

Another use for the money occurred to me then. It could buy my independence – it could be a cushion while I built a life on my own. Then Andy and I would have to meet each other as equals, without this power dynamic between us, where I was dependent on him. He would have to start treating me nicely, since now I could just walk away.

I packed a suitcase and called a taxi. When I arrived at Clara's house, she enclosed me in her arms and made me lunch, then sat across from me at her dining room table while I put my head in my hands and described what had happened. I breathed in and told her my plan to make a fresh start.

She reached out and touched my arm. "Hey, you can stay here as long as you need to, alright?"

I nodded. I had never been more grateful in my entire life. "Thank you so much, Clara. I don't know what I would have done if I couldn't have come here. I don't know how I'll ever repay you."

"Don't worry about that," Clara said. "Just take care of yourself and grow strong again. Then you can be there for other people. You won't repay me, you'll pay it forward."

That autumn, I wrote Andy letters by hand, and delivered them under his office door in the mornings before he came into work.

"Come to me," I wrote. "Give me a sign that you care."

"I don't understand what you want from me," he wrote back.

I explained again and again what he could do to save our marriage, but he kept saying he did not understand what I was asking for. Instead he insisted I should just return home. Things remained unresolved, and over time I began to lose hope.

"Clara?" I asked one evening. "What do you think went wrong with me and Andy?"

She sighed. "The same thing that goes wrong in every relationship, I guess. You recapitulate the damage you've seen your parents inflict on each other."

"Huh," I said thoughtfully. "You think Andy married his mother, and acts like his father?"

"Yep," she responded. "And you married your dominant parent too. You married your mother."

"Oh god," I said. "You think?"

"Yep, both your mother and Andy are incredibly selfish. They make everything about themselves. And they seek to avoid pain by refusing to face what they've done, thereby throwing all the pain and responsibility for the relationship onto you."

"Oh wow. That sounds exactly like what has been going on."

Clara nodded. "Sometimes people choose their damage over connecting with other people. They choose denial, they choose lies, they choose blame, they choose alcoholism as an escape –"

"Wait, but do you think I chose my damage over connecting with Andy? He thinks I perseverate on my past too much."

"You tried to share your past with him, and that's okay. You were trying to show him the deepest scars on your soul, so he could know you and understand you. That's okay."

"Really? I'm not wasting people's time talking about myself?"

"Of course not. No one should make you feel like that."

"But Andy didn't want to hear about it. He said my negativity was the problem in our marriage."

"That sounds like a way to make you shut up. But you can never heal when you hold it all inside. You can never heal when you feel shamed for acknowledging difficult episodes in your life. The people who love you should do better than that."

"But he thought I was trying to throw the pain on him, or somehow blame him for what had happened. He always got angry."

"His anger was the problem, not your efforts to communicate with him."

"But he could not handle hearing about the pain. He said I was causing him pain."

"That's just a way of shutting down the discussion, of making everything about him instead of you. It's okay for things to be about you."

"I never meant to cause him pain or ask too much of him. But sometimes his words and actions hurt me, and I did ask him to confront that."

"That's okay. You should be able to ask him to confront his own words and actions."

"Really? He said I was being abusive by criticizing him."

"No, calling someone out on their cruel behavior is not abuse. That's just asking for respect. And if that respect is not forthcoming, you're doing the right thing to leave."

Andy emailed to inform me: our therapist held the opinion I had drawn him close just to punch him in the face. I had hurt him by leaving.

I felt so guilty. The idea of him feeling pain made me ache all over. I wanted to do anything to assuage it. I wanted to go back to him, comfort him, assure him that I would do anything to make him feel better. I would return home, I would apologize, I would stop nagging him about everything.

Then I stopped. He knew that would be my reaction. He was manipulating me.

I was not punching him in the face. I was just asking him

to be a kinder, gentler, more loving husband. I had called him out on his cruelty – that was not abuse, that was just asking for respect.

The fact that he was making me feel guilty for setting reasonable expectations was the real problem between us. I needed to stop playing my role in facilitating this unhealthy pattern of behavior. I needed to walk away instead of capitulating.

I told Andy he would be welcome at my parents' house for Thanksgiving, as he was still family, but I did not wish him to join me in watching election night with friends in Seattle and I was not interested in sharing a room with him at the neuroscience conference in San Diego.

"Fine," he wrote back.

I arrived in Seattle in early November, relieved to be back home among close friends.

On the evening of the election, I made some snacks and helped gather Rose's children. We went over to Lila's house to watch the results come in.

I held the smallest child they had, a baby of several weeks, the whole night. As the map turned redder and redder, and the commentators did too, my reaction was to exit this world. Everyone else was wide awake, but the baby and I fell fast asleep. It was just too much to process.

When the deciding states had called in their results, we packed up quietly to leave. We had hoped the next generation of little girls and boys would be watching the first female president being sworn into office, but instead they watched their elders exchanging worried looks.

The next morning, I woke up in my friends' spare room,

and the whole stark reality hit me.

I felt like every woman in America, every single one of us, had just slammed our heads against the collective glass ceiling, and we were all lying on the ground with stars circling above.

I went to the bathroom and looked in the mirror. A thirty-five-year-old white female stared back. I imagined my lab, back in England, the faces of the men and women who worked with me. A team of people from five different continents, working together, being led by an energetic woman…. I watched the reflection of my face crumple. Behind that wretched surface, my brain wondered how long this world would allow my beautiful team to continue.

I had thought diversity was the future – that men and women of all races would have a seat at the table, that all our voices would be heard, that power could be shared, that equality and fraternity would rule the day. But now I no longer had faith in that future.

I went upstairs to find my friends Rose and Ryan. All morning, we read the news and hugged each other and cried. We mourned for that bright future that would not be.

The next day, I received an email from Luke, our CANDO project manager. It was addressed to all the investigators on the project and it summarized our entire budget to date, including all staff costs. There were only three women being paid on the project at this point – both technicians and the gene therapy regulatory manager were leaving, having been head-hunted for jobs which paid a lot more money. Of the three remaining posts filled by women, two were problematic. My full-time salary was less than Andy's post-doc, even though I was leading an entire team. I swallowed and let that go, focusing on the other problem.

The only female post-doc not on my team – Erin – was being paid a whole grade lower than every other post-doc. She was making 80% what her male colleagues made. I emailed Andy and Luke.

Luke wrote back that he'd fix the salary grade right away, and make sure backpay was issued too. Later, Andy wrote tersely that he'd see me in San Diego in a few days.

I was looking forward to travelling to the annual meeting of the Society for Neuroscience this year in particular. I wanted to see everyone I had lived with and worked with over the years, to reaffirm our shared values and to grieve the crazy state of the world.

Let's face it: by November of 2016, people were reeling. Our beloved celebrities had been dropping like flies all year, Leicester had somehow won the Premier League championship, the Cubs had somehow won the World Series, Europe was on the brink of falling apart, and a new era of white supremacy had asserted itself in America with the election of Donald Trump.

"I don't understand why people are so upset. It's just another conservative government," Andy shrugged and poured himself a glass of whiskey. We were sitting in his hotel room in downtown San Diego, alongside Jack Fadden, whom we had invited along for the evening. At dinner, I had explained to Jack that Andy and I were separated, and it was his job as our pastor to help us try to patch things up.

"It just seems like you don't want to understand how bad this is," I said evenly. I looked at Jack, appealing to him as a fellow American.

"What's your problem exactly?" Jack asked.

"What's my problem?" I was surprised by his ambivalence. "I thought we shared the same values, and now I'm not so sure. You guys really don't seem very fussed about this."

"What, you think we're not all on the same side here? Of course we are. I voted the same way you did," he stated.

"Fine, but it doesn't feel like we're in it together now."

"What the hell does that mean?"

"Means she's leaving me and she's decided to live on her own," Andy said.

"I've felt on my own for a while now actually."

"Oh really?" Andy replied.

"In what way?" Jack asked.

"Like I said, I'm not sure anymore that Andy shares the same values as me."

"Fine, but what does that mean?" Jack was getting impatient. Andy took a slug from his whiskey glass.

"Well, I once heard him say the n-word," I started. When I had complained, Andy claimed that, as an Englishman, he didn't know he couldn't say that. I wasn't sure why I was bringing it up again.

"He said this, like, in what context?" Jack asked. He laughed suddenly, loudly. "Like, I saw a n****r in the grocery store the other day?"

I stared at him in utter shock and disbelief. We all froze for a moment.

I gazed at these two people who I loved so dearly, and they in turn regarded me, their faces stony. I covered my mouth, which I now could not close.

"Take it back," I whispered, tears pricking my eyes. Both of them were silent.

These two people were no longer my husband and my

close friend, both of whom I loved so dearly. Instead they were strangers – two white men in positions of power, both with skyrocketing scientific careers, one of them with a wife at home who took care of the kids and the other who wanted me to be a wife at home who took care of the kids. They had everything they needed, and they chose to say these words too.

I fell on the floor sobbing, unable to see thru my tears.

"She's hysterical," I heard Andy saying from far away.

"Jesus Christ." I could hear disdain in Jack's voice.

I needed to get myself together. I mopped up my tears with toilet paper and emerged from the bathroom standing on two feet again.

"OK, I'll give you a chance to apologize," I stated.

Both men stared at me, sneering.

"You can go now," Andy said, after a moment.

I walked out of the hotel and onto the streets. People were marching there, calling out for equality and justice. The crowd was gaining strength, and I joined it.

The one thing people in positions of power can't force you to do is stop caring. All they can do is try to shame you into stopping yourself. They can make you feel ridiculous for calling them out, and they can make you feel protected as long as you stand by their side. But they cannot stop the nagging feeling in your heart that what they are doing is wrong. Only you can silence that voice. Only you can decide to be complicit.

A couple weeks later, Andy and I were at my parents' house in Deerfield. It was the day after Thanksgiving, and we were arguing. Andy had posited that my gene therapy was killing neurons, the very cells we wanted to control in order to treat epilepsy.

I have no idea how we had gotten onto this subject.

"The neurons aren't dead. Where are you getting this idea? Some of the viral vectors just express the gene therapy in glial cells. Just because you don't see the neurons responding does not mean they have died, it just means they do not have the gene therapy active."

"Well, that's no good, is it?"

"It's no reason to say the viral vectors kill neurons, when actually we may be able to preferentially control glial cells."

"But we want to target neurons. Neurons," Andy said.

"But wait, is it a bad thing if we're targeting glia?" I ventured aloud. "That would be completely sensible, given the perspective of everyone on the team. I know, from studying glioma, that people with glial cell tumors have seizures. Oliver has been finding that altered glial cell function can cause epilepsy. Gavin recently posited in a theoretical paper that glial cell networks actually set the rhythm for large-scale oscillations in the brain, suggesting their dysfunction is what causes seizures to spread. And you yourself have recorded micro-seizures in localized areas of glial scarring near electrode placements in the cerebral cortex. Glial cells may be the key to treating epilepsy. Maybe we *should* be targeting glial cells with our gene therapy."

"Maybe," he shrugged. "But you don't want your viral vectors to kill neurons."

"Aaah!" I pulled at my hair with both hands. "Our viral vectors do not kill neurons!"

"Well, prove it then."

"Can we do those experiments while we are also testing the functional effects of the gene therapy, at least? To keep the project going?"

"Whatever, I don't care."

"Whatever? This is my time you're wasting here."

"Oh, you just want me to have faith that your viral vectors work?"

"You don't need faith, you saw the light-evoked potentials with your own eyes and heard them with your own ears. We were sitting there together, in Gavin's lab!"

"But those were probably glial cells. The viruses may have killed the neurons. You think I should just have faith that they didn't?"

"No, but you could read more. There is plenty of literature in the field addressing this concern."

"I need to see it with my own eyes. I'm not just going to have faith."

"You know what? The Trust put a lot of faith in us, giving us ten million pounds sterling to support this project. Maybe we should have faith in each other too."

"This is not about faith. This is about science," Andy argued.

"Science is about evaluating evidence and making reasonable conjectures. You're not doing that. I have loads of photographs of neurons, perfectly healthy neurons, after viral transduction. Are you just going to pretend that evidence does not exist?"

"You're –"

"And when we used a different construct, from a colleague, that had a neuronal targeting sequence? And we had neurons responding to light pulses then?"

"You're –"

"You could have some faith in me, you know. You think I would be satisfied if our gene therapy was killing neurons? Do you think I would be pushing this whole thing forward, toward clinical trials, if I thought that was a real possibility here? Do you know me at all?"

"You're asking me to have faith in you."

"Yes, I am."

"Well, I can't do that. I don't operate on faith."

"Oh, honey," I said sadly. "That's your own loss. Don't make it my problem."

"Well, I'm in charge of the project, so we'll just see what happens."

"You should do what you think is best," I said. I had spoken those words a thousand times before. But I no longer believed Andy's decisions were rational. My brilliant husband was burning with rage and that rage was clouding his judgement. He was clearly willing to make a bad call for the project, solely as revenge against me for leaving him.

He had never had faith in the project, and now he no longer had faith in me. Worse, he did not realize he was losing anything, because he had never realized that he had faith at all. I looked at him, alone in his empty world, and I sighed.

This thing faith was difficult. Once it was lost, it would take a miracle to bring it back.

Chapter 19
Magic

Some days later, Andy and I returned to England and got back to work. One snowy evening in early December, we met up for dinner in town to talk through our problems. The conversation devolved into an argument about who was to blame about the demise of our relationship. We stood on the street, quarrelling.

"You broke our vows, by leaving me," Andy accused me, through clenched teeth.

"No, you broke our vows, by refusing to treat me with love and respect. That's why I had to leave."

"You need to do something to fix our marriage. I don't know what to do to make things better."

"Honey, it would take a miracle to bring us back to a state of trust at this point," I said sadly.

"Well, you're the one who knows magic," Andy replied.

I looked at him doubtfully.

A year after the mirror had broken in the trunk of my car, the night before I had moved to Seattle, things were not going well. Despite my skepticism, I did feel unlucky in those days. And I associated it with the car that had brought me there.

It annoyed me to pass my lavender Ford Taurus parked

on the street in my Capitol Hill neighborhood, its wing mirrors now held together with black electrical tape. Slipping another parking ticket off the windshield as I went by, I sighed and continued up the street. I didn't even use the car that much – I always walked or took public transport.

It wasn't that I didn't like Seattle in those early days. I just felt unsatisfied somehow.

I walked up the road – past the bus stop, the karaoke bar, the motorcycle dealer and the strip club, past Bimbo's Bitchin' Burrito Kitchen. I stopped at the door of the neighborhood magic shop, rolled my eyes, and entered. The bells above me jangled.

Inside, I looked around at the books and incense and candles, wondering what the hell I had been thinking by coming in here.

"Hey," I said to the guy behind the counter. "I don't believe in any of this stuff. But if I needed to get a curse off my car, what would I do?"

"OK," said the man. "You want to purify some object in your mind?"

"Yeah, that's pretty much it," I agreed.

"But you don't believe in magic."

"Nope."

He sighed. "I can't really help you then."

"Well, is there something symbolic I could do, to make a fresh start?"

"I don't know," he shrugged. "Circles are useful. You could walk in a circle around your car."

"Is that it?" I asked.

He sighed again. "Sage can be purifying. You could burn sage."

"OK, thanks," I said. I started to walk out the door, but

then I stopped.

"Hey, do you want to sell me anything?" I asked.

"No, I'm not going to sell you anything," he replied, opening a book on the countertop.

"OK, then," I said. I opened the door to leave. The bells jangled again. "Thanks for the advice."

When I returned to my apartment, I poured some of the contents of my spice rack into a bowl, grabbed a lighter, and walked out to my car. This is ridiculous, I thought. I lit the plant matter on fire. It smoldered unimpressively. I shrugged, then walked around the car three times.

I had acknowledged that I held a preposterous belief and chose to cancel it out by believing something equally preposterous. It was absurd, but it sort of worked. I felt better afterwards.

Months later, someone crashed into my parked car and drove off. The vehicle was totaled and had to be towed. I used the insurance money to take Andy on a week-long trip to Barbados. The romantic holiday had solidified our bond and convinced us we wanted to be together. So, seven years after the mirror had broken, I moved to England to chase my love.

It was all just coincidence, with no greater meaning. We both knew this. But now Andy was opening himself to possibility – to magic, to a future together, to giving us another chance.

"You've cast a spell before," he pointed out. "Cast one now, to save our marriage."

I looked around. It was a midwinter evening, and the two of us were walking along the main road through Newcastle, the road that wound past the train station and the hotel where we had held our wedding. It was December again, seven years after I had first visited the city. Snow covered the castle and the cathedral once again, both buildings looming above us at the traffic circle where we stood. To the east of us was the first apartment we had shared, along the Quayside. To our north was the university, where we spent all our time. To the west, up the hill, was Clara's house, where I was staying. To our south was the river and the bridges that crossed it. I felt a terrible pattern had emerged, and it would be difficult to change course now.

"Do you understand," I asked, "That a union is an invisible bond that only holds together as long as both sides want it to?"

Andy tilted his head.

"And each day you act like you don't appreciate that bond, each day you say you'd be fine without that bond – do you realize you are fracturing that bond?"

Andy looked at me, listening.

"Do you recognize that everything humankind has created, including the invisible bonds between us, have been conjured up in our heads?"

"I get that," Andy said.

"Do you agree that what we conjure in our heads – the content of our thoughts – matches reality? In this case, the fact that we turned our love into a legal bond between us?"

"Uh huh," Andy said.

"Do you appreciate that we have overcome this hurdle before? You performed a symbolic act, proposing to me on one knee, and that allowed our love to become real in a new way."

"Yep," Andy said.

"And finally, do you agree that new things become possible when human thought is put into action, within the constraints of the physical world?"

"Sure," Andy said.

"OK." I took a deep breath. "You need to imagine us together, then translate that thought into action. You need to do something symbolic again, something that shows you want us to have a life together. And that will make it possible for us to do so."

"What do you mean, something symbolic?"

I sighed. "Look, magic is only real if you want to believe in it. It's just pretending that you have power over your world. In reality, the only power you have is over your own mind. But that's a wonderful power. Choose to use it, honey. Choose to change our minds. Choose to save our relationship."

"How?"

"First decide that you want something. Then imagine a solution. Then take action. Do something that will change my mind. Help me to trust you again."

"What do you want me to do exactly?"

"Andy, I want you to spin straw into gold."

"What does that mean?"

"I want you to spin the straw of our past into a golden future."

Andy dropped his shoulders. "I don't have a spinner." He sighed. "I don't know how to do magic."

"Andy, throw your pipe into the river and promise me you'll do anything to stop snoring, so we can sleep together in the same bed. Propose to me again, with a new ring that costs almost nothing but means a whole new start for us. Do *something* to set the past to rest and build our future, *something* to create magic in our lives."

Andy shook his head. "I just don't get it. I don't understand what you want from me."

I turned away, exhausted. I had tried to explain as best I could. I had no idea if he couldn't understand or just wouldn't.

Maybe he could not comprehend the power a symbolic act could hold, or somehow did not appreciate the exquisite thrill of sharing a metaphor with another person.

I had asked him to work with me – to find a symbol, held dear to us both, and mold it into a key. With this key, we could unlock the gate to a secret garden where our souls could meet – on another plane of existence, in a dimension we created just by imagining it.

Instead – by default – we diverged into separate universes, existing in parallel but no longer able to reach each other. Our marriage was over.

Chapter 20
Christmas

I went with Andy to Hampstead for Christmas in 2016, after things had fallen apart between us. We had several days of calm and enjoyable civility, but just like our marriage, it couldn't last.

"Why are you even here?" Andy demanded when we woke up on Boxing Day.

I burst into tears. "I love your family and I just didn't want to be alone on Christmas."

"You can't leave me and keep my family."

I was devastated, but I had to admit that was fair.

I went downstairs and sat politely in the living room with Mary. We each had a separate section of the newspaper, and I had made us each a cup of tea. We read in silence, Mary occasionally muttering under her breath, as the guys came downstairs and puttered with their jackets.

Pete left the house for his walk around the heath, yelling goodbye as the cold air poured through the front door to fill the ground floor of the house. I felt Mary's energy crackle, then tuck away again.

A little while later, Andy left the house for his run around the heath. He kissed his mother gently on the forehead and she mumbled incoherently. He turned to me with an angry, worried look, then left.

As soon as the door slammed shut, I felt Mary's energy jump. I turned to her. She looked me in the eye, set down her newspaper, and spoke in a clear, no-nonsense tone. "Alright," she said. "What's happening with you and Andy?"

I took a deep breath and explained that I had lost faith in his willingness and ability to love me and respect me in the way I needed and desired.

"Is that so."

I was not backing down, not with her. "I think our marriage is just like yours and Pete's."

She stared at me coldly. I pressed on.

"Andy is just like his father and they make decisions in the same way. For example, Andy refuses to plan our careers and lives together. He just won't have the conversations with me or take my opinions into account. I feel trapped and I'm not sure all his decisions are in my best interest. I just wish he would listen to me and treat me as an equal, instead of dismissing me and making decisions on his own. Just like Pete just doesn't think about you or take your needs into account sufficiently."

I took a deep breath and went on.

"You need the heat up, since you are recovering from chemo, but he thinks it's more important to save money on gas bills, and for some reason he's the one who gets his way. It's 16 degrees Celsius in here – there's no good reason for that. You guys don't need to save money on utilities and your health is at stake here. He just doesn't care about you or the things that are important to you. He put your paintings under the floorboards of the house, he sold your piano as soon as you got married, and he threw away all your clothing while you were in the hospital. Why did he need to do all that? What does it accomplish other than putting you into a corner?" I could feel my face flaring red-hot. "And he mocks you all the time. Just like Andy mocks me."

She remained silent, looking at me intently.

"I don't want to criticize anyone. But this is the truth. You and I are undervalued and underappreciated and taken for granted by these men."

"That's not true," Mary contended.

"It is true, and it's not said enough," I declared, with growing confidence. "Mary, you are awesome. I know it's a silly American word, but there's no other term for it. For crying out loud, you were one of the first female lecturers at the London Business School!"

She shook her head. "No, I just taught. I didn't do research or anything valuable like that."

"You wrote their textbooks!" I exclaimed. "Teaching students is what brings money into the school. Of course that was valuable."

"It was a long time ago," she said.

"No it wasn't!" I yelled. "I googled you, Mary. They're still using your textbooks. They're on the requirement list for this year's entering business course."

"Well, it wasn't the LSE."

"London School of Economics, London Business School, who cares? Why are you doing this, Mary? What you've done is objectively a major accomplishment, and if you don't feel it's valued, someone is trying to make you feel that way. And I have watched for years as your husband says things that –"

The front door opened and we both froze. A moment later Pete entered the main room with a flush of cold air. We changed gears, fussing over him and making a fresh pot of tea.

Later, I sat back in the chair, knowing we would never

finish that conversation. Pete opened all the mail and always answered the phone; the two of them shared a single email address. With the cancer, Mary wasn't healthy or mobile enough to go to art classes or galleries, so it would be difficult to meet her in public.

I met her eyes, but one was glass and the other may as well have been. I felt I was leaving her to the wolves, but there was nothing more I could do. I was already falling outside the circle. When she hugged me goodbye the following day, I realized it was probably forever.

Chapter 21
Separation

Despite everything that had happened, Andy suggested that we go on two dates every week – one to discuss our relationship and one to discuss CANDO. I told him no on both counts. Our relationship was blitzed and if he wanted my advice on the project, he could put me on the management team.

"I can't put my wife on the management team! I think it would be better if we just chatted once in a while." He smiled sweetly.

"You can't have your cake and eat it too," I told him. "You can't have all the benefits of having me around but give me nothing I want in return."

"What do you mean?" he asked innocently.

"Andy, you can't refuse to acknowledge all my contributions and then expect me to continue giving you all kinds of support. At home or at work."

He stared at me blankly, waiting for me to break.

"Do you even understand how human interactions work?" I walked away, shaking my head.

Later that evening I broke the news to my parents.

"Andy and I are separated," I told them. "I'm not actually living at the house right now."

There was a pause.

"We thought things seemed a bit strange at Thanksgiving," my mother said.

I sighed. "Yeah."

"You'll go back to him, right?" my mother asked.

"I don't know, Mom," I told her sadly.

"Well, we're not taking sides here," my father declared.

"Dad, I'm your daughter. You have to take my side."

There was another pause.

"Your father and I love Andy very much," my mother explained.

"That's fine, so do I, but you have to take my side here."

"Are you sure you two can't work it out?"

"It's not very likely at this point."

"You can try a bit more."

"Mom, Dad, I told you, he's emotionally abusive."

"That's a pretty strong term, there. You can't say that about your husband, about Andy."

"Well, my doctor agrees with that assessment. He even wrote a letter documenting domestic abuse for the court." I had begun visiting my physician every two weeks, to touch base on my life as it slowly disintegrated and to process what was happening.

"I think you're being dramatic, dear," my mother said.

"I wish you would just believe me and take my side."

"This is just the first we're hearing about it."

"Maybe it's the first time I'm asking you to listen."

"Well, if you had told us you were having problems, we would have told you what to do."

"I didn't want you to tell me what to do. And I don't want that now. I just want you to be there for me. Can you do that?"

"Of course, we're there for you, dear. But you should have told us earlier."

"Mom, if you wanted, you could have paid attention. I was alone out here, and maybe I didn't entirely know how to ask for help. If I felt I had a place to go –"

"But sweetie, we had no idea. How could we know? Now you say Andy maybe has a drinking problem – there was no way we could have known this."

"Look, Mom, I don't know. Why does it matter? I just want you to be there for me now."

"You should have brought this up before the wedding. Why didn't you say anything at the wedding?"

"The wedding was a bit of a rush, so I could get my visa. Maybe you should have noticed that, in fact – that I was rushing to get married so I could get a visa."

"We didn't know that!"

"Mom, yes you did. Why else would we plan a wedding in only four months? Don't you remember how important it was that we get married in England by a certain date?"

"That was a long time ago. How are we supposed to remember that?"

"Well, at the time, surely you could have noticed it was strange. And you could have asked at any point if everything was okay."

"Now you're putting this on us?"

"No, no, I'm just saying. The fact that our marriage has been under pressure from the start should not be coming as a surprise."

"Well you were going to have a nice wedding, but you

cancelled the celebration in Chicago."

"Uh, we had a nice wedding in Newcastle. But yes, we did cancel the extra celebration in Chicago."

"Andy announced that he and his entire family were alcoholics and we had better provide a lot of booze. That's why we cancelled the wedding. Your father and I wanted no part in that."

"OK, I didn't know that, although it does sound like the sort of thing Andy would say if he wanted to irritate you. He and his dad may drink a lot, but I'm not sure if they're alcoholics. Anyway, that's not why we cancelled the wedding."

"It is why. It was extremely tacky of him to say that."

"Fine. Wait, I thought you said you didn't know he drank a lot?"

"No, we didn't. We thought he was joking."

"So we cancelled the wedding over a joke?"

"No, the whole thing was becoming tacky. Your father and I wanted no part in that. We wanted you to have a classy wedding. Then, you cancelled the wedding I planned for you and on top of it all, you went and married a man with a drinking problem."

I sighed, waiting for her to finish her thoughts.

"And now you're getting divorced," she continued. "None of my friends' children are divorced. The people I know don't get divorced." She paused for a moment. "You just cannot stop embarrassing me."

"OK, Mom, can I store some boxes with you or what? I need you to help me out for a few months here. I have nowhere else to store my stuff and I don't want to throw it all away."

"Yes, of course, dear. We're here for you. We're always here for you, in any way you need."

"Right, Mom. I know."

Andy emailed me the following day. "Hey, can we meet up? I don't need anything from you, I just want to see you."

"Why?" I replied.

"A paper came out, positing that our entire world is a simulation. I thought it might be interesting to discuss it."

I had read a news article about the study, but I hadn't gotten around to reading the actual paper. The idea sounded intriguing and worth exploring over a pint of beer.

"Alright," I said, and agreed to meet up at the usual pub later that afternoon.

"It can't be true," Andy declared as we sat down. "I just can't figure out why."

He handed me the manuscript he had printed. I paged through it as he sipped his beer.

"Honey, they're not saying they've proven it to be true, just that logic dictates it's highly likely."

"Yeah, I know," Andy agreed. "It's still weird though, right?" The point was that, in any universe where consciousness manifests, like ours, those conscious beings will create systems to simulate intelligent processes, in order to understand them or push them forward or find out what's possible. And no reasonable entity runs only one simulation; they'd run thousands at once, and many of those would in turn create simulations as well – which means the quantity of simulated worlds would quickly outnumber the quantity of actual worlds. So in conclusion it was statistically likely we were living in one of the simulations.

I put down the paper. "I don't know, there's some assumptions about the likelihood of consciousness arising in a real universe and a simulated universe, but they argue convincingly that that problematic variable does not affect the overall mathematics." I sat back and sipped my pint.

"But it can't be true," Andy argued, grabbing the paper.

"Why not?"

"Because, it's too weird."

"Because it doesn't fit with your notion of reality?" He was silent.

I laughed. "You don't like the idea there might be a creator?" I chuckled some more, contemplating the metaphysical implications of the report.

"But this world is not a simulation," Andy complained. "There's matter all around us." This subject was not unfamiliar territory for him. He had studied physics as an undergraduate at Oxford before undertaking a PhD in neuroscience. I only had an amateur interest in the field.

"Well," I countered carefully, "If we were inside a simulation, everything would seem real to us, because we think we're real and everything around us is made of the same stuff."

"Maybe," Andy replied doubtfully. "But we don't live in The Matrix. That's absurd."

"It's not like The Matrix, though," I pointed out. "It's not like our minds are in a simulation and we can escape back to our bodies elsewhere. Absolutely everything is inside the simulation."

"The proposition is still absurd. Our world is an entire universe, not a computer program."

I sighed. "Yeah, you're probably right. We'd be able to recognize signs, surely."

"Of course," Andy agreed. "It would be obvious."

We sat in silence, sipping our beers.

"So what would the world look like if it were a simulation?" I asked, to provoke the conversation further.

We sat there for a while, thinking to ourselves.

"Uh oh," I said quietly.

"What?" Andy asked.

"Time would only move in the forward direction." I took a breath. "It might be theoretically possible to go in either direction, but efficiency would dictate the model only advances." We both swallowed, knowing that a correction of the systemic parameters or a tweak to an earlier event would be made in a separate simulation.

Andy cleared his throat.

"It might start with a few simple rules, then increase in complexity over time."

I nodded, thinking about the big bang, entropy, the expansion of the universe and the number of galaxies within it, the laws of atomic physics giving rise to chemistry, interactions between carbon- hydrogen- oxygen- and nitrogen-based molecules giving rise to self-replicating organisms which then evolved into more complex creatures, and those living beasts becoming aware not only of their own surroundings but of themselves.

"New properties might emerge within the system too," I added, now reflecting on our previous conversation about consciousness – how thought was a strange, matter-less emergent property of biological systems that could somehow interact bi-directionally with the physical world.

Andy nodded, catching my drift. "And such phenomena may provide new methods of processing data, which would allow the simulation as a whole to accomplish more complex tasks."

We nodded thoughtfully, then paused again, pondering other features that might be characteristic of a simulated world.

"Um," Andy said softly. He cleared his throat again. "Detail would get pixelated if you look too closely." We sat quietly, thinking about everything that broke down at a quantum level – how light could act as a wave or a particle, depending on what was convenient at the time; how we could not simultaneously know both the position and the momentum of a subatomic unit, because that would allow us to predict the future perfectly; how uncertainty gave way to downright eeriness at the point one realized one could change reality by merely observing it; and the fact that we actually changed reality all the time with our thoughts and actions.

There was no way around it; we were creating reality just by living out every day. This simple fact was entirely consistent with our world being a simulation.

"If the simulation was being run to solve a problem," I postulated, "It would be really useful to have within it multiple galaxies, multiple planets with life on them, multiple conscious entities on each planet, and the ability for these individual conscious units to interact with each other. That would increase ideological diversity within the simulation, and that would increase the rate of novel idea generation, rendering the whole system more likely to hit on a solution."

"OK, but what kind of problem would this simulation be looking to solve?" Andy asked.

"I don't know, maybe it's just a game to see if we can figure out we're living in a simulation." I laughed, then stopped. "Or if we can find meaning in life afterwards, when all the mystery of the universe has been removed."

Andy sat silently, and I did too.

"You think we're supposed to worship this creator?" Andy asked.

I sighed. "Probably doesn't matter. If you ran 10,000 simulations and one of them manifested entities that worshipped you, would you care?"

"I think that would get my attention," Andy said, chuckling now. "I think I'd be flattered."

I laughed too. "What if everyone argued about what you were like all the time? Tried to say they understood your nature and everyone else was wrong?"

Andy laughed. "That would annoy me."

"Yeah," I agreed. "The whole point of the exercise was to get everyone focused on solving a problem."

"Right," Andy said. "So what problem are we trying to solve?"

"Could be anything." I shrugged. "Figuring out the purpose of our existence would be worthwhile. That either *is* the problem, or a necessary step to solving it."

"So how do we go about doing that?"

"Well, I think it would be sensible to use our magic superpower. The fact that we can create thought and merge on a dimensionless plane of existence with other people, through language."

"Huh?"

"You know, the thing we were talking about earlier. Thought comes from matter, is not itself matter, but can influence matter? And if we put our brains to the task, we can come up with ideas and interact with our world and create things that were not possible before?"

"Maybe." He was still stuck on the basic principles. "But if we're in a simulation, there's no such thing as matter."

"Honey, it doesn't matter what matter is," I said, patting his arm. "You're still real, as much as you were yesterday. Maybe the framework of this world is different than what we thought it was – maybe there's a world outside our world, maybe infinity and eternity are illusions, maybe quantum uncertainty is just a sign that our world is a work in progress – but that's okay. It doesn't change the fact that we're here, and we're still free to find meaning in life. We might just have to create it ourselves."

Andy smiled at me then, his eyes warm and grateful. My heart ached a little bit. He didn't know how much he needed me. He was always talking about how much I relied on him, but he depended on me a lot too, for emotional and intellectual sustenance.

"Hey," he said, easing into a new conversation. "What do you think about this? I have a theory that cerebellar circuitry and cortical-thalamic circuitry are involved in motor learning task consolidation during sleep, but in different ways."

"Uh huh." I gazed at his cunning smile. He knew exactly how much he needed me. That's why he had brought me out here, to run ideas past me, to develop thoughts together like we had always done. He wanted to continue taking, without giving back.

I was pissed off. But I was also interested in his unfinished theory. He was missing some critical motor control circuits, and it would be important to parse the different ways they too might be involved in goal-directed behavior, in order to understand the entire integrated system.

He was watching me, waiting.

"Go on," I sighed. "Let's dig in."

After that night, Andy did not contact me for a month, so I went to meet with a divorce lawyer.

"We have to tell the court why you're separating," she explained.

"Irreconcilable metaphysical differences," I stated. "And he's annoying."

"You need to be more specific," she said, not looking up from her notepad.

"Too much drinking, too few kind words, ignoring my physical and emotional needs, humiliating me privately and in front of people, flirting with other women, and exerting control over me financially."

"These issues sound like more reasonable grounds for divorce."

"I thought the metaphysical stuff was important too."

She nodded. "Best to focus on what the court finds relevant though."

We prepared the paperwork, but I couldn't bring myself to sign it yet.

I emailed Andy, telling him I had been to a lawyer. Our anniversary was coming up, the 13th of April, and I was hoping he would finally realize things were serious and do something dramatic to save our marriage.

But instead he responded that he was jetting to Columbia so he could spend the next three weeks on the beach and in Bogota with his old school friends.

I put my head in my hands.

"You're going to spend our anniversary drinking and doing drugs with your friends, hooking up with women?" I wrote. "Are you kidding me?"

"I have no plans to hook up with women," he wrote back.

I went to the house, missing it too. I lay in the king-size bed, wishing that everything in my life was different.

My neck was stiff and aching. I opened the night-table drawer to search for my tiger balm, to relieve the pain.

My heart stopped. Andy's wedding ring was there, in the drawer.

Chapter 22
Brexit Negotiations

After our conversations in December, I realized there was little chance that Andy and I would get back together. I found myself a room in a house-share down the street from Clara, so I could easily stop by her place for dinner some evenings.

Because I now officially had a separate address, I had to inform the Home Office that my marriage was no longer subsisting, essentially inviting the curtailment of my spousal visa. I informed the CANDO management team and the new director of our institute, asking them to sponsor me for a Tier 2 work visa, as the university had done for me twice before, when I worked with Nick upstairs.

But now Nick was not my line manager – Andy was. He had signed my employment contract and it was up to him whether the project he led would pay to sponsor my visa.

Even without those personal circumstances, it was not a great time to be asking for a visa. Things were different now, with Brexit looming.

In England, in the northern part of the country anyway, I had always been given unkind half-compliments when people heard my accent – "I like America, don't like Americans," people would say, or "You're welcome to visit, but you're not welcome to stay." But academia had been an island of internationalism and courtesy. Now, after the Brexit vote, this toxic mentality had spread to the university. Entering the tearoom, I would hear mocking giggles around the word 'Americans' followed by laughter and silence when I walked in. It was clear I was no longer welcome.

A few people tried to reassure me that I was not the sort of person Britain was trying to keep out. That sentiment only disgusted me, and it showed. Those conversations did not endear me to anyone, or anyone to me.

But I hoped for the best. And in the meantime, I kept plugging away at my work.

I went to visit Lacey, the institute's administrative manager. Her role was to make sure everything was running smoothly in the department and coordinate with other administrative teams on any issues.

I had emailed her to address the problem of my line management through my estranged husband, and she had responded with a request to meet her in her office.

"You can't put this stuff in an email," she told me as she closed the door of her office behind me.

"Well, I just want to make sure we address the issue."

"Yes, of course we will," she said. "But it'll be better to talk about in person."

"OK," I said, and launched into the explanation of how Andy was in a position of power over me as my husband, visa sponsor, and line manager at the university, and he had used this leverage to force me to work on my birthday weekend.

"No, don't say that," Lacey instructed.

"Look, I'm just telling you what happened."

"No, I don't want to hear about your personal life."

"That isn't really my personal life. It's work-related. Also, Andy yelled at me in front of colleagues here at work. That was purely work-related, he was yelling about monkey brain histology."

"That's your relationship."

"No, that's monkey brains. It's separate from our relationship. Not as separate as it should be, but –"

"You're the one who brought your relationship to work, huh? And now you want to make a problem out of it?"

"Are you kidding me? We were married when Andy was put in charge of the CANDO project. The university knew about that conflict of interest, and still made him my line manager."

"No one at the university knew you were married."

"What? Half the institute came to our wedding."

"That doesn't mean anything."

"Sure it does. Everyone knew he was my husband when he became my line manager. I brought up the conflict of interest. But everyone told me not to worry about it."

"Well, he's not your line manager. The institute director is."

"Well then why did Andy sign my last employment contract?"

"No, he didn't."

"Yes, he did. I have the document right here." I showed it to her.

"Well I don't know about that. But he's not your line manager now."

"OK, so the institute director is?"

"Yep, go speak with her. And don't put this stuff in an email again, OK?"

"OK," I agreed. I walked back to my office and archived all my emails.

A few weeks later I managed to set up a meeting with the new institute director, Stephanie, a slim woman with a severe face who horded food in the cold room of her lab.

That morning, Prime Minister Theresa May had called a snap election, calculating it would increase her majority in Parliament. The plan would backfire, leaving her government weakened, in disarray and unable to negotiate any reasonable terms for Brexit. Everyone had just read the news that morning, and we were all in shock at the ill-advised gamble the administration had taken when they already had enough problems of their own creation to deal with.

"My gosh, what was she thinking?" Stephanie enquired as she let me into her office and offered me a chair. She was wrapping up a meeting with Lacey, who stood up to leave. Lacey stood there silently, refusing to give an opinion on the subject.

"Leaders don't always make great decisions," I answered, shrugging my shoulders and taking a seat. The two women exchanged looks with each other, and Lacey left the room.

"Alright, what are you doing here?" Stephanie asked.

"Well, I wanted to talk to you about my grant application. You seem to have rejected the document out of the system."

"This was the first I'd heard about it, this week."

"Well, I tried to set up a meeting with you earlier, but this was the earliest date you were free. I didn't think it would be a problem to submit a grant."

"You have to talk to people at the university about it beforehand."

"I did. I discussed it with the previous institute director, and he agreed it was a reasonable plan. That was only two months ago, before the promotions happened."

"You have to get peer review before submission."

"I did. I sent the grant application along to four professors, including one person who sits on the relevant assessment panel at The Trust. They all said it was great, a perfect fit for the call."

"Well you're not submitting it."

I sat back. This was my best chance to get funding to continue my brain tumor studies. And the deadline was in a few days.

"What should I do?" I asked.

"I don't care, but you can't apply for grants."

"Well, then how am I supposed to build my research program here?"

"If you're looking for a tenure-track position, you're in the wrong place."

I had thought I could not be more surprised by this conversation, but here we were.

"Why not?"

"We're looking to hire more clinicians instead." The National Health Service was underfunded, so clinicians were now being paid academic salaries. They either applied for grants or were paid directly by the universities through the increased tuition fees charged to students.

I sighed. "What should I do then?"

"You should apply for jobs elsewhere."

"What about my job here?"

"The institute doesn't have to keep paying you forever."

"Uh, the institute has to keep paying me for as long as

CANDO goes on. That's in the contract with The Trust, that I'm paid half by the project and half by the institute. And I'm a full-time employee with an open-ended contract. So as long as CANDO continues, I keep both sides of my job. And I'm making damn sure we're hitting our milestones so the project does continue."

"I think you should start applying for other jobs," Stephanie said. "You can go now."

"OK," I said. I walked back to my office and applied for a job at a large pharmaceuticals company.

The institute administrators and CANDO management team had suggested that I meet with Tony, CANDO's lead engineer, to update him regularly on the gene therapy side of the project since Andy and I were no longer communicating effectively.

I gathered my notes, walked over to the engineering building, and knocked on the door to Tony's corner office. He motioned for me to enter and sit down at a large drafting table while he made us each a cup of coffee from a machine on his desk.

"Well, what's the story?" he said, sitting down. "I don't know anything about genetics."

"No problem," I replied. "I'll try to explain everything as clearly as possible."

"OK, then, what are you up to?"

I explained the basics of the gene therapy – how we inserted genetic material into viral vectors and how those viral vectors delivered the genetic material into neurons so those cells could do things they couldn't do before. I explained how the gene therapy would provide brain cells with a single extra protein that would treat the disease or allow a biomedical device to treat the disease. Then I explained how we could modify genetic sequences to encode proteins with new characteristics and how we could add genetic sequences to ensure the proteins were only created in certain cell types.

"I don't know, this stuff is pretty over my head," Tony replied. He was an electrical engineering professor. This was outside his field. I wasn't sure if he really couldn't follow or just wouldn't try. Then I realized how to seize his interest.

The engineers had been trying to get a corporate partner on board with the project since day one, with no luck. But I seemed to attract corporate partners like flies. I had held meetings with half a dozen potential contracting manufacturers to vet their production platforms and validation assays, and now a major drug company with a developing interest in creating and licensing gene therapies for epilepsy had arranged a conference call to discuss the work of my team. Their yearly profits were in the billions and, as one of the ten largest drug companies in the world, they invested a lot in R&D.

"So it could be a three-way partnership, between us and the contracting manufacturer and the large company which would act as an investor then market the drug if it worked."

Tony sighed, as if this were a problem not a solution.

"The only thing is, we need to develop novel gene therapies and novel genetic sequences for cell targeting, so that we have something to license to them." I had learned my lesson about protecting intellectual property after an unfortunate incident with another top-ten drug company. "Anyway I have some ideas about novel gene therapies that could be used to treat epilepsy on their own, without any biomedical device."

"Well, you need the device," Tony said. He did not want the engineers to be left out.

"Well, that's only true if it's an optogenetic therapy," I explained. "There are in fact a number of underexplored genetic targets. I've created an outline proposal for developing tools and testing them." I handed him the document.

"This is outside the scope of the project," he objected.

"Only slightly," I said. "We'd still be developing a gene therapy for epilepsy. If we got some PhD students, we could have some dedicated labor on the problem." The engineering team had loads of PhD students and I had been asking Andy to apply for add-on funding so we could have some too.

"I don't know, we have enough to focus on with the main project," Tony argued.

"Actually, my team is well on-track with our milestones and we could do more if we get a few more brains onboard. I have a talented master's student working with me on another project who would be interested in doing a PhD in gene therapies and a computer programmer interning with me who would be well-suited to develop my proposed Boolean algorithm software to create short synthetic genetic sequences for cell-specific targeting of viral vector mediated gene therapies. It's all useful for achieving our project goals. I just need some support from the CANDO management team here."

"I think we have enough to focus on with the main project," Tony repeated.

"Like I said, my team is well on-track with our milestones and we would love to accommodate some extra work. I know the engineering team is running a bit behind schedule. But because of that, the project as a whole will run behind schedule. Wouldn't it be great if we had *some* therapy for epilepsy by the end of the seven-year project?"

"Not if the therapy does not include a device."

"But developing a gene therapy that could work on its

own would give us something patentable that we could license to a company. Then we build that relationship, and when the device is ready, we license the optogenetic combination therapy to the company as well. This route buys you time."

Tony looked at me doubtfully.

"What?" I asked. "It's a good business plan."

"Maybe you should keep busy with the regulatory paperwork," Tony said.

"Oh, I'm on that," I said, opening the next folder of documents.

"What do you have?" Tony asked, leaning over.

"Well, I gave some thought to our meeting last week, when the CATAPULT people came over."

"That meeting went well," Tony said, smiling. The regulatory manager who worked with me had set up a conference between myself, the CANDO management team, and the UK government-sponsored Cell & Gene Therapies CATAPULT which had consultant services and several clinical-grade production facilities which were not yet up and running.

"The meeting did go well," I agreed. The consultants had decided they could not advise on gene therapies manufacture and validation, as my team was well ahead of them on that, but they could perhaps advise on the regulatory approvals process. This was currently our weak point. The previous regulatory manager Laura and her husband Sam had quit the project after witnessing the spat over monkey brains. Laura's replacement had quit as well, having been offered a better-paying job in industry, but the new guy was diving into the project with fresh energy.

"After the meeting," I continued, "Our regulatory manager and I made a chart of the approvals process, streamlined into the preclinical testing phases and contract manufacturing for test runs of the clinical-grade product."

Tony looked at my chart. "Do you know it's complete?"

"No," I said. "I've never done this before. But we can ask the regulatory agency representatives at our next advisory meeting if we're missing any critical steps."

Tony sighed and looked at the chart again. It was three pages long. "I don't know. CATAPULT offered to consult on it. They said they'd make this chart or look over your version for ten grand. They call it a gap analysis, to assess where there are gaps in your project."

I sat back in my chair. Someone could charge one-third of my yearly salary just to update a chart? I created a document as useful as this one on a monthly basis, alone or with members of my team. I quickly extrapolated the numbers to calculate how much I was being underpaid.

My institute director was right, I needed to get another job.

Excellent news came through. A group of people in the northeast had decided to organize a charity bike ride from Edinburgh to Newcastle to raise money for brain tumor research projects in my lab. They had been so proud to watch a local researcher in the national news, making breakthroughs on cancer, and they wanted to support my team's drug development work. They emailed me to ask if that would be alright. Astounded by their generosity, I enthusiastically agreed to the plan and got everyone together in the lab for a photo, so our supporters could see the whole grateful team.

My institute director might not let me apply for grants, I thought, but she couldn't stop the public from making spontaneous donations in support of my work.

Once a stupid decision is made, it can be difficult to reverse. The viral-vectors-kill-neurons hypothesis stuck. A committee was formed to handle the issue. A meeting was called, between Tony, who was there to watch proceedings unfold; Nathan, who was acting as an ostensibly neutral party although he was closely tied with Andy; Oliver, whom Andy had promoted to lead CANDO's scientific section; and Gavin, who had posited the hypothesis in the first place.

"All right, what is the evidence for and against?" Nathan asked me, after we all sat down.

"There is no evidence for. There is a great deal of evidence against," I stated, and showed a series of powerpoint slides containing the relevant data.

"Do you agree with this assessment?" Nathan asked Gavin.

"Yeah, no one thinks the lentiviral vectors kill neurons," Gavin declared. "Why are we here?"

"You started this whole discussion," Nathan explained. "The project lead and the rest of the management team have decided to take your hypothesis seriously."

"But I don't believe it anymore. I explained before the meeting." Everyone laughed. Gavin had calculated that, with my group undermined, he could purchase viral vectors off the internet and my post-doc would have nothing to do except help with experiments in his lab. He had not calculated correctly – instead he had unleashed a terrible mess, and everyone except me thought it was funny.

"Why have you changed your mind?" Nathan asked, smiling indulgently.

"The data." Gavin gestured at my powerpoint slides, projected on the wall.

"But do we have enough data to make a decision?" Nathan asked slyly.

Gavin shrugged. "Sure."

"Maybe there isn't," Nathan suggested.

"Uh," Gavin spluttered. He was on the back foot now.

"What we've decided to do now," announced Oliver, "Is have your post-docs run some more experiments." He smiled, relishing his new position of power over Gavin, his ancient enemy.

Gavin looked at the table. "Beth's team should be doing all this stuff."

"No, no, no," I said. "My post-doc is busy designing the viral vectors, making them, and measuring their concentration. If you want, we can also measure any levels of toxic by-products in the preparations. It wouldn't hurt to develop those protocols, to set the specifications for the clinical-grade product. But my team cannot also run a bunch of cell death assays. Those experiments are a lot of work. And remember, our staffing is down since the technicians all quit."

"Alright," agreed Oliver. "Gavin's team will make this a priority."

"But the hypothesis isn't true," complained Gavin, who now regretted proposing it in the first place. "And there are more important things to do."

Everyone laughed again. I gave him a dirty look.

At that point, the two post-docs, Georgiana and Erin, were called into the meeting. Oliver announced that he would be acting as their line manager from now on. The two women looked at each other nervously. Gavin and I were both being undermined, right in front of our staff.

We discussed the imaginary problem, the solution to which would be our sole priority from now on. It was decided we would all go home and have a think, then reconvene to discuss the experimental design, so that we could test out a hypothesis that no one really believed.

The post-docs and I showed up to the meeting the following day, notebooks in hand. Nathan, Gavin, Oliver, and everyone else sent their apologies. They were not going to waste their time on this.

I realized I was a sucker for playing their game. But if they wanted more data, I would help collect it in good faith. More data on the safety of a proposed therapy was never a bad thing.

Erin presented her experimental plan. It required Georgiana to make more viral vectors.

"Let's just make sure we have this right, to make the most of both of your time," I said, reaching for her notebook.

"I've already got it sorted," Erin snarled, holding her notebook away from me. She had made it clear, ever since I corrected her paygrade, that she did not want my help with anything.

I withdrew my hand. "OK, but since we're here, it might be useful to talk out the experimental design. After all this work, you don't want the whole experiment to be uninterpretable."

"I'm not taking advice from you," Erin declared. She stood up to leave.

"You have a bad attitude right now," I said. "I'm trying to help here."

She turned and flounced away. "Oh dear," I sighed, watching her walk out the door. I realized that everything would only get worse from here.

A couple weeks later, I was issued a notice from Human Resources. A misconduct report had been filed by my institute director Stephanie and my institute manager Lacey, so HR was formally opening an investigation into my behavior.

There were three complaints. Firstly, Erin had testified that I had bullied her, by saying she had a bad attitude. I had sent her an apology email within minutes of the abrupt end to our meeting and a separate email to the group expressing confidence in her work, but she still filed a complaint. My involvement in correcting her salary to match her male peers seemed to have bothered her for some reason. Clearly, she did not want an ally; she wanted to stand on her own without any interference. In the second case, Lacey reported that I had made false allegations of bullying against a male colleague, which I had later recanted. The bullying allegations were true – there were witnesses – and I had not recanted them, although Lacey had called me into her office again to suggest I recant and to inform me I was asking for trouble by not recanting. Now I understood what she had meant by that. The third complaint was an allegation that I had raised my voice at Lacey during one of our meetings, when I had begged her to say something to a member of staff who was harassing me verbally. That one was true, although I was uncertain it was accurately categorized as bullying. I had just been asking for help loudly.

Glad I had archived my emails, I spent the weekend preparing two hundred pages of documents to submit in my defense. I sent them along to HR on Sunday so I could concentrate on actual work during the week.

HR opened a counter-investigation. I rolled my eyes, thinking how much easier it would have been if everyone had been kind in the first place, and not looked the other way when people were being treated unfairly.

Over the following weeks, the twin investigations stalled under the weight of paperwork, and another tactic was deployed. This one was more direct.

"I will be taking over your research budget," Oliver emailed. "And your staff members will be supervised by me."

At this point, I went on vacation to Italy.

I knew better than to talk to Andy about the situation. As leader of the project, this decision was in his hands. And he was abusing his authority to reassign my contractually-obliged funding to various faculty members, some of whom happened to be on the tenure committee. This was a strategic decision on his part; no one had anything to gain by taking my side when they were being so richly rewarded for taking his.

I received yet another email the following week. The thread had been going for a while before I was copied in. The charity bike ride organizers had sent their first check to the Institute of Neuroscience, and Lacey was trying to redirect it to anyone but me. She had sent it to three different labs, each of whom rejected it and each of whom informed her that money was meant for me. Finally, one of the would-be recipients copied me into the email thread directly so I could wrestle the check from my own institute manager.

When I arrived at the institute administrative office with the documents proving the check was meant for my lab, I was told the money would be held in an account I did not have access to and any further funds would be put there too.

"Is there no rule of law in your country anymore?" I asked, to nobody in particular. Nobody answered.

I met with Luke, the CANDO project manager. We had coffee and I explained the situation to him.

"Yeah, every single last one of you is bloody difficult."

He paused. "They're trying to get rid of me too, you

know. I do everything by the book and it's not very popular."

"But you've run the project on time and on budget for three years now."

"Doesn't matter, they're looking for someone else and as soon as they find someone I'll be out."

"That's terrible. And unfair."

He shrugged helplessly.

"Hey, will you help me with my visa, Luke? I need sponsorship and CANDO is my employer."

"Well, it's actually only half your employer."

A bad feeling stuck in my throat, and I swallowed. "Luke, will you coordinate with HR to sponsor me for my visa so I can continue work on this project?"

"Uh, I'm not sure how to do that."

"Luke, it just means calling HR and saying the project will cover the costs. It should be fine, I'm named in the grant as having a critical role in the project, leading the development of the gene therapy."

"Maybe the institute could sponsor your visa."

"The project really should sponsor me."

"I think you had better talk to someone in the institute." He knew perfectly well my institute director would not sponsor my visa, after pulling my grant applications and telling me to get another job and filing a spurious bullying claim against me. But his response made clear that he was not going to throw me a life preserver to help me out. He would just let me drown.

I nodded, realizing that his own requirement for self-preservation was preventing him from being able to fight for someone else.

I emailed the CANDO management team to object to the seizure of my lab budget, the reassignment of my staff, and the decision not to sponsor my work visa.

Tony replied, cc'ing the entire CANDO management team.

"Stop arguing, Beth," he wrote. "We can meet face-to-face but we're not going to write this down."

I sighed. I realized that put me on the back foot, as every conversation turned into a he-said-she-said situation, while emails created documented paper trails. That was exactly why they refused to communicate this way, insisting on meeting in person instead.

I prepared to go to Tony's office for another meeting with him. I groaned loudly and repeatedly while I gathered my notebooks into my bag, and my officemate Barry spun around in his chair.

"What's going on?"

"Sorry, I didn't realize I was grumbling. I didn't mean to distract you."

"It's no problem. Are you doing alright?"

I smiled at him. "Thanks for asking, Barry. I'll be okay."

"You don't look so great lately." He paused. "Sorry, I know you're not supposed to say that to a person, when they're already having a hard time."

I laughed. "Friends can tell the truth, that's okay."

"You're going to another CANDO meeting, are you?"

"Always another CANDO meeting these days." Barry and I went for a beer every few weeks, he knew what was going on and how stressful it was.

"You know," I said, thinking out loud. "I'm not sure how much worse things can get."

Barry scratched his head. "They sure are throwing a lot

at you."

"I'm meeting with Tony again this morning, and I honestly don't know what to expect. I just can't read this guy."

Barry nodded. "Some people are really tough that way."

"You know, the last time I met with him, he asked me if I was scared of him?" I laughed, remembering. Tony had such a friendly, smiling face. It was a weird question, and I had laughed at the time too.

"What did you say?" Barry asked.

"I said no, of course not."

"What was his reaction?"

"I don't know. He seemed disappointed."

"Huh."

"It almost seemed like he wanted me to be scared of him, come to think of it."

"Well, for crying out loud. What are you supposed to be scared of?" Barry chuckled. "I mean, what else can they do to you, that they haven't already done?"

I laughed and gathered my bag. "Exactly."

I knocked on the door of Tony's office on the top floor of the engineering building, and he let me in. As usual, he offered me coffee and made some for himself.

I accepted the beverage and asked if CANDO could sponsor me for a work visa.

"No, I think you should talk to people in your home institute about that."

"Well, I would like support from my project."

"I'm not really in a position to make this decision."

"Right, my husband is the lead of the project. He's not exactly in a proper position to make this decision either."

"He's not making the decision."

"Who is? No one will tell me."

Tony shrugged.

"I'm just looking for an independent advocate here."

"I'm not in your institute. This needs to be handled locally."

"But Andy is the person in my institute who is acting as my line manager. And there's a conflict of interest there, as we have discussed before."

Tony shrugged again.

"If I don't get sponsored for a visa, I'll have to leave the country."

"That's too bad," Tony said. "We'll miss you." It didn't look like he would.

"But I wanted to push the project forward," I said sadly. "And help CANDO get to clinical trial."

He smiled gently. "Your team has already been successful. You've produced the gene therapy and a plan for the clinical trial. So maybe it's a good time for you to move on."

"But I'm not ready to move on. I want to build on the foundation I created here. Normally if you're successful at your job, you get to stay. And there's so much more I'd like to do here."

Tony tilted his head, a warm look in his eyes.

"The Boolean algorithms for creating cell-specific targeting sequences –"

"I think Nathan might take that forward." I knew that already. Nathan had mentioned after our last meeting that he had some collaborators who would be interested in the project and well-placed to take it forward. I could either join them or be left by the wayside.

"But the novel gene therapies to treat epilepsy –"

"Gavin is already working on that." I nodded. I knew

that too.

"My other work is yielding drug targets related to cellular metabolism which may have implications for normal brain function as well as understanding brain tumors. Basically, I think glial cells or interneurons might rely on fatty acid metabolism and related strategies for energy production. It would explain why the ketogenic diet works for some types of epilepsy. I would love to do that research too. If I had the support and a visa, I could push it forward. It would provide a really interesting sideline to CANDO."

"I think Oliver will be pursuing that project." I looked down, knowing this already. I had asked Oliver to support a grant application I was preparing on this subject, and now it appeared he would be taking the project forward himself instead. Over the past couple of years he had borrowed a number of reagents to test out the hypothesis, but repeatedly insisted that he had gathered no data to add to our grant submission. But then I had found out from a student in his lab the experiments had been successful. Oliver had loads of data on the study. Now he would not speak to me or meet my eyes – when I saw him in the hallway, he would take a sudden turn, tucking into an office or a lab.

"What am I supposed to do now then?" I asked.

"I think it would be great if you could continue to consult for the CANDO project," Tony replied, the warm look still in his eyes and the small smile still on his mouth.

"But, would I get paid for that, or how would I be credited?"

"I think it would be useful for you," Tony said. "But we couldn't pay you if you didn't have permission to work in this country."

"And there's no way for you to help me out with that,

help me get a visa."

"No, I'm sorry about that."

I cried a little bit, and Tony waited until I sniffled. Then I nodded and stood up to leave.

"I won't tell anyone that you cried," he said. "This meeting can be a secret between us."

"I don't care if people know I'm having a hard time," I responded. "I think this is a normal reaction."

"Still, I won't tell anyone," he said, smiling. "Come on, let's hug it out."

I don't know why I agreed to this, except that I needed human comfort in that moment and he seemed to be offering it.

Tony drew me in, with his arms around me. Then he patted my bottom with the palm of his hand. I pulled away, but he pulled me toward himself again, sliding his hands up and down my body, along my breasts, along the curves of my ribs, from my armpits down to my hips.

I stepped back, appalled, quickly said goodbye, grabbed my jacket, turned around and walked out.

I was in shock as I walked back along the path to the Institute of Neuroscience. When I pushed open the door to my office, tears began running down my face. Barry was chatting in the doorway of the office next door. He saw me arriving and rushed over, shutting the door behind us.

"What happened?" he asked.

"Turns out, they could take more from me." I told him what had happened. Barry listened to me with jaw-dropping concern.

"What are you going to do?" he asked when I finished the story.

"I think I'm going to go home for a little while."

"I think that's a good idea," he agreed.

My jacket was still on, to brave Newcastle's summer weather. I picked up my bag and left the building. For some reason, I walked east instead of west and I ended up at the house I had shared with Andy until eleven months ago. I unlocked the door and let myself inside.

There were several greeting cards on the fireplace mantle. Andy's birthday had been two weeks ago. I looked at them – one was from his mother, one was from his old school friend Joel, and one was from Evelyne. I read them each, one by one. Evelyne's card was a revelation.

"Congratulations on your birthday and your professorship, BIG A!" the card read. So, Andy had gotten his tenure within his timeframe after all – on the back of the project we had created together. But that was not everything. Evelyne had continued writing. "I hope you will be nicer to me now. And not incidentally (!), I hope you will find a big new love in this new year of yours."

I set down the card. Stunned, I trudged upstairs and lay on the bed. Then I sat up again and walked downstairs, to look at the garden. I was disappointed to find that Andy had given no effort to its care in the months since I'd been gone. The roses, which had always looked so beautiful, were in dire need of pruning. The leaves were black with fungal infection, seed pods were left to harden, and cobwebs hung between the branches. It was as if he didn't care about beauty at all.

My cell phone rang. It was the Newcastle University occupational therapist Deborah. She explained that one of my colleagues had reported an incident and she had to ask if I was alright.

I told her in detail what had happened: the CANDO management team was taking my lab and my projects without my consent and now one of them had decided to touch my body without my consent as well. She asked if I was thinking about suicide and I said no.

I had an appointment set up with my doctor during lunchtime that day, so I walked over there. He too asked if I was thinking about suicide.

When two independent parties ask this question in the same day, it's best to consider it carefully.

I thought about my lab mice and the customized scoresheet we used to assess their health. That could be useful as a guide. These days, when I looked in the mirror, I saw that my face was stretched with exhaustion, my eyes were sunken, and my hair had lost its luster. That gave three points. A point for lethargy and a point for my recent 5% loss in body weight made five. Euthanasia criterion was 11, but only with the reasonable conjecture that terminal illness was involved. A mouse could easily reach five after getting attacked by other mice, then fully recover, as long as he was separated from his aggressors. That was applicable to my situation here. I told the doc I would be okay.

Later that evening, I called up my parents.

"It looks like my life is falling apart in the UK," I told them. "I'll be returning to the states."

"Well, it'll be wonderful to have you back," my mother said.

"Uh, Mom, you know how you said you'd be there for me, in any way I need?"

"Yes, of course, dear. Anything at all. You just ask."

"Well, could you buy me a car?"

"No, we'll give you money."

My parents had never given me money before, in my entire adult life, and I did not want any now. That could become a habit, one I did not wish to have. I just wanted a single discrete object – a gift and a symbol that they were there for me, the way lavender Ford Taurus had allowed me to be there every weekend for them.

"I'd prefer you just buy me a car. Just the same kind as before, a simple used but reliable four-door sedan. I know it might cost a few thousand dollars, and also I might not be able to pay you back for it this time."

"Yes, of course. That's fine."

"Really? That's great. This is amazing, actually. Thank you so much."

"Of course, dear. We're here for you."

"This is just fantastic. So it'll be there for me when I get home?"

"Yes, it will. We'll get something reliable, like the Ford Taurus. And it'll be here for you when you get home."

"Oh my gosh. Thank you so much."

I hung up the phone, feeling so much better. My parents would be there for me. They would help me land on my feet. I almost cried with joy.

Chapter 23
Nothing Left

"So everything I built will just be taken away from me."

"It's not yours, really. It belongs to the university," Anna explained, in her role as deputy director of the institute.

"Right, but I worked hard all these years in good faith, thinking I would continue to have a job here."

"Your visa is being curtailed because your marriage to a British National is no longer subsisting." I knew this – I was the one who had contacted the UK Immigration Service and I was the one who had initiated discussions with the university visa coordinator months ago.

"Right, but I could be sponsored for a work visa."

"The university does not have to do that for you."

"It was no problem when the university did it for me twice previously."

"That was before. The CANDO project does not have to sponsor you for this work."

"What the hell is going on? I consistently contributed more than anyone to CANDO, alongside my brain tumor work and several other productive collaborations. I reached every project milestone, stayed in line with every regulation, tried to be a supportive mentor and colleague at all times, applied for grants regularly, published well, was invited to speak about my work at conferences, won awards for my research – does all that mean nothing?"

"The university will not be sponsoring you for a visa."

"It doesn't matter that my name is written into the grant with a defined role? That I have an employment contract through 2021?"

"No, to stay on the safe side from a legal standpoint, the university must advertise the position openly. You would have to beat out all other candidates in order to be sponsored for a visa."

"That's fine, advertise the position. Few people in academia have ever done what my team has already accomplished. If anything, I'm far more perfectly suited for this job than when I first started. No one else applying for this post will have led a group to make a preclinical gene therapy, test it out, devise a strategic partnership for subcontracting the clinical-grade product, set out the specifications for manufacture and validation, and start the process of applying for regulatory approval. Bring it on! I'll apply for the post and I bet you I'll earn the position fair and square."

Anna sighed. "We would have to advertise the job for six weeks."

"Yeah, let's go! This should have been started months ago."

"Well, it has not been started yet and you would have to go back to your home country. It could take months to sort out – and Beth, it's not certain you would get the position."

I heard what she was saying. I was not going to keep my job, even if I jumped through every hoop. My ex-husband was leading the project and he wanted to punish me for leaving him. Stupidly, I had thrown all my efforts into this project and had continuously demonstrated progress, thinking it would help my career. Now the remainder of the ten million pounds sterling had come through, and everyone was going to leave me in the ditch, instead of letting me keep pushing the project forward.

And then it hit me. They didn't want to continue pushing the project forward. They had no intention of advertising this position and ensuring the gene therapy platform would progress toward the assortment of potential new treatments for epilepsy that I had proposed. Those guys would take the money for themselves, while everything I worked for would stall. I put my head in my hands.

"Are you going to be okay?"

"I don't know. I think I'll have the energy to start over, but I've got to find a place to land. I want to keep doing science. But I've been applying for jobs for a couple months now, with no hits."

"You'll find something," she said lightly. But it didn't seem possible. I was overqualified for some positions and underqualified for the rest, in both academia and industry. Nothing was a good fit, except the only obvious path from here, a tenure-track faculty post at an American university, and those were hard to come by.

I was going to end up working as a post-doc again, or in a grocery store or a bridal shop. At any rate, doing what someone else told me to do. I started to count how many months I could survive on the twenty-five grand my grandfather had left me. I decided the answer was about ten months, realistically, with rent and food and student loan repayments and public transport costs and water and electricity and gas and internet.

"If I run out of money, I guess I'll just jump off a bridge," I murmured, lost in thought.

"Don't you dare say that!" Anna snapped at me, through clenched teeth, before remembering her medical training and her aristocratic poise. She spoke more calmly. "No, don't do that."

I was taken aback, but then I realized she must have thought I was emotionally blackmailing her or something. I shook my head. "I'm sorry, I just got caught up in my worries. I shouldn't have thrown that on you."

She stared at me coldly.

My mind wandered, remembering long ago when my main luxury in life was library books, read in the breakroom of the pharmacy or in the tiny office of the bridal shop or underneath a blanket during my few waking hours at home, in the converted front parlor of an old house in central Illinois that rented at $100 a month, where I lived when I first moved on my own as a teenager, working two jobs to put myself through college.

"Have you ever read Somerset Maugham's 'Of Human Bondage'?" I asked.

Anna shook her head. "It's about people with money problems," I explained, "And how it all just gets worse and worse until they just give up. I guess it's a common thing to think, when panic sets in. But I'll be alright. I'll just keep going, as long as I can. I've lived on very little money before, I can live like that now."

Anna had a blank look on her face, like she did not understand what I was talking about or whether it was even a justifiable concern. I wondered how to bridge this gap spreading like a chasm between us. Obviously a viscountess would never understand being worried about having enough money to get by. Anna's husband had been at the helm when Northumbrian Bank crashed and burned at the beginning of the last recession. The government had bailed out the corporation on the taxpayer dime. They didn't lose anything personally from that mess – not their own wealth, not their sprawling estate in the country, not his seat in the House of Lords.

"When you're a star they let you do it," a certain person once said.

Anna set her notebook aside and spoke. "There is one thing we could do."

"What's that?" I asked.

"Well, if you want to resign, you could perhaps be given an *ex gracia* payment."

"A payoff?" I asked. "But I'm not resigning, I'm being pushed out."

"But you could resign instead. We could have a meeting to explore this possibility, if you like."

"I guess we could discuss that option."

She agreed to set up the meeting. Everything seemed to go well, and they offered me 10,000 pounds sterling – about 13,000 dollars at the current conversion rates. I went out to celebrate with two friends, a bit pre-emptively it turned out.

A few days later the contract appeared in my inbox. There were several gag clauses sprinkled throughout. The terms stated that I could not make any disparaging comments about Newcastle University or any employee there. The money would be rescinded and I could be sued further if I spoke at all about my expertise, my data, or what they had done to me.

I refused to sign the settlement. I accepted my dismissal instead. I would rather be poor and free to speak about my life and my research than have that dirty money. After all, who else would take the etomoxir work forward?

"Now you know what it feels like to be a person with dark skin."

I looked at Renata – her warm smile, her perfectly coiffed hair, her easy grace – and underneath, her passionate focus on cancer research and marathon training. All this strength and brilliance that she presented to the world was hiding a truth which simmered closer to the surface than she normally let on. Centuries old but still very much alive, shared by a billion other souls in Africa and throughout the African diaspora – a certain knowledge was pumping through her heart, telling her that injustice was a fact of life, that anything and everything could be taken from you and it didn't matter where you wanted to live or what you wanted to do with your life. That knowledge reminded her that your direction in life would instead be chosen for you – by others, by circumstance.

My student was teaching me. I nodded, becoming aware of something I had not realized the true scope of before. The perils of life when other people decide the rule of law does not apply to you. As a white American, I had never, ever felt what that was like.

Renata's family had moved from Ghana to the United Kingdom during the 1990s for a different life. She excelled in school at every level, immersing herself in a master's degree program in cell biology and beating out 24 other students to win this prestigious PhD studentship. She was enormously clever and highly-skilled, and she deserved that shot at success. And now, her life too was being decided by others and by circumstance. I understood she was concerned about her own future. I put aside my own worries for the moment.

"You're not going to slip through the cracks, you know," I assured her. "Your PhD studentship was awarded by the university. It's not tied to me. You will continue to be a graduate student here and you can continue to do cancer research. Ethan will agree to take over as your primary supervisor. Your project will take a slightly different turn, but you will get that PhD as long as you keep working on it."

"But I want to pursue this project," she said. After all, she had begun to make it her own.

"Realistically, that's not an option anymore," I replied. It was incredibly unfair for us to be split up, when we had created a team to tackle this problem. But I could not give away everything I had left. I had to take care of myself. "I'm taking the resources that I brought to Newcastle with me. They don't belong here anymore – they will stay with me."

She looked bereft. But I knew she'd be alright.

"Renata, your first year of training opened a lot of options for you, especially related to your work with Ethan on tumor imaging and metabolite analysis. You've already launched into that, and there's plenty left to do. The best strategy for you is to move forward with the strongest supervisor and the strongest project you can find. There is no doubt in my mind – Ethan is that person and his proposed metabolite analysis is that project. The best part is, you'll still be looking at fatty acids in brain tumors."

I realized, the least I could do now was ensure Renata would stay on track, not fall by the wayside too.

"OK," she sighed. "Let's talk to Ethan."

A few days later, we held a meeting. I had chatted with Ethan first, to discuss the situation in detail. He looked disappointed but unsurprised.

"People are vicious around here," he said.

"I've started to notice that," I replied.

"This is too bad. I was looking forward to building our collaboration."

"I know, me too. There were a lot of possibilities. But what do we do about Renata?"

"Well, she collected enough data on the metabolite content of these tumors in her first year to keep her busy doing analysis in her second year," he answered. That had been my assessment as well.

"Then what? How does it move forward?"

"Well, there's some historical data on metabolites in human brain tumors. This group in Bristol has been trying to get me to analyze this huge dataset for ages now. She'd be well-trained to tackle that in her third year. And by then we might be set up to do human MR imaging and spectroscopy too."

"That's fantastic," I said. "This project could really go somewhere."

"Yeah, like I said, I had really hoped to build our collaboration. I'm doing mostly brain stuff now."

Ethan suggested another meeting, with the new head of Cancer Drug Discovery. The former director, Professor Harold Norwich, had retired shortly after refusing to support my research. Harold's replacement, Professor Simon Hancock, was more interested in the project and agreed to meet with us a few days later. He had already met with Renata, and showed they were good buddies by sociably asking about her marathon training. Then he turned to me, saying he was sorry to hear about my situation.

Then he explained, smiling, that he had an idea to rescue the project. He suggested that he could take over my resources – my precious cell cultures and the animal model I had created in Seattle, my ideas, my corporate partnership – everything I had brought to Newcastle and built there. That way, he could continue working on the etomoxir project after I was gone.

I pointed out that no one at the university, including him, had experience working on adult brain tumors, syngeneic rodent models of cancer, primary neural stem cell cultures, that particular drug or the biochemical pathway it targeted. And it was not okay for them to swoop in, after my ten years of work, taking over the project right when it was beginning to soar.

He started to object.

"No," I responded through clenched teeth. "You cannot take everything I created and keep it for yourself. You are not stripping me of my resources and taking them as your own."

Simon tilted his head and looked at me silently, with interest.

I cracked my knuckles. "This isn't the fucking British Museum."

"Whoa." Simon leaned back in his chair. "Hey, it was just a suggestion, alright? Take it easy. We'll come up with an alternate project, OK?"

"Yeah, I thought we had already agreed on one," I said in an even voice.

"Yeah, yeah, alright," Simon said, waving his hands. "I'm just here to be supportive."

Everything was being taken away from me. I had worked so hard, for so many years, and it didn't matter. I was going to lose everything I had built.

My visa would expire and no one would do anything about it. I would shortly be homeless, jobless, kicked out of the country I had tried to make my home. I would have to go back to America, while my CANDO colleagues took my equipment, lab space, funding, and staff posts for their own. I simply had to accept it: I had no control over my life whatsoever. I was being left to the winds and there was nothing I could do.

I came home each night, exhausted, back to the house-share down the street from Clara's house, where I now lived. Each night I microwaved a meal in the kitchen and took it upstairs to my little bedroom, where I could eat while watching YouTube videos at the desk, before going to bed early. The only upside to my life at this point was that I got massive amounts of sleep.

One night that summer, I woke up in the darkness and sat up. My eyes adjusted and my vision cleared. I was not alone in the room.

Sometimes, in times of stress, people hallucinate. It's called an acute psychotic episode. And I was having one. An enormous figure stood in the room, next to the window. There was plenty of light from outside, as if the moon and all the stars were shining.

For some reason, the bathroom sink was in the corner of the bedroom, on the far side of the window; it normally sat in the same corner, but in the washroom, which was behind me. It was like the sink was pasted into the wrong room. The rest of the wall appeared continuous, everything in its customary place. Except that towering figure, in long white robes.

"Believe!" it bellowed.

Oh Christ, I was having a combined auditory and visual hallucination. I didn't feel scared, just baffled. I looked the figure up and down. Then I noticed one of its feet, a cloven hoof, like that of a large goat, protruding underneath the robes. That didn't seem right. The good guys were almost certainly not supposed to have feet like that. I looked up again at the face but it was blank, eyes like nothing had ever existed at all.

"Believe!" it bellowed again.

I sat there, patiently observing the phenomenon. This hallucination was telling me to believe – but in what exactly? The illusion, whatever it was supposed to be, was clearly not to be trusted. Its physical presence was suspect and its demand for faith was vague and unconstructive. Furthermore, this was not the best time to drop my habitual skepticism, considering the stress I was under and the likelihood that my mind was simply playing tricks. I concluded this experience did not provide any reliable or useful information, and therefore should not lead to any alteration in my philosophical framework or subsequent behavior.

"Believe!" the figure bellowed a third time. Then it disappeared.

That was weird, I thought. I lay my head down on the pillow and fell asleep.

I went to Clara's house the following evening. We sat at her dining room table again.

"Are you okay?" she asked.

"Not really," I replied honestly.

"Think of everything you still have," she told me.

"I have nothing left." I lay my head down on my arms and cried.

"Nothing? Are you sure?" she asked gently.

"No marriage, no home, soon no lab and no staff and no job and no visa and no country to live in. Definitely no trust in anyone anymore. Oh, and possibly my sanity is going too."

"Are you sure you have nothing left?" Clara pressed.

"I guess I have you, you're still here." I lay my head on its side and looked at her.

"That's right, see?" She reached out and held my hand.

"And I guess I have faith that everything will turn out okay."

I suddenly sat up straight in my chair. Clara stared at me, surprised.

"Wait, what did you just say?" she asked.

I began to laugh through my tears, and she began to laugh too. After losing everything, I had found the only object remaining at the bottom of the barrel.

There it was, undeniably. Faith. It was tiny, but it was all I had left.

Chapter 24
A Fresh Start, Maybe

A few days later, with my divorce petition issued and permission to remain resident in the United Kingdom revoked, I flew back to the United States. I wanted to see my parents and hug them, eat familiar food and sleep in the familiar house.

My dad picked me up at O'Hare and drove me back to Deerfield.

I wanted to sleep for days and days, but there was no peace. My father had converted my old bedroom to his office, so whenever I napped there, he woke me up by rustling papers and using the computer. Whenever I crashed on the couch in the basement, my mother suddenly needed to use her exercise bike there. If I fell asleep in the den, within moments, one of my parents would come in to read or watch tv.

With rest not being an option, I decided to work on job applications and wrap up business back in Britain. Exhausted, I realized that some time had gone by and I hadn't checked my email in days.

But the house did not appear to have a wireless signal for laptop use. All of the computers in the house seemed to be ancient lumbering macintoshes connected by ethernet. My mother claimed to have a wireless router though.

"I had a guy set it all up," she said. "If it doesn't work, you should fix it."

"I'm not going to mess with your stuff," I said, exhausted. "I'm just gonna go find a public network."

It was August in Chicagoland and the one-mile walk to the public library rendered me exceedingly sweaty. In my dazed and fatigued state, I had not even bothered to put on antiperspirant.

The cold cycled air of the Deerfield Public Library felt refreshing on my skin. I wandered around, searching for a comfortable desk and chair. I spotted an empty one across the way from an attractive guy.

Forgetting about my complete lack of makeup or deodorant, I sat down and pulled out my laptop. Self-awareness kicked into gear a minute later, and I realized there was no chance this man would speak to me in my current state. Well, at least I would get some work done.

"Beth?"

I looked up. Not only was this guy speaking to me, he knew my name. I stared at him for a long time, blankly.

"Freddy!" he yelled excitedly. And then it dawned on me. My high school best friend's high school boyfriend.

He was much better-looking than he had been in high school, when he had been a scrawny teenager on the football team. He had filled out and his face had a masculine stubble. He was dressed casually but well, in a shirt and khakis. His skin was tan, Italian ancestry dominating his appearance. Across from me now, he gave a mischievous grin. I wondered if he possibly remembered standing in the high school cafeteria that afternoon, with his arms around my waist, telling me he was in love with me. That moment came flooding back into my mind. How had I resisted this guy before? I must have been really mad at him.

"Fredrico Castiglione," I said slowly. "Oh my god. What have you been doing all these years?"

"Uh, I'm a neuroscientist," he said. "I work at Abbott Labs. Just here doing some writing today."

"That's crazy!" I exclaimed, much too loudly for the library. "I'm a neuroscientist too!"

"What?" he laughed. "No way."

We quickly caught each other up on where we had done our degrees, the places we had lived and worked over the years, the research we had done, whom we had dated. Why he had stayed in Chicagoland (to be near family and friends) and what had brought me back to Deerfield (the recent divorce and a readiness to start fresh).

After an hour of chatting, we went back to our work, although we kept looking up at each other and smiling. I didn't really have much email.

"Abbott Labs, huh?" I ventured. "Do you like working there?"

"Yeah, I do," he said.

"Maybe I should apply."

"You should, to make more opportunities for yourself. I'll forward your CV along if you want. But you shouldn't move to industry if it means stepping back into entry-level lab work. I bet you'll get a faculty post somewhere. With what you've been doing, I think you're exactly the kind of person who should be directing a research program. Some university will see that."

"Thanks," I smiled. "Hey, do you want to get out of here and grab a drink or something?"

"Yeah, definitely," Freddy said, closing his laptop and grinning at me.

We walked outside, to his car. He no longer had the

black Mustang that he had in high school. He clicked to open the doors of a green 2007 four-door Buick. I loved that he had grown so sensible over the intervening years.

I climbed into the passenger seat and remembered again that I had not exactly dressed for a date when setting out that afternoon.

"If I had known I would be going out, I would have put on some makeup," I said lightly.

Freddy paused, his hands on the steering wheel, the car not yet in gear. He breathed in and spoke carefully. "You're just as beautiful as you always were," he said, turning to look at me.

My heart actually fluttered. Was it going to be this easy? Could I just fall in love again, like that? Maybe live in Chicagoland, get a job here, raise kids and everything?

The evening flew by. We talked for hours. Then he drove me home, and we kissed each other in the front seat of his car, in my parents' driveway, like we were still in high school.

Freddy asked me out again. In the meantime, we emailed each other, talking about my life abroad and his life in the suburbs where we grew up.

"You're a fire in the hearth and I'm a gust of wind blown in when the door is flung open," I said. "Does that make you nervous, or does it just make your tinders crackle?"

"I think you know," he said. "Us being together will be like a house on fire."

We met for pizza in Highland Park. The hours passed like they were nothing. The only awkwardness was when Freddy pointed out a man across the restaurant, with whom he had gotten into a fight the previous year.

"Like an actual, physical altercation?" I asked.

"Yeah," he said. "Only problem was, when I went to punch him, he ducked, and I hit his friend instead. His friend had nothing to do with it."

I wondered if I was about to be collateral damage in a return mistake.

"No, no, no," he said. "That's all in the past." Still, I felt slightly insecure until the man left, without noticing us.

After dinner we walked along the lake, enjoying the balmy evening. We chatted easily, breathing the night air. Suddenly, he turned and kissed me again, deeply.

"Let's go back to your place," I said, in a husky voice.

We arrived at his apartment and I looked around. The style was distinctly bachelor-esque, with a brown leather sofa and a big flat screen tv.

I swung around to watch him setting his keys down on the dining table, next to a red mug. I walked over, incredulous.

It was what I had thought it was. #MAGA, it read in large white letters.

I picked up the mug and laughed. "Is this a joke?" I asked.

Of course it was. We were scientists, we were on the same page with reality.

"No," he said.

"Oh crap," I said, putting it down. "I guess I just assumed we had a lot more in common than we did. What made you do it? What made you vote that way?"

"I don't want to pay as much in taxes," he said. "And I think there should be fewer regulations on industry, instead of all this environmentalism."

"Uh huh," I said. "Do you think you will actually pay less tax with Donald Trump as president?"

"Yeah," he said.

"And do you think you personally have more to gain when industries are given more freedom to pollute?"

"Well, yeah, we all have a lot to gain when industry is less restricted. It helps the economy grow."

"Um," I said. "I think the tax plan underway may not end up working in the interest of your income bracket, and your risk-benefit analysis for industrial pollution may be incorrectly weighing the impact of toxins and carcinogens in the air and water which affect all of us."

"Ooh, are we talking science again now?" he asked, as a way to lighten the discussion. I looked at him and wondered what to do. There had been such a build-up that I was reluctant to walk away.

I paused, feeling our dynamic. Yep, the chemistry was still there, the attraction between us not much lessened. He was smiling at me.

I sighed. "Do you understand that what you voted for, what it means for society, reveals a whole different way of viewing the world from me?"

"Yeah, of course."

"And do you think that's okay?"

He shrugged.

I just looked at him.

He smiled. "Could we put aside our differences?"

I smiled too, despite myself. The guy had such an easy charm. "Guess we could try." We wrapped our arms around each other and forgot about anything but our bodies pressed together.

Freddy emailed me the next day. "I just had to write to thank you for our date. Who knows what the future holds, but last night was so special, and I'm grateful that we got to share that time together."

I wrote back to him. "Thanks for your sweet words. I really enjoyed the time we spent together too. I'm glad we had the opportunity to get to know each other better after all these years."

I hesitated, wondering how to word my feelings diplomatically. "You surprised me in a lot of ways," I added, without being specific. "We may go our different ways, but I'll certainly remember you fondly."

I thought that was a good way to end it, but a few days later he wrote back, asking if I might want to meet up again.

I thought of his baffling vote, his worrying propensity to get in a fight, his attempted cheating episode on his high school girlfriend, my friend, so many years ago. I thought of all that, and I wondered if I could trust him with my heart.

"You are such a warm and engaging and attractive and intelligent guy," I wrote. "But I'm not sure I trust your instincts. Sometimes you say or do things impulsively, without thinking through how your words or actions or vote might damage other people."

I needed to know how he would respond. I needed to know if he understood that his decisions sometimes hurt other people and whether he was able to accept that fact. I wondered if he was like my husband, or if he was a different man – if he could take responsibility, if he would listen to my words of wisdom and experience, if he might be open to growing his heart and his mind with another person.

"Bitch," he wrote back. And like that, it was over.

Chapter 25
Tensions in Europe

My first attempt at post-divorce dating a complete disaster, I flew back to the UK. I'd decided to visit some friends then travel around Europe while waiting for job opportunities to manifest in the states.

I had hit rock bottom, surely. Things could only get better from here. And not every attractive guy I would meet would end up being a Trump supporter.

Upon arriving at Heathrow, I was placed in the detention pen, holding a white sheet of paper stating there was a warrant outstanding for my arrest.

My mouth hung open as the officer latched the gate. I had never been arrested before. Things were not getting better. It seemed they were still getting worse.

I sat down in a hard plastic chair, between a Brazilian woman and a Nigerian man. The two of them stared at me openly until finally, the woman spoke.

"What are you doing in here?" she asked, blinking. "You're white."

"Uh, it's just a misunderstanding," I explained, wishing the guard had not taken away my American passport.

They continued to stare at me. I continued to speak;

babbling seemed the most natural response in this situation. "My visa was curtailed because of my divorce, but I should be allowed to come back to this country for a short time as a visitor. I guess they just assumed that I overstayed my visa, but then why would I be showing up at Heathrow? It's definitely just a misunderstanding."

The Brazilian woman sighed and stretched her long legs. "Mine's just a misunderstanding too."

"Mine's a technicality more than a misunderstanding," the man chipped in. "It's always one or the other."

The officer approached, and we fell silent. He motioned to the man beside me and demanded that he produce some documents that had been emailed to him by the Home Office.

"There's no wifi signal here," the man said, motioning to his phone. "I can't put it on the screen."

The officer shook his head. "I'm not going wait for you forever."

The man began to tremble slightly, and the officer walked away.

"I think I can set up a wifi hotspot from my phone," I said, poking at the settings. The woman with the long legs leaned over me, advising. After a few moments, the man found his documents and called the guard over. The guard took one look at the phone then told the man to call the person he would be staying with. They needed to have a little chat.

As the man frantically dialed friends and relatives, the woman turned to me and shared her story. She had come over here for a job. She hoped her misunderstanding would be sorted out and she would not be sent back to her home country after having set up this work with her new employer. She was quite looking forward to the gig.

I wondered how she seemed able to take it all in stride.

Most people I knew would be jumping up and down demanding immediate resolution. I mentioned this to her. She sighed.

"Just remember," she told me, "When you get out of here and your life returns to normal, just remember that some people will never have the luxury of your normal life, where you aren't put in detention for a misunderstanding. Remember what it feels like to dip your toe into these waters."

"I'll remember," I told her.

"Because now you know what it's like to be a brown person." These were nearly the same words Renata had said to me earlier in the year, when everything I built, everything I cared about, was being taken away from me. The words cut me like a knife all over again, an agonizing combination of my own pain and my unintentional complicity in others'.

The guard came over holding my precious navy-blue passport. I stood up as he unlatched the pen. Before exiting, I turned around.

"I'll remember," I promised her again.

Grateful for my freedom, I got on the bus and headed to Oxford, then Cambridge, then Peckham in South London, visiting the diaspora of friends – scientists and artists – I had met in Newcastle.

Two friends, a Lithuanian couple, had decided to move back to eastern Europe, as Vilnius now felt like a more safe and stable place to raise their family. Two other friends, a Polish couple, were staying, even purchasing a house together to solidify their lives in the UK. Everyone was in motion, and unsure of the direction they were taking.

Each place I went, I found a common sense of worry. In each place, we took long walks with the dogs, cooked meals together, drank wine and talked late into the night. We shared our concerns about what was happening in the UK and in our home countries.

I took the train north and caught an EasyJet flight from Newcastle, having booked the round-trip nearly a year earlier, when I couldn't possibly have known my life would completely fall apart. But the timing was perfect – I was happy to spend two weeks in Crete right then, writing job applications on the balcony of a stucco cottage in the dry hills west of Heraklion. Some afternoons I lay on the beach under a melon-colored umbrella and every evening I watched the yellow moon rise over the quiet valley. I rented a car for a few days and whipped around the mountain roads with the windows rolled down and the radio blaring euro pop music. I had applied for fifteen faculty positions across the United States and now I could let my mind sit still for a little while.

I returned to England. After the drama of recent months, I had grown nervous to revisit Newcastle, holding out a glassy-eyed certainty that while I was in town my department head would burn down the institute for the insurance money and frame me for it, just to cause me extra trouble. On my last visit, I had refused to stay in the city for any length of time for this insane reason. After my holiday I felt more relaxed, less paranoid. It would be nice to have one last stopover in the place I called home for nearly seven years.

When I arrived, I was held up at immigration again. Newcastle Airport didn't have a detention pen, they just put me in a chair off to the side while they checked the rest of the passengers in the queue.

I sat and thought of all the times I had been welcomed home at this airport – from holidays, from scientific conferences, from visits to see friends and family. But that was before Brexit. Now, Her Majesty's Customs and Immigration Service was called The Border Force.

"Things have changed," I observed as the border officer finally stamped me into the country as a visitor.

"Things do," the man replied, not looking up.

Once back inside the country, I got to work. I needed to wrap up some projects from the past couple of years that were nearly ready for publication. I met with Georgiana, the post-doctoral researcher who had worked in my lab before everything was seized by my colleagues.

We were both still in shock that no effort had been made to sponsor me for a work visa. But of course, certain individuals had a lot to gain personally if I had to leave the country: specifically, over half a million pounds sterling in lab equipment, funding, and staff posts that had been awarded to support my research program. If I could not live and work in the country, all of that was up for grabs. In this post-modern world, contracts didn't matter anymore. Only power did.

Georgiana was relieved that she herself had been able to keep her job and that we would still be getting our papers out. But she glumly reported that in recent weeks she had been placed under a new supervisor who did not understand her skillset, our department head had already made a move to commandeer some of our equipment, another senior professor within the department had taken over our budget and other researchers were making themselves at home in our lab space. Sophie had quit months ago, making it easier for the vultures to reassign that technician post under another professor. I nodded, too numb to feel anger. Georgiana confessed that she had gotten pregnant, to do something more valuable with her life. That cheered me up greatly and I hugged her congratulations. Her previous project had given me no end of grief, but now she going to create a new human being and that made me want to burst with joy.

After a few hectic days spent on tables and figures, I flew out of Newcastle again. I was done with that place. I had moved to Britain years ago because I wanted to live in Europe. Now that Britain would no longer be part of Europe and I was already no longer part of Britain, I decided to spend some damn time in Europe.

Days later I stood in the arched remains of Devin Castle, on a cliff above the confluence of the Danube and Morava rivers, south of the point where Czechia, Austria and Slovakia meet. The September sun shone on my shoulders and the bleached-white stones. In the following weeks, elections in Austria and the Czech Republic would yield two new far-right anti-immigrant governments in Europe, added to the nationalist fervor which had already overtaken Poland and Hungary and had threatened to take over France and the Netherlands earlier this year.

Here in Slovakia, but further east, NATO was on watch as Russia conducted their once-every-four-years ZAPAD exercise on their western front. During the previous exercise, in 2013, they had left troops stationed outside their borders after the military games were complete; these were used the following year as a front-line force during the invasion of Ukraine. Eastern Europe looked in worry at these exercises now, as battleships filled the Baltic Sea, fighter jets bolted across northern airspace, and hundreds of tanks sat ready in Kaliningrad, mirrored by hundreds of tanks behind the Russian border on the other side of the Baltic states. Accounts differed regarding the number of troops stationed in Belarus during the exercise; Russia claimed them to be below the international limit of 13,000 while NATO estimated closer to 80,000. Accounts also differed as to whether these troops were removed after the war games were complete. At the castle, I chatted with some US army boys who were on leave and travelling around Eastern Europe. They showed no nervousness, unlike my friends in Estonia, Latvia and Lithuania, whose families were not far away in Ohio but surrounded on all four sides by a large aggressive neighbor who had been a subjugating force within living memory and was currently occupying nations to the south.

The next evening, after a long walk encircling the city, I ate supper at a café in Bratislava's old town, not far from my hotel. I sat at a table outside, watching couples walk past in the warm evening air. As I finished my glass of wine and gathered my things, I spotted a man looking at the menu. He noticed me standing up.

"Is the food good here?" he asked, in a sociable way.

"Yeah, it was pretty good." The guy was quite attractive.

"Is that an American accent I hear?" he asked. His own voice had a slight Texas twang.

"Yep, it sure is."

"Nice to travel halfway around the world and hear a familiar sort of voice."

I smiled. "I wouldn't mind having another glass of wine, if you want company."

"Of course," he said. We went back to my table and sat down. The waitress came by, disappointed to find she still had customers. It was only 8, but the street was quieting down. We ordered drinks and he ordered food as well.

"Mark," he said, by way of introduction.

I shook his hand and introduced myself.

"Are you on holiday here?" he asked.

"Sort of," I replied. "I lived in the UK for a few years, but I'm getting divorced. So now I'm travelling around Europe for several months before moving back to the states." I mentally applauded myself for managing to harness my story into a few short sentences.

"Cool," he said. "I work three weeks on, one week off, so I travel a lot."

"Are you in the military?"

"Used to be. Served in Iraq. Now I repair industrial equipment. Involves a lot of trekking around, so I use my airline miles and hotel points during my week off each month."

That sounded like a neat way to live, even if it meant not really having a permanent home. I wondered how long a person could go on like that.

"What do you do?" he asked.

"Oh, I'm a scientist." He asked what kind of research I did, and I explained that I was trying to find a way to slow the growth of brain tumors.

"Not a climate scientist then."

I raised my eyebrow. "Why? You got something against climate scientists?"

"Nothing in particular, just don't trust 'em."

"Oh dear," I murmured. It was happening again.

"What?" he asked, grinning. "Do you just trust all other scientists, automatically?"

I sighed. "The job of a scientist is just to understand our world. We get paid regardless of what we find is true. So, generally, yeah."

He looked skeptical. I continued. "Meanwhile, it should probably be noted that climate change deniers have a lot to lose if their position is proven false. Industries want to continue processing fossil fuels unregulated by environmental protection laws. And they won't be able to do that if there is a public understanding of climate change."

"But there is a public understanding of climate change," Mark said. "We have our own eyes and ears, you know. And it's been hard to miss, the past few winters have been bitter cold on the east coast."

"Yeah, that's because the ice caps are melting. The Atlantic Ocean is getting a massive influx of freezing water every year – a chunk of thawing ice the size of Wyoming."

"I thought you said the planet was warming."

"Have you looked at a temperature map? The most northern and southern regions are much colder, while the land and sea near the equator has been heating up."

"So?"

"That means parts of the world, especially Europe and North America, will be cold as storms form over the North Atlantic. But once all the ice melts in a couple decades, there will be nothing left to reflect sunlight back into the atmosphere and nothing left to melt cold water into the oceans to counteract the warming. Then the planet will really start to heat up."

"Is that right."

"Yeah, it is."

"Well a lot of climate scientists disagree with you."

"Only those who are paid by oil companies to say so."

"No, I think there's broad disagreement about the issue."

"Nope. The stats say 97% of climate scientists believe in human-induced climate change."

"Oh really?" Mark had a challenging look. "If that's true,

then how come the people in charge do nothing about it? They must know what's real. They have access to all the information."

"Of course they know what's real. But think about who's in charge. Rex Tillerson, the Secretary of State? Of course he knows that climate change is real. It's his whole business plan." I explained how Exxon Mobil, under the direction of their former CEO Rex Tillerson, had made deals with the Russian state-owned oil company Rosneft to drill in the oil-rich north pole. These people are sitting on half a trillion dollars of oil reserves with no way to transport the stuff, I pointed out. Collapsing the Paris Climate Accord will buy time for the ice caps to melt, making access easier. In government, Rex Tillerson undoubtedly acted behind the scenes to trigger the US decision to withdraw from the agreement. Now, I asserted, the State Department under his leadership will probably find a way to nullify the sanctions that prevent the partnership moving forward.

He looked at me doubtfully. I stood my ground. "These are the people we should distrust – the people making money by lying about climate change, the people actively destroying our world to serve their pocketbook."

He shrugged.

"Don't you understand?" I argued. "We're still fighting the Cold War, on a warming planet. You are refusing to notice this massive risk to the security and economy of our country. And you would rather stand back and let it happen rather than admit you made a mistake and supported the wrong people. But the stakes are too high to ignore. We are literally handing over our territory, in the form of our coastal cities. The Russians don't have coastal cities to lose, but we do."

"If that stuff's true," he ventured, "Then what are we

supposed to do about it?"

I stared at him. "Use your vote. Elect people who don't have giant glaring conflicts of interest."

He rolled his eyes. I knew what was coming and I was right.

"As if Hillary Clinton didn't have conflicts of interest," he said.

"Look, I'm not going to defend her ties to Goldman Sachs, if that's what you're getting at. But if you care about that stuff so much, why did you vote for a person who put a bunch of Goldman Sachs executives into his cabinet?"

"But her foundation is a front for money laundering."

"And what do you think Donald Trump's real estate business is?"

He shrugged again.

"I'm not sure why you want to talk about Hillary Clinton's alleged financial misdeeds while ignoring Donald Trump's alleged financial misdeeds. That money he has 'pouring in from Russia'? You don't care? You don't want to ask what they're getting in return? It seems you would rather just focus on Clinton's private email server, which by the way was never hacked, so maybe it wasn't such a bad idea for our national security. Meanwhile you ignore the fact that your man Donald Trump has literally given away state secrets."

"I think he's doing what's best for the country."

My face was growing hot but my voice was steady. It was difficult to be around someone who would let the world burn rather than admit he had made a mistake.

"The guy could start a war with one of his ill-considered tweets," I asserted.

"That seems unlikely," Mark demurred.

"His terrible leadership has already ceded power to

other nations, especially China and Russia."

"What, are we gonna go to war with China and Russia?"

I shook my head. He seemed completely unaware of the military build-up in the South China Sea and right here in Eastern Europe, perfectly willing to ignore the daily nuclear brinkmanship with North Korea.

"We can just agree to disagree," he averred, giving me an easy smile. "Would you like another glass of wine? We can find something else to talk about."

After dinner, we exchanged contact information. I figured, hell, I'm moving back to the states and I'm clearly going to keep meeting republicans. Might as well try to understand them.

Mark told me about his ancestry search in villages near the Tatra Mountains, the reason he was visiting Slovakia on his week off. He sent along his leads and we tried to reverse-engineer the mistakes of nineteenth-century clerks at Ellis Island, to identify the surnames of his great-great-grandparents and their towns of origin. We agreed to meet up again in Budapest later in the week.

Mark got the date wrong, and texted me on Thursday evening instead of Friday. "Where are you?" he demanded, expecting to find me at the chain bridge crossing the river that divided Buda and Pest.

I rolled my eyes. Like most men, he didn't listen well. I had informed him I had a skype date arranged later that evening with friends back home on the west coast, but he hadn't paid attention. When I received his text, I was sitting at a bar after a day of exploring the city, not expecting a rendezvous.

I messaged him back to let him know where I was, in case he wanted to join me for a quick sandwich. He found me at the tavern, sat down and ordered a beer.

"How did the ancestry search go?" I asked.

"Total disaster," he replied. "No one speaks English out in the countryside and I didn't recognize any family names in the graveyards I visited."

"What a mystery," I said. "What do you do now?"

"I don't know," he said. "Look to the future instead?"

I smiled at him.

He asked me if I wanted kids. My smile faded.

"Not really," I answered. "I prefer my freedom." It was true – I wanted my father's life, with long productive days at the office followed by long relaxing train rides with the newspaper, not my mother's life, with two screaming kids in the backseat and a career stalled behind the more urgent concern that everyone was fed and clothed.

"You're gonna regret it later," Mark declared.

"No, I don't think I will. You don't think I can live with my own decisions?"

"OK, maybe that choice is right for you," he said doubtfully.

"Yeah, I think it is," I replied. "Anyway, to have kids, you really need a partner who is supportive and reliable and willing to share the workload. I've not had the privilege of having one of those."

"Unlucky," he said. "What are you going to do instead of building a family?"

I gestured widely. "Explore the world, I guess."

"You're gonna get stuck on travelling," he replied, grinning. "It's addictive."

"I think that's already happening." I had to admit, this

adventure was pretty fun.

"But women who travel a lot are undateable."

"What?!"

"Like, you can't stay in one place and you get restless."

"Why is that a problem?" I asked, with an edge in my voice.

He shrugged. "Just, people notice that you're willing to walk away."

"Yeah, that doesn't sound like a bad thing," I said evenly. "Problems seem to show up when people assume I'm just gonna keep sitting there and taking it."

"Oof," he said. "I've walked into it now. You know yourself, woman."

"Look, I've gotta go," I said, signaling for my bill.

"You won't let me get your drink?" he asked.

"No, I told you before. I won't let anyone buy me anything until we've established a non-favor-trading-based relationship. And then it's best to take turns treating each other."

"You're no fun. I wanna take you somewhere."

"You're not taking me anywhere. I'm going where I please."

He grinned at me and paid his bill as well. We walked to the river before parting ways, me toward a cheap aparthotel to the east and him toward the Hilton in the city center. We agreed to meet up again the following night for a proper date.

After I skyped with my friends, an email pinged into my inbox. It was from Mark.

"Looking forward to meeting you at the chain bridge tomorrow," he wrote. "I promise not to ask too many questions about your divorce again."

"No worries about the questioning," I replied. "And I'm

quite accustomed to men suggesting I don't know my own mind or what's best for me, saying that I'll regret not having kids or that I spend too much time alone. I'm happy doing what I want to do, regardless of other peoples' opinions, and I'm sure I'll find like-minded souls along the way."

"To start," he wrote back, "I wasn't judging you at all. I completely understand your perspective as I don't have kids and I'm not interested in having them either. I was talking about prodding you about your divorce and having to restart your life."

"Again there is no reason to keep insisting that was a problem," I returned. "You asked, I answered, it was fine. However I did find it patronizing when you said 'you'll regret it later' about having kids and when you said that women who travel independently are 'undateable'. But you did not succeed in making me feel like shit. I'm happy with myself and my decisions and I don't really want to argue further. I'm just explaining what went wrong so you might be more respectful in the future."

"Hey," he wrote back the next day. "I think I'm gonna grab a boat ride this evening instead. Later."

I read his email in the afternoon, while standing among the ramparts of Buda Cathedral overlooking the Danube River. Later that evening, after an early dinner by myself on the west side of the city, I walked across the bridge, imagining a parallel universe where I was a more agreeable woman.

But the moon is beautiful whether you're alone or not. I realized I had done the right thing to stand up for myself, even and especially if it drove the other person away. I texted Mark. "I just watched the moonrise from the chain bridge, it was stunning. Too bad things didn't work out – it would have been a romantic evening. Anyway, take care of yourself and have a good trip back."

He texted back. "I'm looking at the moon now. I kind of wish it worked out also."

I didn't *really* wish it had worked out. It was blindingly apparent we weren't right for each other. "No, it's better everything fell apart," I replied. "There might be chemistry, but you drive me absolutely nuts and I suspect you feel much the same about me."

I thought that would end it, but Mark sent me a long email the following day. He still did not apologize for his rudeness in judging my life choices, but he admitted that he regretted working too much and not having kids, which I took to mean he was projecting his life disappointment on me.

Then he wrote some nice things about me and said he wished he had met me at the chain bridge. He still wanted to buy me dinner and lend me his jacket. I shook my head, reading this. He just did not understand that I wanted to spend time with a guy, not become indebted to him. He stubbornly pretended to be unaware of the well of anger that often arose when such a debt was not repaid.

I sighed. He wanted a certain dynamic and he was not backing down. I told him I was not willing to meet but was happy to keep in touch over email. He was flying back to the states, and he asked me to share what I had seen and heard and smelled so far during my travels. I liked the way he asked the question, and I allowed the sensory overload to wash over.

I recounted the sights for him, the modern art in Czechia, Slovakia, and Hungary. At the Moravian Gallery in Brno: abstract paintings, light and shadow around geometrical shapes. I told him about the cubes like skyscrapers, hard and smooth; other shapes curved like guitars or violins, their hollow centers aching for sound and their edges just curved enough to force another glance. Others more recognizably human, skin on hands that could almost be touched. At Galéria Nedbalka in Bratislava: the suggestiveness melted into visceral form, a biological familiarity warped to arrive at a metaphorical truth, that underlying or arising from all this flesh and blood is another reality, and we don't know which way around it is, whether it created us or we created it. I described figures in the fields, figures in the woods, blood-red guts exposed inside a figure, a yellow dress with no figure inside, a Madonna without a dress against an azure-blue sky, both beautiful and blasphemous. I told him how, at Mucsarnok in Budapest, the floor dropped out and what remained was unnerving, otherworldly – lost people with lost traditions; unimaginable and inaccessible landscapes; herds of ominous dark raincoats drifting silently, moving nearly imperceptibly, in an otherwise empty room; impossible shoes without owners; the bowels of buildings turned inside-out to show our own patterns of movement; and sex. Sex as mere suggestiveness, titillation, a naked body on a bed turning to face the room with a beckoning look. Sex as violence, Tarquin overpowering Lucretia, or instead, her subduing him. Sex under moonlight, timeless like the stars. Sex in the daylight, faces turned upward, smiling.

I told him about the sounds... At the jazz club: the screaming of the trumpet, fast fingers on the piano, the softness of the brush on the drums and the thumping rhythm of the bass. At the apartment: the sound of Dirty Three's Horse Stories coming from my laptop at dawn to cover the sounds of drilling elsewhere in the building. At the Terror Haus: head-achingly loud heavy metal in the offices and torture rooms of the Nazi and Soviet headquarters alongside dizzying wall-after-wall arrays of photos, victims and perpetrators, their innocence and guilt undifferentiated from each other by appearance or expression. In the labyrinth underneath Buda's castle and cathedral: the sounds of Verdi's 'Un Ballo in Maschera' disorientingly appearing then abruptly cutting out, leaving no sound and no light except for the candle-torch in the endless darkness underground. Walking back to the apartment after midnight: the crackling thrill of Budapest at night, the chatter of people still in the bars, the ticking of the streetlights, the quiet rustling of the wind; a busker in the warm underground of Bajcsy-Zsilinszky metro station playing House of the Rising Sun, his fingers creating heat from the strings.

Then I described the smells... the mildly sulphur scent of the thermal springs at Rudas Bath, overpowered by the scent of roses or lavender whenever another female body joined the pool; the Ottoman stonework lit by the reflecting water; the sterile symmetry of the baths broken only by the differing temperature and saline content. I explained the sick taste at noticing the word 'migrant' scrawled above a public trash can, with an arrow pointed inside. I told him about the odors of cities too, in central Europe, especially in the warm months. It's the combination of diesel and old stone buildings and the sweat of bodies and a warm soft humidity even when the skies are clear and blue. All the cities along the Danube, I said, from Bavaria to Romania, hold the same soil and water, so of course they smell similar. The taste of grapes only changes gradually over land too – drier and bolder further south, sweeter and richer in the north, where the sugars cannot fully ferment. But something remains the same, a shared root. That's why I wanted to travel through Europe, I explained, to understand all the similarities and differences, all the common roots and the profound divergences.

"Let's meet up," he emailed. "I'll come over on my week off next month."

"No," I replied, annoyed at how responsive he was to the physical imagery after ignoring my other point.

Still in Budapest, I walked to the Jewish Quarter, and found a café near the synagogue that served strong coffee and excellent pastries. After receiving my order across the counter, I realized no table was free. I noticed a young guy with a friendly demeanor and asked if I could sit with him.

"Ahmed", he said, shaking my hand and gesturing to the empty chair across from his own.

We went through the basics – what pastry we'd ordered (chocolate-ganache, chocolate-hazelnut), where we're from (America, Egypt) and why we're in Budapest (on holiday, of course – but with an undercurrent suggesting that neither of us could be at home right now).

"What do you do for a living?" he asked.

"I'm a scientist. I study brain tumors," I told him.

He set down his fork and swallowed. "My mother just passed away from a brain tumor," he stated.

"I'm so sorry," I said, setting my fork down too.

"I'm glad someone is working on it."

We looked at each other for a long moment, both of us unable to eat, then continued our conversation as we polished off our coffee. Eventually we stood up and stepped out into the sunshine together.

"Which way are you going?" I asked.

He pointed west. "This way. I have a few errands to do."

"I'm going that way too," I said.

"Mind if we walk together?"

"Of course."

"Do you want to meet up later tonight?" he asked as we started up the street.

"No," I said. "I just want to spend some time by myself."

"Do you want to exchange information?" he asked, knowing the answer.

"No," I said. "I just want to exist in the moment right now."

"OK," he said. "Since we're not going to see each other or talk to each other again, I'm going to tell you what I do." He stopped, and I turned to face him.

"I'm in the army."

I raised my eyebrow.

"We're your allies," he said.

I lowered my eyebrow.

"Are you stationed in like Syria, or Iraq, or Yemen, or the Sinai Peninsula, or where?" He frowned. "Never mind," I said. "I get it. You can't tell me."

He sighed. "The thing is, I'm on leave because I needed to be. When my mother died a couple weeks ago, I couldn't square how devastated I felt by that with how I wasn't supposed to feel anything when I killed someone." My heart froze, even though this was the most human thing I had ever heard anyone say.

He continued. "I just started to think, who are these guys? Are they really that different from me? Or do they just think they're fighting to protect their families and their culture too?"

I looked at him and thought how hard it must be for Muslims to fight against other Muslims in all these crazy wars dreamed up by the men in charge. But shouldn't everyone feel this way about opponents, understanding they have their own motivations for fighting too?

Ahmed was right, most people involved in these wars are not really in charge of their own destiny, every day they're just doing what they can to get by. And yeah, that means taking sides with whoever you think is most aligned with you. Do we, as Americans, take the appeal of sovereignty into account when we allow our government to invade other nations, bomb their cities, install new regimes, and let global corporations decide how their natural resources are allocated? And do we think about the cost to our moral standing, or to the rule of law that we depend on too?

I emailed Mark a couple days later. "Did you kill people when you were serving in Iraq?"

"What? No. I repaired vehicles," he replied. "Why are you asking?"

"No reason," I said.

"You think about things too much," he said.

As if that's a bad thing.

Chapter 26
Freedom, And Being Followed

The trees were changing color. As the bus wound through the Croatian countryside, I leaned my head against the window. Each little village set among the hills had an identical church, matching the autumn leaves – yellow, with a fiery-red roof and a dark green steeple. The picturesque villages repeated, again and again, until we reached Zagreb. It felt like ages since I had been to Croatia, holidays on the coast in what felt like a more innocent time. But it really had not been that long – only a year and a half since Andy and I were swimming in the sapphire-blue seas of the Adriatic and hiking the hills above the walled city of Dubrovnik. A few seasons go by, life changes indelibly.

I wanted more than anything to be back at home doing science, but that was not an option right now, so I had to enjoy my freedom. Funny, what I would have given a year and a half ago to have a few more days or weeks to explore the Balkans. Well here I was, and I had to admit I was happier than I had been in a long, long time.

The previous evening in Ljubljana, I had taken the last cable car to the fortress, set on a rocky cliff in the center of the city. The place was deserted, the bars of the former prison cells flickering with the unsettling illusion of prisoners and the sound of water leading to a hidden grotto in a corner turret. Outside, bats flitted round the treetops above the stone walls. A wooden hanging bridge led across a waterless moat, and further the footpath diverged into two trails – one east, one west. I headed west and suddenly there was no light at all, only forest. The woods grew darker and darker, the trees denser and denser, and the air between them turned white, a chalky smell overpowering the scent of pine. I normally have a strong sense of time, but the moment held indefinitely, suspended within the obscurity of fog. After a while I reached the bottom of the hill in another part of the city, in a quiet residential area. I continued walking – past cafés open late, couples chatting in various languages; past more residences, dim lights in the upper windows; past the slumbering zoological gardens, past dismal train lines, past a thumping rave in a warehouse near Tivoli. Then I circled back, feeling like I would never be tired, and packed my bag for another journey.

  Each time we reached a border, the bus would stop and everyone would de-board, stand in line to be stamped out of one country and then stand in another line to be stamped into the next country. Then everyone would pile back on the bus, the last few stragglers finishing their cigarettes and stamping them out. It felt like going back in time – before Schengen, before Union. But not everyplace is Schengen over here, and Union is something not everybody wants.

  In Zagreb I found myself at the Museum of Broken Relationships. It was therapeutic, and I tried to think of a solitary artefact of my own that would symbolize the dramatic buzz of endless possibility and tragic breakdown that characterized my marriage to Andy. I couldn't think of a single thing. I was living out of a suitcase and just did not have much physical stuff. What a challenge, I thought, to reduce a lifetime's worth of emotion into a single solitary object. I decided to think about this question more – choosing an item might aid my sense of closure.

In Belgrade I stayed near Kalemegdan Fortress. The surrounding gardens were sunny and parklike, but the older structures, especially those underground, felt unnervingly creepy. Tucked under the hill, the source of water in the Roman Well has never been traced – there is no spring and no physical connection to the Danube or Sava Rivers that meet nearby. For a long time, the space was used as a dungeon where prisoners were left to die, and the well, fed with flesh and blood over the centuries, spawned a new life form – a little crab that exists nowhere else in the world. Even the churches felt eerie – under the gold-painted icons of one chapel sat an altar made of weapons; chandeliers comprised entirely of artillery shells hung from the ceiling. I shuddered at the terrible potential of human nature. Later I met up with a friend for brunch and a ramble through the city.

"We were wrong," she explained sadly, recalling the war during her childhood. Serbian forces had sought to overtake the other Yugoslav states, and Western forces had undermined their struggle for dominance with bombings of her hometown, Belgrade. But my friend was westernized, having done her studies in England, and not everyone in her country felt the same way as she did. Judging by the words on the street and in the newspapers, it was clear that many of her compatriots remained staunchly nationalist, anti-NATO and anti-EU. "We took the offensive, but the world response that resulted now justifies our defensive stance," my friend explained. I nodded, understanding.

Some days later, I arrived in Sarajevo. It's a sprawling

city, nestled in the mountains of Bosnia and Herzegovina. While Slovenia and Croatia, sitting along the Adriatic Sea, retain their Venetian merchant identity and Roman Catholic faith, and Serbia, further east, celebrates its Slavic and Orthodox influences, another era held its traces here. The long tail of the Ottoman Empire extended through time into this valley – there were mosques on every street, muezzins calling out for prayer, bistros and teashops and craftsmen and vendors packed into the bustling souks, winding roads filled with people and bicycles and cars and cats, and huge cemeteries spread across the hills, dotted with identical white markers – Muslim graveyards filled with the lives that NATO could not save. These hills were covered in the same dazzling autumn colors, but here they were filled with landmines too. The core of the Balkans pumped rich blood, the knife still stuck deep in its heart.

I took a tour of the city and surrounding region with Earl, a guy about my age who kept a website about his hometown and showed people around too. He told me about being kidnapped during the war as a child, described the progress of the war chronologically, and drove around the places that played critical roles in the four-year siege.

I had grown to realize that everyone had a perspective in these parts, defined by their own identity and history. I asked Earl what side he was on.

"Funny story," he answered. "Of my four grandparents, one is Muslim, one is Jewish, one is Orthodox Christian, and one is Catholic. It all cancels out."

"So what are you?" I asked.

"I don't believe in any of that stuff," he replied.

I laughed. Here was a man who saw his complex country as it was, unadulterated by wishful thinking, personal bias, or ulterior motive. He knew this land and he knew its people, as well as he knew himself. Even more, he understood the weight of history, the depths of absurdity, and the breadth of possibility in his nation, and he loved it all. If the world were a better place, he would be the president of a more united Bosnia and Herzegovina.

We discussed the alliance between Serbian government officials and the leader of Republic Srbska, a breakaway region of Bosnia and Herzogovina, as well as Russian-backed efforts to sow discord in neighboring countries. It was the one-year anniversary of the attempted coup in Montenegro, but peace stubbornly continued to reign in the region. War was too recent here, in living memory, for people to fall back into it again easily. It was the rest of Europe that was worrisome, Earl pointed out. They didn't know what they were stumbling into, by turning against each other. Here in Bosnia, he said, we know it is best to stay neighborly despite any simmering resentments.

We got along and decided to keep hanging out that evening. Over dinner, we talked about our hopes and dreams and plans for the future. I said I thought I might rent a place near the beach in southern Spain so that I could write. In recent days I had hatched a plan to tell my stories. Earl encouraged me to put pen to paper.

After dinner, we walked across the city toward the central fountain, where we would go our separate ways. Earl turned to face me.

"Your husband was an idiot to let you go."

I looked at him, wondering what sort of fresh hell this man would bring to my life if I let him in. He took a step backwards, sensibly, rather than approach me further.

"You think so?" I asked, feeling skeptical.

"Yes, I do." Earl took a deep breath. "You'll have a

happier life without him though."

"Maybe," I said, looking at my toes.

In Montenegro I rented a car and drove across the mountains to the sea. I rolled down the windows and blasted euro pop music and let the car climb through the switchbacks. When I arrived at the seaside, I bought a bikini and flip-flops on end-of-season sale, and spent days lounging in the late-season heat on the beach. Then I took the inland route, amongst the hills, from Budva to Kotor Bay, the little Skoda building layers of dust from the road still under construction. Finally, descending into the cove at dusk from the high mountains, my jaw dropped. They say Montenegro is the land of fairy tales, and it's true - every surreal story you have ever heard, and many you have not yet heard, have a home in the hidden corners of this place.

Each night I sat on the balcony under the stars, looking out over the quiet bay and shaded mountains. In the mornings I drank coffee and watched fishermen casting their lines from the pier. In the afternoons I drove around, exploring the concealed towns and imposing hilltop fortresses around the inlet. One day I parked on the side of the two-lane road and found a tunnel leading to stone steps, which took me downhill past iron gates and bougainvillea until I hit the seafront. This was the tiny town of Perast, comprised of seventeen palaces, sixteen churches, a stunning belltower, and several waterfront cafés overlooking two picturesque islands a kilometer away in the middle of the glittering bay, each crowned with a fifteenth-century stone monastery. I sat basking in the sunshine at one of the cafés with a glass of white wine, chatting with two Belgian girls. Walking back to the car, I found that special item, the token symbol that would give my relationship closure.

Solitary exploration was nothing new. Before this trip, I had wandered the streets of London, Paris, Rome, Edinburgh, Berlin, Madrid, and a dozen other cities alone at night, without my heart so much as fluttering in fear. I had always felt safe in Europe, more so than in the states. I felt a sense of belonging, of security – and a comfortable anonymity. It was the people who knew you who could hurt you, and people who knew you best who could hurt you the most.

Mark emailed me again, asking if he could meet me on his week off next month. He would not give up on me now. He wanted to try again, he wanted to take me somewhere. I sighed, sick of that language and the deeply-rooted misogyny that was underneath it.

"Your proposal is just not appealing to me," I wrote back. "To 'take' me somewhere implies that I am some object. There is sense of agency on your behalf, and none on your partner's behalf. That's what people mean when they talk about a power imbalance between the genders. Some of us would rather come together as equals."

"Look, I don't know what kind of guys you've run into," he replied. "But I'm not like that. There's no expectation of retribution or anything. I just want to spend time with you."

"Why?" I asked.

"You're a beautiful, intelligent person, passionate about what you do," he answered. "In fact I think you're a glowing ball of energy. Maybe there are sexist people in your life who don't appreciate you enough. I just want to protect you from that."

I sighed. How easily the person who wishes to be a protector could become the person one seeks protection from. I did not want protection, or any form of dependence.

"Ugh," I responded. "Your desire to protect me from sexism is sexist. The whole point is I want to live in a world where I don't need a protector."

"You know what your problem is?" he sent back. "You just don't understand that men are different from women. We are bigger and stronger and more inherently violent. Nature made us this way, and so there can never be equality."

"Are you kidding me?" I asked.

"Look," he said. "There's no getting around nature. I'm not going to apologize for the way things are, no matter what you say."

"I didn't ask you to apologize," I wrote. "You're feeling defensive for some reason. Is it because you're happy to stand by and say that society can only be as good as our base nature? Because you're happy to live with an aggressive social order while simultaneously identifying as a 'protector' of women? What does that mean, anyway? That you get to be someone's hero, predicated on the fact we live in an unjust and violent world? You get to be the good guy in someone's life?

"I think that ultimately, at a deep subconscious level, you are okay with the whole situation – you have no desire for things to change, because if they did, you would lose your identity as someone who could or would swoop to the rescue. After all, there are no good guys without bad guys – you need them to define yourself. The good guys are protectors, the bad guys are perpetrators, and women must always remain damsels in distress, in need of rescue. You like those definitions because they make you the hero. You are complicit. That's why you're defensive. So yeah, maybe you should apologize. For refusing to believe in a better world, when this one serves you perfectly fine."

"I don't know what kind of better world you imagine,"

he replied. "Utopia doesn't exist, it's a fantasy, and any time we gain in equality we realize there is some other group that has been disregarded. There will always be someone who feels oppressed."

"So why even try to change society?" I prompted.

"Exactly," he agreed. "Even if we do, there will always someone complaining."

"Uh huh, people will complain when they are assaulted, or raped, or killed – either individually or disproportionately as a group."

"And people have a right to do so."

"Do you understand that women's lives are filled with fraught and potentially violent situations? And that we almost never find justice for crimes against us? Do you even know what we go through?"

"I've experienced violence in my life," he said. "Not sure if you know what that's like. Do you feel personally that you have too?"

"Uh, yeah," I said. "Do you even get what I'm saying here?"

"What was it exactly?" he asked. "Looks, feelings, conversations?"

I leaned back, reading that. Wow, do men just not know what our lives are like? They think we are just misinterpreting words or looks? Perhaps every single one of us should just explain it to them?

"OK, here goes," I wrote. "I've been catcalled and groped in public more times than I care to remember. I have been followed by men - some silent, some yelling loudly - on foot, on bikes, in cars. Sometimes they grab me. One time I was locked in a room and another time I was locked in the back of a car, and both times I had to escape. But I did not leave unscathed.

"In high school, a boy whose desk faced mine in a horseshoe arrangement put his hand down his pants and masturbated while staring at me, and when I raised my hand to say something the teacher shut me down. She told me not to say such dirty things, and when she turned away again, he smiled at me and continued. I felt powerless as the whole class watched this scene.

"When I was in college, I was sexually assaulted at a party. One of my closest friends was in the room at the time, but she did nothing as I tried to fight him off and she is no longer my friend.

"Two years later a friend of my neighbors broke into my house and tried to rape me. I woke up and he was on top of me. In that moment, not physically strong enough to fight him off, I negotiated with him, eventually consenting to a minor deed which left me with less damage to my body but more complicity in the act. Over the next few months, the guy tried to break into my house repeatedly. I spent so many sleepless nights that year yelling at him to stop drunkenly scratching at the locks on the door that connected our neighbors' part of the house to ours. My roommate always stayed at her boyfriend's place, so she didn't know what was happening. I grew exhausted, spending every night awake protecting my home and my body. I told my friends and my neighbors and they didn't believe me, so I did not dream of trying to get the police to believe me.

"That's why women do not report these things. It's a waste of time and no one believes us anyway. If I reported every damn time I was groped or worse, I would have spent most of my life in police stations, reliving these shittiest of moments. Instead I've decided not to care. I spend my time instead thinking about the neural correlates of consciousness and the biochemistry underpinning brain tumors. I got graduate training in neuroscience, earned a PhD in stem cell biology, did post-doctoral research in enzymology and genetics. Then I started my own lab, surrounding myself with people who respect each other, build each other up, and help each other achieve their dreams.

"And then everything was taken away from me. A group of men and women took away my funding, my lab space, and my momentum to continue. They used my visa status, which changed upon my divorce, as a tool to get rid of me and seize everything I had built. And then one of those men felt me up during our last meeting, just groped me as if he wanted to prove that everything of mine was for the taking. I reported it, but no one did anything. That man kept his job and I lost mine.

"So yeah, that's what I've lived through, along with a thousand other moments I want to forget. It's been a distraction from what I care about and it's caused me at times to distrust the people I love. It's what has made me into a person who cannot bear to see someone in pain or someone else refusing to take responsibility for the pain they've caused."

"Thank you for sharing that with me," Mark wrote. "I really hope you know that not all guys are like that."

"Fine, but you should know that every woman has had run-ins with guys like that and lives with the damage. It adds up to the fact that our entire society is living with this damage."

"That's a pretty messed-up way of viewing life, don't you think? Maybe you're being too negative?"

There is nothing I had grown to dislike more than someone telling me I was being negative, as if everything would be sunshine and rainbows if I just shut my mouth.

"I think I have presented an accurate view of reality, actually," I wrote. "I showed you my damage so you would understand what a privilege it is to walk through life and every social interaction without the weight of personal and historical context. It's your decision whether you accept that or not."

"There's no point in complaining," he wrote back.

"But there is," I stated. "Women are suffering, don't you see – these stories we are telling, these heavy secrets we are carrying around, all the mild aggressions and all the outright violence, it's coming out. Every woman on earth is a glowing ball of energy right now. And we need men to be stronger - not to be our 'protectors', just to be decent human beings and acknowledge you haven't been doing so. You guys have each been pretending to be a hero in your own story, while allowing others in your midst to be villains. Then you walk around oblivious to the destruction around you. We're sick of pretending every single caustic event that happens is just some big misunderstanding. It's time you guys take responsibility."

"I have never done anything to anyone."

"I get that you feel that way. But you have."

"What the hell are you accusing me of?!"

"Complicity, my friend."

"I feel like you think my vote represents some greater harm to you personally." He oozed bitterness.

"Yeah, absolutely," I declared. "The lives of women change, depending on whether society extends us rights or not – reproductive choice, the right to vote, equal protection under the law, and faith that we're not liars when we report a crime. The people you've helped to elect are trying as hard as they can to shut down women's health centers, with the effect of women dying of preventable diseases and being burdened with children against their wishes. Then they have stripped healthcare subsidies needed to care for the resulting kids, stripped wage protections that allow underprivileged women to rise from poverty, and on top of everything, they have made it socially acceptable to grab us and socially acceptable to pretend it's not a big deal."

"There were plenty of other reasons to vote for that ticket."

"Maybe you voted for other reasons, but the fact is: you fucked over my entire gender last November. So you don't get to fuck me too. I view you not as a potential partner, but as an aggressor. You have caused me harm."

"I have done nothing to you personally."

"Well, you haven't impressed me much. You want to be a protector of women? Protect our rights."

"There's a feisty liberal. Meow!"

"You know what? Last time I checked, the rights to life, liberty, and the pursuit of happiness were American values, not 'liberal' ones – for everyone, not for the few. I understand: you like me, except for my feminist stridency. But bear in mind the intellectual persistence that you admire otherwise is the same that led to my politics. Perhaps you may have noticed that I am otherwise able to take things in stride. But misogyny is dangerous, to my body and my career and my life. So I take it enormously seriously and I will not date someone who votes to take away my rights, whether you understand what you're doing or not. Pretending ignorance is no longer a valid excuse. I have no desire to stand for that bullshit any longer.

"The truth is: I'm Lilith, not Eve, and I would rather wander the world alone than spend time with a man who acts or speaks or votes as if I am subject to his dominion.

"How many women feel this way? How many would do so if they felt it was an option?

"You know, I hate that we even have to have this discussion. I have no wish to teach you feminist theory. You'll just think I'm trying to brainwash you anyway. So I give up. You're a smart guy, you can evaluate things on your own. But if you're looking for intellectual exercise, try it out. I hope you might gauge 'liberal' women for the content of our ideas – not just the shrillness of our voices, the discomfort we provoke, and the nasty things people say about us without shreds of evidence."

A few days later, I drove to Albania. About ten kilometers after the border crossing, I reached a roundabout and waited as a man with three cows traversed the intersection. I continued driving on the empty roads, noticing small clusters of graves, each gathered around a single tree. There was a long history of blood feuds in this country, long-simmering territorial disputes, and a distressing tendency for Muslim people to be pushed here from their home nations elsewhere in Europe.

Approaching Shkoder, the traffic increased – men on rusty bicycles and men pushing ancient wheelbarrows, poor women with cows and even poorer women without cows, roaming gangs of stray dogs and a horse pulling a wooden cart filled with onions. But despite the desperate poverty, everyone was kind and easygoing. I walked to a restaurant a few blocks from where I was staying and was given a lump of goat cheese to nibble as my meal cooked in a giant wood fireplace along the wall.

I spent the next day browsing through the town – fruit markets, shops, museums and cafés. At a gallery, I walked alongside a series of black-and-white photographic portraits taken a century earlier, stopping at one depicting a married couple. His arm lay on her shoulder; she held two guns while he held a sword and a knife. They both looked straight ahead, ready to face the world together. Afterwards I went for a walk, and I thought about the two of them a lot.

The following day, I lounged along the lake with a picnic lunch, watching birds fly overhead, bare mountains in the distance. Pomegranate trees grew lushly here. The fruits split open, over-ripe, in the late October sun.

I returned my rental car and took a bus through Kosovo, past the old city of Prizhen, to Macedonia. I spent a couple days in Skopje, the capital, where every poet, saint, and politician has a statue in his honor. The local elections were on the day I arrived, and after dinner I wandered the streets, finding the epicenter of music and fireworks and drums and honking cars to be the square next to my hotel, where political victory was being celebrated. No one seemed to know which party was gaining power and which was losing it, who was open to integrating the Muslim minority population and who was more ethno-nationalist, who was corrupt and who wasn't. It didn't matter, they were trusting someone new and it was exciting.

Mark emailed me. "Hey, I'm flying to Athens and I'll be there this coming week. You're there too, right?"

My heart stopped. Early on, I had told him about my itinerary, describing how I would travel south through Eastern Europe, reaching Greece in November. I now regretted this openness. I was suddenly glad my father had proposed meeting me in Athens – having expressed jealousy when I travelled to Rome earlier in the year, he was not about to miss the enormous history of Athens as well. I had been very much looking forward to seeing him, but now I was relieved too. I had never sought out a protector, but as Mark himself had pointed out, this is the world we live in. I proudly emailed him that I would be spending time with my father over the next week and he could leave me be. I had told him several times I hadn't wanted to meet, and now he had better stay away.

My dad was in the hotel lobby when I arrived. I had called him on my way from the airport, after arriving from my stopover in Istanbul. I gave him a huge hug. It was wonderful to see a familiar face, and I suddenly realized I had not done so in months. I popped my suitcase into the room and we went downstairs to have a drink at the bar.

"Dad, I have news." I was absolutely boiling over with excitement. "I found out a month ago, but I wanted to tell you in person. I got an interview. For a faculty post at the University of Mississippi."

He gave a short dismissive bark and rolled his eyes. "You can do better than that."

My smile faded. I sat back, stunned. "Dad, it's a big American university," I told him. "They have strong research programs in physiology, neuroscience, cellular systems and molecular biology. They have a large clinical neurology department, and they've just created a new cancer research center, with several new buildings to support the expansion of basic and clinical research. The university medical center in Jackson and the town itself – they're really happening."

He shook his head with disappointment, thinking of me moving to the southern states.

"Dad, I don't know what's wrong with you, but there's nothing wrong with Jackson. I wish you would stop making me feel like shit." He stared at me, appalled.

I gave him a long hard look. "This is not cause for disappointment. It's actually a fantastic opportunity – a chance to do my research in a place that might be really supportive."

"Fine," my father said. "Good for you. I hope it works out."

I sighed. It would be impossible for this evening to go worse. I decided to get something else over with now too.

"Dad, I've been going through a lot lately," I started. "Not just the divorce and everything at work. But everything that's happening in the world – Brexit and Trump and this insane build-up to war and the incredible racism and misogyny on public display these days."

My father sat quietly, looking at me.

I took a deep breath. "Things have really hit a nerve with me this year," I continued. "There's just been too much symmetry between global events and events in my own life. And so I've been confronting a lot of pain all over again, and, well, I realize it goes way back."

He said nothing, and just sat there with his hands folded on the table.

"Dad, you know how Mom used to come into my bedroom at night and yell and beat me and dig her fingernails into my skin? She was so upset all the time, and she didn't know how to handle it, and she took it out on me. She made me handle pain because she couldn't."

My father was silent. He knew I had taken the brunt of frustration and anger all those years.

"But Dad, she didn't just find comfort in lashing out. There were times she also asked me to provide her comfort. When you would not let her into bed, she came into my bed and she asked me to hold her and touch her."

I had never said it out loud before. I had no idea what would happen.

My father sighed and looked down. "I know I wasn't there for either of you enough," he said quietly. "That put too much pressure on your mother, and she in turn put too much pressure on you."

He paused and took a deep breath, then looked up at me. "I'm sorry."

My jaw dropped. All those years, all that pain – it just eased, like the entire weight of the world had begun to lift off my shoulders.

"Dad, thank you for saying that," I said. "Thank you for understanding what happened and acknowledging the pain. Thank you for sharing the burden with me. I needed that."

I leaned back in my chair, exhausted. We made plans to meet up the next morning for breakfast and a day of exploring. I went to my hotel room with an incredible sense of relief.

We spent a few sunny days exploring excavation sites scattered around the city, then a cloudy day at the archaeological museum. We gawped, fascinated, at the myriad displays in glass cases, calling each other over when we felt a click of understanding that tied geography to history and human nature in the past to the present. We had to be ushered out when the museum closed, both of us gazing back longingly at the Antikythera Mechanism through the closing door, as if a few more minutes or hours would be enough. That evening, as we pored over maps on my laptop in my father's hotel room, my mother called up.

"Beth's here," my father said, after chatting with her as he did every night. "Do you want me to put her on?"

He handed me the phone. My mother was chewing some food.

"Your father told me that you've been having some nice conversations together." She spoke in a dangerous tone.

"Um, yeah," I replied. "We're having a good time. We went to a museum today."

"Uh huh," she said, with audible snarkiness. "And he also told me you have an interview coming up in Mississippi.

That's *interesting*."

I waited for her to congratulate me or wish me luck. She didn't. I shrugged and handed the phone back to my father. He listened quietly then hung up the phone.

The next day was sunny again so we hiked up the hill to St George's Chapel. On the way I unraveled stories about my travels, but my father seemed distracted and anxious. When I stopped talking in the middle of a sentence, he didn't seem to notice. That irritated me, but I let it go. He always acted distant from me after he had spoken with my mother. Seamlessly I began to let him pace the conversations and choose the subject matter instead.

The following day was sunny, so we decided to visit the Acropolis. On the way back, we passed a row of cafés across the way from the Agora and decided to have dinner there.

As our appetizers arrived, several cats came over to beg for food. I was in the middle of telling a story and I ignored them. My father leaned down to coo at them, ignoring me.

"You probably shouldn't feed the cats, Dad. They're strays. The restaurant won't want to encourage them." I leaned alongside the table to talk to him, trying to get his attention, since he was not listening to me. I looked up and noticed the waiter standing a few feet away, arms crossed over his chest and a stern look on his face.

"I'm sure the cats belong to the restaurant," my father said, obliviously. He picked some food off his plate and gently fed the two kittens below him. Other, larger cats swarmed in, and the waiter ran over to our table, yelling and scattering the animals out of the patio area. Then he reprimanded me sharply and at length. My father laughed at my undeserved public humiliation.

After the waiter walked away, one stray remained

sitting below us as we finished our meal. It stared up at my dad.

"What a sweet cat," my father tutted, tilting his face and blinking at the creature. "Isn't she sweet?"

"Uh, I think that's a tomcat," I pointed out. "And he's not sweet, he's clearly a psychopath. Nice cats blink back at you. This cat isn't blinking."

The animal turned its head and stared at me hatefully for a moment, then turned back to face my father. He squinted at the cat and the cat stared back at him, unblinking. My father prepared some more food from his plate and dropped it on the ground. The tomcat ate the food greedily, then strode over to another cat lounging a few feet away, on the other side of my chair. The tomcat put his jaws around the poor neck of the other, and within seconds shoved himself inside and started pumping away. The little cat underneath mewed and struggled helplessly, but the tomcat was bigger and stronger, easily holding the other down. The rape scene was painful to watch. I felt the vomit rise in my throat and I turned away. My dad leaned over the table to watch.

"Oh, they're friends!" he exclaimed, still looking. I thought I would not be able to hold back my food, and I covered my mouth. My father continued to make conversation as I barely held it together.

After another half an hour, I signaled the waiter for the bill. I was irritated and exhausted. But the waiter ignored me. My father took the bill out of his shirt pocket and waved it at me.

"I have it already," he said, and tucked it back into his pocket. My shoulders slumped but he kept chatting. Finally, after another half an hour or so, he paid the bill and we got up to leave.

The entire week we had walked side-by-side as we

explored the city. Often the sidewalk would narrow, forcing one of us to walk in front. Each time, I slowed, assuming we would switch turns. Each time, my father came to a complete stop and I came to a complete stop and we would both stand there waiting patiently until I would finally go in front of him. This significantly increased our travel times and brought every conversation to a stop.

That night I finally lost it – the path kept narrowing, my dad kept having me walk in front and he kept following me. The feeling of having someone right behind me finally broke my defenses. I walked quickly, not speaking. When the path narrowed again, we both came to a stop and I refused to go. My father stood there waiting, for a full minute, not saying anything.

"Go in front!" I yelled, finally.

"No, you go ahead," he replied.

"Go in front!" I yelled louder.

"No you go ahead," he said again.

"I don't like you following me."

"I'm just walking behind you," he said.

"I don't want you following me like that," I repeated.

"I have no way of knowing this, you should have spelled it out," he replied.

"Did you notice me stopping, waiting for you to go ahead half the time?"

He shrugged.

"It should have been clear from the body language. When we were walking, every time we came to a stop I expected us to trade spots so that each of us could walk in front and set the pace. That's how people walk together, not one person always following the other."

"You should have just said you didn't want to be

followed."

"I did say that, by slowing to a stop and gesturing." I was losing patience, having to explain this simple point. "It's not normal to refuse someone's gestures and make them uncomfortable."

"Well, you should have spelled this out," he replied. "You can't expect me to read gestures.'

"You know what? That's a lot to put on me. You could put in some effort and figure out how to behave properly so as not to make people uncomfortable."

"No, you're the one who needs to use your words and say something." We had reached the hotel and were now arguing in the hallway near our rooms.

"Dad, even when I did say something, you still wouldn't go in front of me."

My father gave me a long, ugly stare.

"And making me spell out exactly how you're making me uncomfortable makes me feel weak and vulnerable. Why do you need me do that? Why can't you just engage in normal behavior?"

He shook his head dismissively, not saying anything, as if trying to make me feel I was making a big deal out of nothing.

"Dad, why can't you just notice when you are making someone uncomfortable?"

"Fine," he said, and walked away.

I went into my room and closed the door, feeling panic wash over me. Instead of being sensitive to other people, my father was forcing me to spell out my own feelings – to relive my damage and explain it to him, to go through my own pain just to convince him to cause less pain toward others.

I thought of all the times I've been followed, and why it made me uncomfortable. I reached into the core of fear and agony in my psyche which had been slowly becoming more accessible in recent weeks and months. Now the memories exploded like a volcano, horrible experiences spilling into my consciousness like lava, their flames wracking my body for hours.

I finally fell asleep at dawn, and a couple hours later, my father knocked on my door asking if I wanted to go downstairs to breakfast together. I was unshowered and not in the mood to spend the day at museums with him again. I stood in the doorway, muscles in my face contorted, eyes burning and hands clenched in fists. He didn't notice, or pretended not to.

"Shall we go down to breakfast?" he asked cheerily.

"No," I said evenly.

"You aren't hungry?" he asked.

"I'm not doing okay," I replied through my teeth.

"Oh, your stomach is upset," he said confidently.

"No," I said. "You asked me to spell it out and so I've been thinking about how to explain it to you better. You need to know exactly how you were making me uncomfortable, so I'll spell it out for you.

"I don't like being followed. I told you, a man followed me to Athens – took a transatlantic flight even after I told him to leave me alone. I have been trying to avoid him all week. And over the years, I've been followed by men, driving close behind me, walking close behind me, grabbing me from behind, groups of men laughing and grabbing me, each taking their turn. Men alone, following me with their dicks out and their hands on their dicks, heavy-breathing men on public transport, following me off the bus at my stop, dirty men on the subway, pressing against me or pressing against other women, and it's impossible to say anything because the terror dries your throat, because you know if you do say something the guy will turn to you and smile and make it clear he's remembering your face and then follow you later and other men just never seem to notice. And if they are the ones doing it, making you uncomfortable, they just act like it's some big misunderstanding instead of just accepting they did something creepy."

"I don't want to hear all this," he said. "You could just say you didn't want to be followed."

"This is not a failure of communication on my part. You really need to pay better attention to people's reactions to your behavior." It was clear he had no intention of starting to do this.

"So are you coming to breakfast or not?" he said.

"No," I replied. "I'm just going to spend the day on my own."

On the flight back, my father routed himself through Amsterdam to check out the Rijksmuseum and I routed myself one last time through Newcastle to pick up my things and say goodbye to Clara. He and I would meet again at Schiphol in a few days' time. But on the flight from Newcastle to Amsterdam, I ran into Gavin. He was headed to the Society for Neuroscience meeting in the states. I wasn't going this time around, because I wasn't sure if I was a neuroscientist anymore. I was heading back to Chicagoland. Connecting in Amsterdam, I had forty minutes to find my father and catch my transatlantic flight. But Gavin and I had some unfinished business. I took him by the arm as he exited the plane, and spoke quickly.

"Hey, Gav," I said. "I know you didn't lead the charge to destroy my lab and my career."

"I'm really sorry about everything that happened," he replied, sighing.

"Doesn't matter now," I said firmly. "The important

thing is that we get the data out. We need to show that our gene therapy worked."

"Yeah," he agreed. "Fair enough."

"Great," I said. "Now I need your data on the functional testing and the neuronal survival rates after the cell cultures were treated with the viral vectors. We can add those data to our validation assays."

"I should be able to get that together," he said.

"And I need you to make sure the project covers the costs of publication, including open-access fees so everyone can read this publicly-funded research."

"Fine, yes," he said.

"And one more thing," I added. "We watched the cells switch on the red fluorescent protein under live time-lapse imaging. Those constructs work, and they work really well. The reason you didn't see any glowing neurons under your microscope after treatment with those particular viral vectors was because you had the wrong settings on your scope. That's the reason you could trigger spikes, even though you didn't observe the fluorescence. Like I said time and again, you need to adjust your peak excitation and emission wavelengths to each construct."

"Yeah, okay," Gavin replied. He had built his own microscopes, he knew this stuff. It was the basics. He had just tried a short-term solution to explain why things weren't working. Undermining me was just easier than troubleshooting at the time. But now he had begun to realize what had gone wrong.

"Bye, Gavin."

"Bye, Beth."

"Good luck with everything," I said sincerely.

"Good luck to you too." Gavin paused. "I hope you find

a nice life out there."

"Thanks," I said, and I flew back to the United States.

Chapter 27
Right Back Where I Started From

My father and I arrived at O'Hare and took a taxi back to Deerfield. When we arrived, my mother was in a state. She had bought a freezer to store my DNA samples, but it had defrosted and she had moved the boxes to her own freezer.

"This is actually the second freezer to break down," she explained in a harried voice. "I didn't want to worry you, but this keeps happening."

It wasn't that big of a deal. The important thing was my cell cultures, which were useful in themselves and for initiating tumors for drug testing studies. And those cells were being stored in liquid nitrogen tanks in multiple locations around the United States.

"Mom, it's fine. The DNA samples shouldn't go through too many freeze-thaw cycles, but if you got them into another freezer pretty quickly, they'll be okay."

I didn't even care about these samples personally. They were CANDO-related and I had nothing to do with that project anymore. I had left a copy of everything at Newcastle and taken a copy of everything with me – before I left, I had not had time to deposit the samples in a public repository. The team was legally obliged to do so as a condition of our publicly-funded research, but I knew that no one else would do it, so I'd decided to store the samples until I could get it done myself. Scatter-brained during this hectic year, I'd sent the samples to my parents instead of other scientists.

"You should take a look at the freezer," my mother ordered. "Go to the basement."

I set my things down and went downstairs to look at the freezer. I had assured her it was safe to store these samples in the regular freezer – they would not contaminate anything. But since she wanted to get a separate freezer for them, I had requested that she get one that reported its temperature, stayed below -20 degrees, and did not require regular defrosting if the door was kept closed. This one had no temperature reading, no sealing to keep the cold in, and a sticker on it saying it needed regular defrosting.

I sighed. Since my mother had assured me there was a freezer to store my things, I had optimistically returned from the last leg of my journey with precious tissue samples on dry ice from a collaborator in London. This new material definitely needed to remain below -20 degrees, which would not be possible with the current setup.

I had trusted my parents. They had received half a million dollars when my grandfather passed away, so I thought they might have bought a decent freezer fitting my specifications to store my things. I wished they valued my work enough to do that. I trudged upstairs.

"Mom, could we get a new freezer?" I asked, but she was already on the phone with the appliance catalogue spread out on the kitchen table in front of her.

"Can I order the cheapest freezer you have?" she spoke into the receiver. I shook my head and touched the button to hang up the landline.

"Mom, let's talk about the specifications first."

"No, we need a freezer right now and I'm going to get you one!" Her tension put me on edge and make my blood feel like it was crackling with electricity.

"Mom, the DNA samples are in the freezer right now. I'm putting the new tissue samples in there alongside. There's no risk of contamination. Lab animals are cleaner than ones on farms."

"No, that's not the problem," she said. "I promised to get you another freezer for your things."

"They're in the freezer now. They're okay. If we're going to get something else, more long-term, we should talk about the specifications first."

"I was going to buy you a freezer but you hung up the phone," she said, her voice rising alarmingly.

"I know, Mom, but you asked for the cheapest freezer they have. That's not the most useful way to start the conversation. That way, you'll end up with a third freezer crapping out."

"Now you're swearing at me! I'm just trying to get you a new freezer! And I didn't ask for the cheapest freezer they had, I asked for the most expensive freezer they had!"

"Mom, that's not what you said."

"It is, you just didn't hear me correctly."

"Mom, those two words do not sound alike. I know what you said."

"No, I definitely asked for the most expensive freezer they had."

"Mom, that's ridiculous. No one would say that. You're great at getting deals on all kinds of things, you always have been. Obviously we'll get the cheapest thing that meets the specifications."

"No, I want to get you the most expensive thing!"

"Mom, that's not helpful. I just want the right thing. It's okay to get the cheapest version that fits the bill."

"No, you need something expensive!"

"No, I really don't, Mom." I was getting irritated, with all this reinterpretation of my words. "Look, a dripping electrical appliance sitting on a carpet in the basement there is a fire risk. This is not just about my stuff, this is about your safety too."

"Oh, you don't want all your things to go up in flames?" Her eyes lit up weirdly.

"Mom, I'm worried about you and Dad more than my stuff. Let's make sure we can store this stuff in your home without a fire risk."

"I asked for the most expensive freezer and you hung up the phone."

"Mom, you're lying. You did not say that word."

"No, you're lying. And accusing me of lying."

"Mom, it doesn't matter. I just wish you wouldn't lie."

"I'm not lying. I wanted to get you the most expensive freezer."

"Mom, stop lying. I'm sick of the lies."

"What lies? Now there are more lies?"

I sighed. There were so many lies, much bigger lies.

My father busied himself with dishes in the sink. My mother looked at me with a challenging expression.

"Mom, I've been confronting a lot of things about the past lately. And I think it's time we face up to what happened during my childhood."

"What happened during your childhood?" she asked, her face hard.

"Mom, you yelled and hit me a lot. You said a lot of unkind things about my face. And Mom, you came into my bed."

"I did no such thing."

"Mom, you did. When Dad kicked you out of the bed you shared, you came to my bed. You made me spoon you and touch your breasts. You told me that's how you're supposed to treat a woman."

She was silent.

"You came to me for comfort. It was not right that you did that. I was a child and you should have been there for me instead of making me be there for you." I shook, describing this.

"I was there for you!" my mother cried out. "You're remembering it wrong. I came into your bed when you were sick, so I could hold you when you were coughing."

"Mom, that's not what happened."

"It is. It is what happened."

"Mom, that doesn't even make sense. No one gets into bed with a coughing person and puts their arms around them. Anyway, you certainly didn't."

"No, I'm sure that's what happened."

I looked at my father. He had finished with the dishes and he was standing at the sink, facing us.

"I don't know what happened," he said. "Your mother says one thing, you say another."

"Why the heck would I be saying this, if it weren't true?" I asked. "This is not pleasant for anyone."

My parents both looked at me.

"Beth, we're always there for you," my mother said. "Why do you need to hurt us?"

"Mom, I'm not trying to hurt you. I just want you to come to terms with what you've done."

"Beth, we've done nothing to hurt you. We're doing everything we can to help you," she said.

"I know, Mom. Thank you for agreeing to store my boxes. And the freezer stuff too." Then I remembered something – the car, my freedom. My heart rose. That gift meant so much to me. For them to help me out like that, it meant the world to me. I turned and walked to the garage, connected to the kitchen by a door a few steps away.

There was only one car in the garage, their car. I closed the door and turned around again.

"Um, Mom? Dad? Were you going to buy me a car? I realize it was a big thing to ask but –"

"You'll get a car," my father said, enunciating each word threateningly, "When and if I think you deserve one."

"I thought it would be an unconditional gift," I said. "I thought you would just –"

"Your father meant that you can go pick one this weekend," my mother said.

"That's not what he said," I pointed out.

"That is what he said," my mother stated.

"No, it's not. He just said something completely different. He said I'll get a car when and if he thinks I deserve one."

"That's not what he said," my mother insisted. I looked at my father, whose face was a blank.

Mere seconds had passed, and they were pretending to have no memory whatsoever of what had just happened. As if the past could have held anything at all, as if it didn't define every single inch of the present. As if there was no such thing as absolute truth and no possibility for shared understanding among human minds.

I took a deep breath.

"You know," I said, "I've begun to notice how happy I am when I'm not around you or Andy."

My mother was silent.

"Both of you always said I was depressed – or, more accurately, that I am depressing and negative. But I only feel that way around you and him. Life has its ups and downs, but only around you two do I feel lost in a pit of despair."

"That's not a very nice thing to say," she replied. She started to cry. "You're so hurtful. Why do you want to hurt me?"

"Mom, you've hurt me a lot over the years. All I'm doing is saying so."

"Why can't you just put the past behind us? Why do you need to keep bringing things up?"

"How about this – Why can't we talk about it? Why do you make me feel guilty for bringing it up?"

"You're so hurtful!" she cried out. "Why are you doing this to me? After everything I have done for you, this is how you repay me."

I paused. "Mom, you need to accept what you've done. You need to stop making me carry all the pain – you need to accept holding some of it yourself."

"Why are you trying to make me feel pain? You are horrible, horrible." Her face twisted terribly. "Why are you doing this to me?" she demanded again.

"Mom, I'm asking you to share the burden." I sighed. "Pretending this stuff didn't happen, pretending like I am the one hurting you by asking you to admit what you've done – maybe that makes you feel better, but it doesn't make things okay. You're leaving me with all the pain. You need to take that on."

"Stop, just stop," she cried, her face in her hands. But my patience and mercy were finished. It was time for her to face what she had done.

I flew to Jackson, Mississippi. I had a job interview and a future to look forward to.

When I stepped out of the airport, I was met by warm sweet air and a red Mercedes-Benz. The head of the department was a kind-faced, energetic blonde woman in her fifties, the president of the American Biochemical Society.

"Katie," she said with a smile, holding out her hand.

"Izi," I replied. I had decided, with all the changes in my life, to change my name as well.

"I'm gonna be rude and leave you to settle into your hotel room for a few hours until dinner," Katie said. "I've got some work I need to catch up on." This arrangement suited me perfectly. I could practice my one-hour seminar talk scheduled for the following afternoon.

"So," said Katie, as she pulled onto the road. "What's your story? Do you have a partner who's looking for a job as well?" It could be tough for two academics to find jobs together in the same city, and often universities would evaluate both partners, considering the whole team as a potential hire. I thought of Andy refusing to apply for that professorship at UCL, saying I would only have a chance at a lectureship as his spouse. I laughed inwardly with the realization that he could have gotten a leg up on a faculty post in America as *my* spouse.

"No, I don't have a partner," I replied. "I'm actually in the process of getting divorced. That's why I'm looking to move back to the states."

"Ah yes, a divorce, I got one of those too," she said. "And I've lost a partner."

"Oh my gosh, I'm so sorry," I said. "Life finds all sorts of ways to be hard."

"It sure does," Katie said. Then she smiled. "Well, let me tell you all about the university and what it's like to live in Jackson, Mississippi."

Over the following two days, I interviewed with each member of the Department, as well as some of the clinical neurosurgery staff who were interested in collaborating with academics who had ideas on new treatments for patients.

I told them about my early interest in psychology and neuroscience which had evolved into an interest in cell biology and biochemistry. I told them about my graduate work identifying the cell-of-origin of glioma; changing normal neural stem cells into cancer cells and transplanting them into mouse brains to make the first accurate laboratory model of that tumor; resolving the paradox of how aging leads to both lost regenerative potential in the brain and increased risk of cancer formation there. I told them about discovering the metabolic fuel requirements of normal neural stem cells and glioma cells, and how that research had yielded novel drug targets for treating brain tumors. I told them about my work developing gene therapies for epilepsy and devising ways to modify specific brain cells genetically, about cultivating project-tailored business plans, working with corporate partners, meeting with regulatory agencies to seek approval for human clinical trials, and the efforts to achieve funding to support my work. They asked about my managerial experience, my teaching and mentorship experience, my interests and my travels and the collaborations I had formed along the way. I enjoyed speaking and breathed easily here, feeling like I was finally at home.

After my seminar, I went out to dinner with a few members of the faculty. The previous night, Katie had taken me to a little restaurant with a bar and open kitchen, a jazz man at the piano and people who knew each other gathered around him. This evening, some other professors took me to a steak and seafood restaurant where the fish fritters and fried green tomatoes were recommended. I had never tried real fried green tomatoes, and I was pleased to find they were amazing. I grinned, chatting easily with the group. At one point, my divorce came up and everyone agreed they had either done it or thought about doing it, and I felt normal for the first time in ages. An older couple – both retired emeritus professors – sat at a table nearby, and the senior professor at our table politely excused himself to go speak with the two gentlemen, since they were old friends of his. It felt like such a small town, a welcoming community. I ached to be a part of it.

The next afternoon, I drove around town with a local real estate agent to look at houses in Belhaven and Fondren and neighborhoods further afield. The department had set up the tour as a way to introduce me to the city. As we chatted, I looked out the window at the diners, taverns, tapas bars and other eateries, locally-owned coffeeshops and independent grocery stores, yoga studios, libraries and museums – a town with an easy authenticity that popular coastal cities lacked, like Portland felt ten to fifteen years ago. With a light-rail system, the place would be absolutely perfect. I found myself imagining a life in Jackson but tried to stop. I could not get too attached to this dream – my fate was still not in my own hands.

I flew back to O'Hare and returned to Deerfield. When I entered the house, my mother was in a state again.

"I wasn't lying to you," were her first words as she opened the door.

"Mom, I don't want to talk about it," I replied, setting down my suitcase and taking off my jacket.

"I wasn't lying to you," she said again.

"Mom, let's not talk about it for a little while. Let's have some food and some rest and take some time to process. I'm going upstairs." I changed into my pajamas and came back downstairs, hoping for some food. I was starving.

"I wasn't lying to you," my mother repeated.

"Mom, stop. I can't take this anymore."

"You need to believe I was not lying to you."

I slapped her. My right hand connected just above her left ear. Then we both stared at each other, horrified.

"What have you done?!" she cried out.

I couldn't say anything.

"What have you done?!" she shrieked.

My father came running into the room. I turned to him. "Hit me," I said. "I hit Mom, so you need to hit me back."

He stared at me, his face twisted with an ugly gaze. "I'm not going to do that," he snarled. Then he snorted with disgust in my direction.

He and my mother had hit me a thousand times, slapping me across the face with a bare hand exactly as I had just done, or beating me with household objects. Why would they do it to me as a child, but not do it to me as an adult now? I felt bereft and confused.

It was not okay, what I had just done. There needed to be some kind of punishment. If my parents would not provide it, then an objective third party would have to do so. I called the police. My father grabbed the phone and hung it up. They called back immediately, and I explained what I had done.

A few minutes later, several police cars showed up on our street. Small town, nothing else to do. Six officers entered the house, two of them taking my statement, two of them taking my mother's statement, two of them taking my father's statement. All in general agreement about the argument and who had hit whom, they handcuffed me and took me to the station.

"We have to do this, if one person hits another person and it's reported," the arresting officer said.

I nodded. He snapped my mugshot with a digital camera and turned to the computer.

"Hey, why are you already in the system?" he asked.

I looked at him, confused.

"Have you been arrested before?" He looked at me curiously, as if he were suddenly wondering how many times I had hit someone before.

I shrugged, just as perplexed as he was. Then it dawned on me that my marital separation-induced visa curtailment, which had been entered into the system as an illegal immigration event, leading to my detention at Heathrow, must have been shared with law enforcement agencies in the United States and probably across Europe as well.

The officers had me remove the drawstring from my pajama pants. Then they ushered me to a cell. I lay down on the bed and waited for hours while the State's Attorney decided whether to press charges. I breathed heavily, in stunned bewilderment, wondering what was going to happen with my life.

"The State's Attorney called back," said the officer, as he unlocked the cell. "They're not pressing charges and you're free to go."

"What does that mean?" I asked.

"It means you're not being charged with a crime, you don't have to go to court and you don't have to post any bail."

"OK," I said. I had still done something wrong. But it had been decided it was within the range of normal – hurtful, certainly, but not bad enough to be called a crime.

I asked the officers if I might stop at the house to grab my suitcase and my tote bag and then get a ride to a hotel. They agreed.

My mother ran to the door when we arrived. It seemed like she wanted to talk to me or touch me or something but I kept moving. One officer kept her company while the other one went upstairs with me to grab my bags. It appeared I would be living out of a suitcase for a while longer.

"I will be back within one year to pick up the rest of my things," I said to the officers in front of my mother. I would later email my parents with an inventory of items I had left with them and that same timeframe, so there was written documentation – no need for any further muddled discussion.

I looked at my mother one last time, then left.

Later I lay awake in bed in the hotel room, thinking about what I had done.

My brother used to say to me, "You're always the fucking martyr."

Well, I wasn't anymore. I had finally stopped taking all the slings and arrows, and as soon as I did, I became the kind of person who hurts someone else. I had taken on so much pain that I drowned in it, losing myself.

The social worker at the Deerfield Police Station called me a few days later and I explained the whole thing more clearly than I had before. The abuse I endured as a child and the fact my mother would not confront it, the ways she had hurt me and how much I wished she would just admit it already. Our family dynamic, including the way my mother acted toward my brother – telling him that she treated him nicely because he was a guest in the house, even though he had been adopted when he was only a few days old and he was as much a part of the family as anyone else. How my mother always grew angry whenever the two of us children laughed and played together, jealous of conversations that did not include her. How she turned us against each other and isolated us with humiliating personal ridicule. How she lied so readily and frequently about her words and actions that as a child I had taken to testing the accuracy and comprehensiveness of my memory against a tape recorder. Zooming to the present – what had happened on the night I arrived back in town. Why, how, when, where, under what conditions I had slapped my mother and how badly I felt about it. How I was so glad I had called the police right away, so they could objectively evaluate the situation. How relieved I was that my mother had not developed any bruises. But the fact that my action was still not okay.

"Do you have somebody else you can talk to?" she asked.

I thought of my friends in Seattle, and how they'd always been there for me. "Yes," I told her.

I took a taxi to the airport and flew west.

Chapter 28
Moving Out West, Again

"Of course you're welcome to stay," Rose said, hugging me when I showed up on her doorstep. "That's what a spare bedroom is for."

"But I don't have anything to give you in return."

"Well, you could spend time with me and the kids," she said. "That would be helpful. Or you can just eat our food and sleep in the basement, for as long as you need."

I burst into tears and cried harder than I had for ages.

"Oh, Boo," Rose said. "It's alright. You're home now."

I celebrated Thanksgiving with my new family – the family I chose because they welcomed me when I was so desperate. Rose's family was happy, healthy, kind, thoughtful, sweet and welcoming. They always tried to love and care for each other, even when it was hard.

I went to see Lila and hug her too. She didn't always recognize pain or know what to do when she witnessed it, but she had always loved me and she had tried her best.

A couple weeks later, there were protests at the unveiling of the civil rights museum in Jackson, Mississippi, when people who did not celebrate those values overshadowed the proceedings. Several days later, Alabama made the decision to place a civil rights lawyer in the senate rather than an accused pedophile. The South had showed it could lead the way to a new, revitalized America, and I was overcome with pride for the place I hoped would become my home.

It didn't matter that many people had voted for the flawed and hate-filled person. The way democracy works is clever – even a slim majority can decide the outcome of an election. The brilliant thing about the whole setup is that individuals do not have to be right all the time; it was possible for a group of people to make a better decision than any one person on their own. Such an ingenious information processing system can provide a robust method for human progress in this world.

I enjoyed being at home among friends. I drank American beer, cold and crisp, with bitter hops. I realized I had gone seven years without hearing any Creedence and I corrected that problem. I hugged my friends' children and I hugged my friends too. I met with Cynthia and Skye and we talked about a million things, like how much we've changed since we met and how much we've stayed the same and how we keep on going.

Although I enjoyed being among close friends and those I now considered family, I also needed some time alone to process everything. Somewhere I could hear the train whistling when I left the window open at night. Somewhere with clear skies, to remind me there were a trillion stars out there, all waiting to be counted.

I hugged my friends goodbye and moved to Colorado. I had no idea what I would do with my life, but I was sure I would figure it out there. When I walked out of the airport and saw the purple foothills of the Rocky Mountains rising into white capped peaks against the flawless blue sky, I knew I'd made the right decision. I remembered the only other time I'd seen the Rockies, when I moved out west to Seattle on Highway 90 – Helène and I, sitting in the front seat of my lavender Ford Taurus in awed silence for half an hour as the mountain range grew bigger and bigger, more and more violet, through the windshield, before either of us could even think of something to say. I'd found a path then, and I'd find some path from here too.

    I rented a car for a few days to get oriented in my new surroundings. Suddenly I could not believe it was possible that I might have spent the rest of my life on that fusty little island across the ocean. I belonged in America, driving around with the radio blaring, windows down and wind in my hair no matter what the season was. I was glad that everything fell apart - my marriage, my visa, my job, my whole life over there, just so I could start fresh, with fresh air. A mile up, and light as a bird.

    Every morning, I woke up with a nosebleed, the deferred pain from my sinuses radiating along my jaw and causing my teeth to tingle. The dry high-altitude air contained less oxygen, and my body was blocking the rest by producing mucus and blood clots. On top of that, I started exercising, which I had never done before. The fitness room in my big American apartment complex had fancy weights and treadmills, mats for doing stretches and sit-ups. My heart beat more steadily, more strongly, than it had in a long time.

    Earl emailed me to say that he had cashed in all the bitcoin people had paid him for tours over the years, and the first thing he had done was buy a house in southern Spain. He offered to purchase me a plane ticket so I could come over. It sounded like a lovely situation that would inevitably be difficult to extract myself from, just like England had been. I explained to him that I did not want to feel indebted to him for his generous offer of hospitality. I wished we could just travel in the states for a little while – as equals, each of us paying our own way. He responded, insisting that I should not feel indebted and I should just come over.

It was the same as always – he wanted to decide and he wanted me to accept. But now that I could imagine a better way to live, I wanted nothing less. I sighed and went for a walk.

I had forgotten how aggressive men are in America – accelerating their cars at stop signs then braking sharply to make me feel nervous, swerving toward me on their bicycles to watch if I would dart out of the way, criticizing my shopping choices as I stood in line at the grocery store, opining on my age while standing on the street corner waiting for the light to change, frankly assessing my body as I ate a burger at the bar, yelling vulgarities as I walked down the street. After getting settled in town, I mostly stayed inside for the next month; it was distracting to venture interactions with the outside world when I had so much to concentrate on.

I made a plan. I had enough money to last through April. Then I would use my last $2,500 to open a bank account with a line of credit. I would purchase a used SUV, throw my mattress in the back, get myself a national parks pass and camp out until something worked out. In the meantime, I'd explore Colorado – the hot springs, rivers, mountains, sand dunes, rock formations, fossil-rich cliffs and ancient dwelling sites that were still a secret to me.

If I didn't get the faculty post, that would be okay. I'd

start a new life, one that didn't involve science at all. I'd continue to write and I'd continue to live.

If I did get the faculty post, I'd run the final preclinical experiment with etomoxir. If it worked, I would try my hardest to bring this promising new cancer drug to clinical trial. If it didn't work, I would go back to the drawing board and try my hardest to find something that did. Whatever happened, I would keep going and I would keep trying to do something good in this world.

My parents didn't invite me to Christmas. My mother emailed to say I probably had a lot on my mind and she hoped I was doing well. Her cousin, one of her closest friends, invited me to the extended family gathering. He was deeply involved in the religious community at his church. I told him I was having a tough time these days, confronting the abuse I had suffered as a child and coming to terms with my relationship with my mother. I hoped he might have some warm response, but he didn't reply at all. Catholics are good at turning their heads away upon hearing allegations of child abuse.

My father emailed me a couple weeks after Christmas. He wanted to tell me that my mother had developed bruising around her eye a week after I had hit her. He told me about it in detail.

Before Christmas, he said, the therapist had advised not to share this information with me, but he and my mother thought it was a good idea to do so now.

I wasn't sure whether to believe them or not. I didn't want to believe them, and they had lied to me so much over the years. Also, I desperately hoped it wasn't true. I wasn't sure if I could handle it.

"Could you send pictures please?" I asked. What I actually wanted were the photos of me and my dad in Greece, photos of my family at the holidays, anything but this.

My father sent photos from a week or so after the incident. My mother's face was stretched and rigid, with an appearance of great unbearable pain. There was no swelling but there was a dark bruise around her eye.

I hated myself so much. At least I had called the police when it happened. That was the right thing to do. But they had decided not to punish me, even though they knew what I did. I had told them I had slapped my mother and she had told them all about it too. She didn't have redness and bruising at the time, or the following morning, but maybe they hadn't evaluated it correctly. I called Rose, since she was a doctor. She explained in detail how bruising works.

"If there was a serious injury, it would have shown up right away. The police would have seen it," she told me. "Sometimes blood gathers, and that shows up later. Old people bruise really easily."

I still hated myself, absolutely hated myself.

"It's awful, what happened. But if there was no bruising right away, it was not a serious injury. And they said it's all better now – it got better before Christmas, right?"

"Yeah," I agreed. "But that doesn't make it okay."

"No," she said, sighing. "No. But are you okay?"

"No," I replied. "I hurt someone."

I lay in bed for days, trying to come to terms with what I had done.

I could be impatient and I could be unkind. I sat with that for a little while, waiting for the pain to go away, wishing the bad feeling would degrade.

But it would not. It stuck there. I had hurt another

person, and that fact would never go away. I would have to live with it.

All I could do was vow to try harder, and never allow myself to hurt someone again. I needed to remember there were people who loved and supported me, and that I could be strong enough to love and support others. I couldn't just give up – I had to try harder.

I prayed for strength and then I found it within myself.

My mother wrote to explain that she had lied to me so I would trust her again – if she had admitted what she had said and done, I would have lost faith in her, and she thought what I really needed was to trust her again, so she had lied to cover her actions. It was necessary, she explained – she was not hurting me, she was doing what was best for me, and I should come back to her.

I didn't know what to say, so I didn't respond.

I started writing on mid-winter's day. I listened to classical music in the mornings, turned the radio down low in the afternoon, and switched to jazz in the evenings. I wrote about my life until I had nothing to write about anymore. Then I cut out half my stories, to keep them for myself.

Everything that had been clogging my brain was now released onto the paper. Chaotic fragments of conversations, discarded to streamline the narrative, fell out of my mind, grew light and floated away into the clear blue skies. I mourned the loss of completion and clarity, feeling the past was now a jumbled confusion the way everyone else always described it.

The whole process was cathartic. With every page, a new realization hit me. When I got to the part where I had to confront what I had done, I stopped. I had so much trouble, thinking about how I had slapped my mother, the first action in my life I could not justify at all.

I stopped writing for a while and just read back through my journal. My own words, written earlier that year, ripped my heart out.

"Is it too much to expect of someone, not to do something hurtful because it is easy or it feels good in the moment? I understand that people don't always realize when their actions hurt someone else. But if someone slips up and does something hurtful, they have to own it. They have to recognize the pain they cause and ask for forgiveness. Nothing less is acceptable. That is simple human decency, and yes we all deserve it. Every single one of us needs to do better."

Damn. My own words.

I had to say something to my mother. And to Andy. I had to say I was sorry for hurting them. You have to treat others as you want to be treated yourself.

But that is where the responsibility ends. You do not have to be a martyr. You do not have to stick around and keep being treated like shit. You have every right to get out and grow strong on your own, avoiding the people who have caused you pain in the past. Then, one day, you might be strong enough to help others who are hurting too.

Martyrdom is letting the bad guys win. It's the way by which good-hearted people ease their own pain, by accepting the sins of others. But the goal is to eliminate sin from this world completely. And to do that, we need to confront bad behavior and work toward achieving justice. Those who have been hurt must be gentle yet firm. Those looking the other way need to start realizing their role in facilitating evil and stop being complicit now. And those who have hurt others need to live with the pain of their own actions.

That was a tough realization, but a useful one.

After forty days, on 31 January 2018, I finished writing my story. I felt a great sense of completion and I sat out on my balcony to watch the full moon rise.

I no longer had any need to fear the void.

Acknowledgements

I would like to thank my dear friends who read the first version of this book, providing hugs and kind words of support: Amy Farrar, Deborah Hamilton, Deb Guirl, Hyon Rah, and Thomaie Hilaris, I'm not sure what I would have done without you. I am incredibly grateful to Viva Obscura for greenlighting my book and to everyone else who made it possible to publish this work, particularly Brooke Warner, who provided amazing mentorship and support during the publication process. I am also extraordinarily grateful to have found The Lighthouse Writing Community in Denver, which provided time, space, and a wealth of feedback. I am especially grateful to Lisa Peterson, Laura Miller, and Dan Manzanares at The Lighthouse for their encouragement and instruction. And finally, I would like to extend my immense gratitude to those who stuck with me throughout my toughest year, especially Sam Slater, Nora Kochie, Jay Weiner, Karolina Rygiel, Anne Gruenewald, Carmen Skager, Amy and Dustin Key, Kristina and Philip Tilker, and Geraldine Wright; to others who gave up on our friendship when I asked too much; and to the wonderful people I met along the way. All of you hold a special place in my heart.

www.ingramcontent.com/pod-product-compliance
Lightning Source LLC
Chambersburg PA
CBHW021352290426
44108CB00010B/205